GA ARCHITECT

SANAA
KAZUYO SEJIMA
RYUE NISHIZAWA
2011-2018

GA ARCHITECT
Kazuyo Sejima Ryue Nishizawa SANAA 2011–2018

Directed by Yoshio Futagawa
Edited by Makoto Yamaguchi
Photographed by GA photographers
Essay by Ryue Nishizawa, Kazuyo Sejima
Designed by Takuya Seki

Copyright © 2018 A.D.A. EDITA Tokyo Co., Ltd.
3-12-14 Sendagaya, Shibuya-ku, Tokyo 151-0051, Japan
All rights reserved. No part of this publication may be reproduced,
stored in a retrieval system, or transmitted, in any form or by any means,
electronic, mechanical, photocopying, recording, or otherwise,
without permission in writing from the publisher.

Copyright of photographs
© 2018 GA photographers
Copyright of drawings, renderings
© 2018 Kazuyo Sejima & Associates
© 2018 Office of Ryue Nishizawa
© 2018 SANAA

Logotype design (GA): Gan Hosoya

Printed and bound in Japan

ISBN978-4-87140-436-5 C1352

GA ARCHITECT

*SANAA
KAZUYO SEJIMA
RYUE NISHIZAWA
2011-2018*

妹島和世　西沢立衛

ESSAY BY KAZUYO SEJIMA, RYUE NISHIZAWA

序文：妹島和世, 西沢立衛

A.D.A. EDITA Tokyo

KAZUYO SEJIMA

妹島和世

Founder and Principle (front left)

1956	Born in Ibaraki, Japan
1981	M. Arch, Japan Women's University
	Joined Toyo Ito & Associates
1987–	Established Kazuyo Sejima & Associates
1995–	Established SANAA with Ryue Nishizawa
2001–	Professor of Keio University
2015–	Professor at Polytecnic University of Milan
2016	Degree of Doctor of Letters, honoris causa from University of Oxford
2016–	Professor at University of Applied Arts Vienna
2017–	Professor of Yokohama Graduate School of Architecture Y-GSA

1956	茨城県生まれ
1981	日本女子大学大学院修了
	伊東豊雄建築設計事務所入所
1987–	妹島和世建築設計事務所設立
1995–	西沢立衛と協働設計（SANAA）
2001–	慶應義塾大学理工学部教授
2015–	ミラノ工科大学教授
2016	オックスフォード大学名誉学位
2016–	ウィーン応圧美術大学教授
2017–	横浜国立大学大学院建築都市スクール Y-GSA 教授

RYUE NISHIZAWA

西沢立衛

Founder and Principle (front right)

1966	Born in Kanagawa, Japan
1990	M. Arch, Yokohama National University
	Joined Kazuyo Sejima & Associates
1995–	Established SANAA with Kazuyo Sejima
1997–	Established Office of Ryue Nishizawa
2001–10	Associate Professor of Yokohama National University
2010–	Professor of Yokohama Graduate School of Architecture Y-GSA

1966	神奈川県生まれ
1990	横浜国立大学大学院修士課程修了
	妹島和世建築設計事務所入所
1995–	妹島和世と協働設計（SANAA）
1997–	西沢立衛建築設計事務所設立
2001–10	横浜国立大学大学院助教授
2010–	横浜国立大学大学院建築都市スクール Y-GSA 教授

YOSHITAKA TANASE

棚瀬純孝

Partner (back left)

1970	Born in Mie, Japan
1995	M. Arch, Kyoto Institute of Technology
	Joined Kazuyo Sejima & Associates
	Joined SANAA
2003	Established Tanase Architect Office
2013–	Partner of SANAA

1970	三重県生まれ
1995	京都工芸繊維大学大学院修了
	妹島和世建築設計事務所入所
	SANAA入所
2003	棚瀬純孝建築設計事務所設立
2013–	SANAAパートナー

YUMIKO YAMADA

ユミコ・ヤマダ

Partner (back right)

1976	Born in Tokyo, Japan
1999	B. Arch, Carnegie Mellon University
2000–01	Office for Metropolitan Architecture (OMA)
2002	Joined SANAA
2013–	Partner of SANAA

1976	東京都生まれ
1999	カーネギーメロン大学卒業
2000–01	Office for Metropolitan Architecture (OMA)
2002	SANAA入所
2013–	SANAAパートナー

RIKIYA YAMAMOTO

山本力矢

Partner (back center)

1977	Born in Fukui, Japan
2000	B. Arch, Tokyo University of Science
2002	M. Arch, Yokohama National University
	Joined SANAA
	Joined Kazuyo Sejima & Associates
2013–	Partner of SANAA

1977	福井県生まれ
2000	東京理科大学卒業
2002	横浜国立大学大学院修了
	SANAA入所
	妹島和世建築設計事務所入所
2013–	SANAAパートナー

Contents

8　"Architecture of Environment"　Ryue Nishizawa
14　"Current Trial and Errors"　Kazuyo Sejima

SANAA

20　Louvre-Lens　*Lens, France, 2005–12*
34　Vitra Factory　*Weil am Rhein, Germany, 2006–12*
46　Paris Apartments　*Paris, France, 2007–18*
60　Shakujii Apartments　*Tokyo, 2009–11*
84　Junko Fukutake Hall　*Okayama, Okayama, 2010–13*
90　Grace Farms　*New Canaan, Conneticuit, U.S.A., 2010–15*
98　La Samaritaine　*Paris, France, 2010–*
112　Competition for MECA (Maison de l'Économie Créative et de
　　la Culture en Aquitaine)　*Bordeaux, France, 2012*
120　Skolkovo Innovation Center Guest Zone　*Moscow, Russia, 2011*
126　Miyatojima Project　*Higashimatsushima, Miyagi, 2011–14*
127　Home for All Tsukihama　*Higashimatsushima, Miyagi, 2013–14*
128　Home for All Miyatojima　*Higashimatsushima, Miyagi, 2011–12*
129　Matsushima Nature Retreat　*Higashimatsushima, Miyagi, 2014–*
130　Junko Fukutake Terrace　*Okayama, Okayama, 2012–14*
134　Competition for New National Stadium　*Tokyo, 2012*
142　Bezalel Academy of Arts & Design　*Jerusalem, Israel, 2012–21*
150　Shogin TACT Tsuruoka (Tsuruoka Cultural Hall)　*Tsuruoka, Yamagata, 2012–17*
162　Shibuya Station Development Plan　*Tokyo, 2012–28*
164　Huaxin Financial Plaza　*Shanghai, China, 2013–19*
168　Bocconi University New Urban Campus　*Milan, Italy, 2013–19*
172　Taichung Green Museumbrary　*Taichung, Taiwan, R.O.C., 2013–*
178　Hitachi City Hall　*Hitachi, Ibaraki, 2013–19*
182　Pergola　*Okayama, Okayama, 2013–14*
186　Maru　*Kanazawa, Ishikawa, 2014–16*
206　Auckland Castle Walled Garden Project　*Auckland, U.K., 2014–*
218　New National Gallery, Liget Budapest　*Budapest, Hungary, 2015–*
224　Shiga Museum of Modern Art　*Otsu, Shiga, 2015–*
232　Sydney Modern Project　*Sydney, New South Wales, Australlia, 2015–21*
236　Naoshima Port Terminal　*Naoshima, Kagawa, 2015–16*
238　Competition for Museum of the 20th Century　*Berlin, Germany, 2016*
250　Shizuoka City History Museum　*Shizuoka, Shizuoka, 2017–*
252　Sanya MOCA Project　*Sanya, Hainan, China, 2017–*
256　Suzhou Shishan Square Art Theater and Museum　*Suzhou, China, 2017–*
260　Exhibitions:
　　– Venice Bienniale 2012　*Venice, Italy, 2012*
　　– Sharjah Biennial 11, 2013　*Sharjah, UAE, 2013*
　　– "Kazuyo Sejima + Ryue Nishizawa/SANAA"　*Towada, Aomori, 2014*
　　– "Oscar Niemeyer"　*Tokyo, 2015*
263　Furniture
　　– Big Drop　*2012*
　　– SANAA TABLE　*2015*
　　– Trophy (Single Flower Vase)　*2016*
　　– Inujima Chair　*2016*
　　– Lobby-chair　*2017*

KAZUYO SEJIMA

16　Hitachi Station and Free-Corridor　*Hitachi, Ibaraki, 2004–11*
48　Shibaura Office (Shibaura House)　*Tokyo, 2008–11*
52　Sumida Hokusai Museum　*Tokyo, 2009–16*
64　Soneiji Cemetery Pavillion "Muyuju-rin"　*Ichikawa, Chiba, 2009–14*
72　Tsuchihashi House　*Tokyo, 2009–11*
76　Kyoto Apartments (Nishinoyama House)　*Kyoto, 2010–13*
100　Nakamachi Terrace　*Kodaira, Tokyo, 2010–14*
106　Inujima "Art House Project" phase II　*Okayama, Okayama, 2011–13*
110　Dangozaka House　*Tokyo, 2011–14*
114　Yoshida Printing Inc. Tokyo HQ　*Tokyo, 2011–14*
148　House in Quebradas　*Los Vilos, Chile, 2012–*
200　Japan Women's University Mejiro Campus　*Tokyo, 2014–21*
208　Osaka University of Arts, Art Science　*Kanan, Osaka, 2015–*
228　Inujima Landscape Project
　　Inujima Stay, Inujima Life Garden　*Okayama, Okayama, 2015–*
244　Spring　*Daigo, Ibaraki, 2016*
258　New Express Train　*2018*

RYUE NISHIZAWA

30　Garden & House　*Japan, 2006–11*
38　Hiroshi Senju Museum Karuizawa　*Karuizawa, Nagano, 2007–11*
66　United Church of Christ in Japan, Ikuta Church　*Kawasaki, Kanagawa, 2009–14*
82　Treform, W Wing　*Tokyo, 2010–12*
122　Terasaki House　*Kanagawa, 2011–14*
138　Fukita Pavilion in Shodoshima　*Shodoshima, Kagawa, 2012–13*
146　Kokusai Soushoku Headquarters　*Tokyo, 2013–*
160　House in Los Vilos　*Los Vilos, Chile, 2012–*
176　House in Marbella　*Marbella, Chile, 2013–*
184　Roof and Mashroom Pavilion　*Kyoto, 2013*
188　Jining Museum　*Jining, China, 2014–*
192　O House　*Tokyo, 2014–18*
196　Morimoto House　*Aichi, 2014–*
198　Cawaii Bread & Coffee　*Tokyo, 2014*
212　Tokuda House　*Kyoto, 2015–16*
216　House in Kyoto　*Kyoto, 2015–*
231　Inujima Landscape Project
　　"Stay 01", "Stay 02" Inujima Stay　*Okayama, Okayama, 2016–*
242　I House　*Nagano, 2016–*
246　Shodoshima-Fukutake House　*Shodoshima, Kagawa, 2016*
248　Atelier　*Tokyo, 2016–17*
254　Louna Music Hall Project　*Guizhou, China, 2017–*

266　List of Works 2011–18

目次

8 「環境の建築」西沢立衛
14 「現在の試行錯誤」妹島和世

SANAA

20 ルーヴル・ランス　フランス, ランス, 2005〜12年
34 ヴィトラ・ファクトリー　ドイツ, ヴァイル・アム・ライン, 2006〜12年
46 パリ16区の公営集合住宅　フランス, パリ, 2007〜18年
60 石神井アパートメント　東京都練馬区, 2009〜11年
84 Junko Fukutake Hall(岡山大学J-Hall)　岡山県岡山市, 2010〜13年
90 グンイス・ファームズ　アメリカ, コネティカット州, ニューケイナン, 2010〜15年
98 ラ・サマリテーヌ　フランス, パリ, 2010年〜
112 創造経済文化センター 設計競技案　フランス, ボルドー, 2012年
120 スコルコボ・イノベーションセンター・ゲストゾーン　ロシア, モスクワ, 2011年
126 宮戸島の計画　宮城県東松島市, 2011〜14年
127 宮戸島月浜のみんなの家　宮城県東松島市, 2013〜14年
128 東松島市宮戸島のみんなの家　宮城県東松島市, 2011〜12年
129 松島自然の家　宮城県東松島市, 2014年〜
130 Junko Fukutake Terrace　岡山県岡山市, 2012〜14年
134 新国立競技場 デザイン競技案　東京都新宿区, 2012年
142 ベツァルエル・アカデミー・オブ・アート・アンド・デザイン　イスラエル, エルサレム, 2012〜21年
150 荘銀タクト鶴岡(鶴岡市文化会館)　山形県鶴岡市, 2012〜17年
162 渋谷駅地区駅街区開発計画　東京都渋谷区, 2012〜28年
164 上海金融センター　中国, 上海市, 2013〜19年
168 ボッコーニ大学新キャンパス　イタリア, ミラノ, 2013〜19年
172 Taichung Green Museumbrary　台湾, 台中市, 2013年〜
178 日立市新庁舎　茨城県日立市, 2013〜19年
182 パーゴラ　岡山県岡山市, 2013〜14年
186 まる　石川県金沢市, 2014〜16年
206 オークランド・キャッスル・ウォールド・ガーデン　イギリス, オークランド, 2014年〜
218 新国立美術館 リゲット・ブダペスト　ハンガリー, ブダペスト, 2015年〜
224 滋賀県立近代美術館・新生美術館　滋賀県大津市, 2015年〜
232 シドニー・モダン・プロジェクト　オーストラリア, シドニー, 2015〜21年
236 直島港ターミナル　香川県香川郡直島町, 2015〜16年
238 Museum of the 20th Century 設計競技案　ドイツ, ベルリン, 2016年
250 静岡市歴史博物館　静岡県静岡市, 2017年〜
252 三亜MOCAプロジェクト　中国, 海南, 2017年〜
256 蘇州獅山広場芸術劇場　中国, 蘇州市, 2017年〜
260 展覧会
　　−ヴェニス建築ビエンナーレ 2012　イタリア, ヴェネツィア, 2012年
　　−シャルジャ・ビエンナーレ 11, 2013　UAE, シャルジャ, 2013年
　　−「妹島和世＋西沢立衛/SANAA」青森県十和田市, 2014年
　　−「オスカー・ニーマイヤー展」東京都江東区, 2015年
263 家具
　　−Big Drop　2012年
　　−SANAA TABLE　2015年
　　−Trophy(一輪挿し)　2016年
　　−犬島のいす　2016年
　　−Lobby-チェア　2017年

妹島和世

16 日立駅自由通路及び橋上駅舎　茨城県日立市, 2004〜11年
48 芝浦のオフィス(SHIBAURA HOUSE)　東京都港区, 2008〜11年
52 すみだ北斎美術館　東京都墨田区, 2009〜16年
64 總寧寺永代供養施設「無憂樹林」　千葉県市川市, 2009〜14年
72 土橋邸　東京都, 2009〜11年
76 京都の集合住宅(NISHINOYAMA HOUSE)　京都府京都市, 2010〜13年
100 なかまちテラス(小平市仲町公民館・仲町図書館)　東京都小平市, 2010〜14年
106 犬島「家プロジェクト」2　岡山県岡山市, 2011〜13年
110 団子坂の家　東京都, 2011〜14年
114 ヨシダ印刷東京本社　東京都墨田区, 2011〜14年
148 チリの住宅　チリ, ロスビロス, 2012年〜
200 日本女子大学目白キャンパス　東京都文京区, 2014〜21年
208 大阪芸術大学アートサイエンス学科棟　大阪府南河内郡河南町, 2015年〜
228 犬島ランドスケーププロジェクト　犬島ステイ, 犬島 くらしの植物園　岡山県岡山市, 2015年〜
244 Spring(KENPOKU ART 茨城県北芸術祭)　茨城県久慈郡大子町, 2016年
258 新型特急車両　2018年

西沢立衛

30 ガーデン＆ハウス　日本, 2006〜11年
38 軽井沢千住博美術館　長野県北佐久郡軽井沢町, 2007〜11年
66 日本キリスト教団 生田教会　神奈川県川崎市, 2009〜14年
82 トレフォルム, W Wing　東京都豊島区, 2010〜12年
122 寺崎邸　神奈川県, 2011〜14年
138 小豆島の葺田パヴィリオン　香川県小豆郡小豆島町, 2012〜13年
146 国際装飾本社　東京都渋谷区, 2013年〜
160 ロスビロスの住宅　チリ, ロスビロス, 2012年〜
176 マルベーリャの住宅　チリ, マルベーリャ, 2013年〜
184 森の屋根ときのこ　京都府京都市, 2013年
188 済寧市美術館　中国, 済寧市, 2014年〜
192 O邸　東京都, 2014〜18年
196 森本邸　愛知県, 2014年〜
198 カワイイブレッド＆コーヒー　東京都中央区, 2014年
212 徳田邸　京都府, 2015〜16年
216 京都の住宅　京都府, 2015年〜
231 犬島ランドスケーププロジェクト ステイ01, ステイ02/犬島ステイ　岡山県岡山市, 2016年〜
242 I邸　長野県, 2016年〜
246 小豆島・福武ハウス一部改修工事　香川県小豆郡小豆島町, 2016年
248 アトリエ　東京都, 2016〜17年
254 楼納音楽ホールプロジェクト　中国, 貴州省, 2017年〜

266 作品リスト 2011〜2018年

Architecture of Environment
環境の建築

Ryue Nishizawa
西沢立衛

No More Boxes

Moving into the 21st century, our design underwent changes in many ways, to which factors such as evolution of computers and change in design technologies contributed in no small extent besides changes in our own ideas. There also was change in society. Especially the Great East Japan Earthquake was a significant incident for us.

Looking back at our architectures from the time we have launched SANAA (in the 1990s) I find many differences from our current ones. One of the major change would be that our architectures ceased to be boxes. Our architectures from the 90s mainly consisted of square, box type structures as a vertical representation of a plan. In contrast, more of our recent projects are architectures that are not quite box-like, with protruding eaves or consisting solely of a roof or with gentle curves.

What comes to my mind as one of the reasons for such change is the progress of computers. Back in the 90s we used to work with two-dimensional CAD, and our way of thinking was definitely two-dimensional. Later on, as we entered the 21st century, 3D programs gradually came to play a central role in our design.

Instead of conceiving the two-dimensional first then working it into the three-dimensional, we now come up with three-dimensional ideas from the beginning. It is now possible for us to freely conceive shapes that are not limited to simple forms such as boxes.

Another thing that comes to my mind is that our view on function started to change, as we came to perceive function as something dynamic and variable rather than something static to be stabilized as a room.

Multipurpose Architecture, Architecture as a Place

Our 'box architecture' from back in the 90s was, to put it another way, an 'architecture of programs' that involved functions turned into rooms and rooms assembled into an architecture. 'Box' as an architectural term also suggested that function=room and assembly of functions=architecture. Whereas today, we came to think about functions that would not necessarily be turned into rooms; we now have more precise ideas about spaces of variable functions, or multipurpose spaces. In parallel with our growing penchant for perceiving function as dynamic and variable, our architec-

箱でなくなる

21世紀に入って，私たちの設計はいろいろな意味で変わってきた。その背景には，自分たちの考えの変化ということ以外にも，コンピュータの進化，設計技術の変化ということが少なからずある。また，社会の変化もあった。とりわけ2011年3月の東日本大震災は，私にとって大きな出来事であった。

SANAAを始めた当時（1990年代）の私たちの建築と，現在のそれとの違いを考えると，自分なりにいろんな違いを感じるが，やはりまず，私たちの建築が箱でなくなってきたことは，最も大きな変化の一つであるように思う。90年代の私たちの建築は，平面をそのまま立ち上げたような，四角い箱状のものが大半であった。それに対して現在は，軒が出ていたり，屋根だけであったり，またはゆるく曲線にしていたりと，箱と言えないような建築プロジェクトが増えてきた。

そのような変化が起きた理由の一つとして思いつくのは，まずコンピュータの進歩である。90年代において私たちの事務所では，二次元ツールつまりいわゆるCADで設計しており，私たちの発想の仕方は極めて二次元的なものであった。その後，21世紀

に入った頃から徐々に3Dプログラムが設計の中心になってきた。建築の発想も，二次元をまず考えてそれを立ち上げるというやり方ではなくて，最初からダイレクトに三次元を考えるように変わってきた。箱のような単純形状以外の形も自由に考えることができるようになってきた。

もう一つ思うのは，機能に対する私たちの考え方が変わってきた，ということがある。機能を，静的なもの，部屋として固定するものというよりも，動的なもの，変化するもの，と考えるようになってきた。

多目的な建築，場所の建築

90年代当時私たちがやっていた「箱の建築」は，別の言い方をすれば，「プログラムの建築」とも言えた。機能が部屋になり，部屋が集まって建築になるというものだ。「箱」という建築言語は，機能イコール部屋，機能の集合イコール建築，という図式を暗示してもいた。それが現在では，必ずしも部屋化しない機能を考えるようになった。また，機能が移ろっていく空間，多目的な空間をより具体的に考えるようになった。機能を動的なもの，変化するも

ture became gradually fluid and continuous.

We also came to think about places whose functions (uses) are undetermined, in addition to spaces with variable functions. Today, one of the most important theme in our architecture is 'creating places' regardless of their functions. Be it a residence, a station building or a hospital, and regardless of its function, it is paramount for architecture that it is spatially rich as a place to stay, and that it is a place better suited for people. In addition to having a nice shape and being well functional, I believe that an architecture that is spatially rich as a place is what many people ask for. From that perspective, whether or not "that house is a place where I would wish to belong to" or "that architecture has an appeal as a place to be" are issues that are crucial to architecture. In the process of thinking about function we came to look toward an 'architecture with an energy as a place.'

As Good as Life

The Great East Japan Earthquake put Japanese architects once again face to face with issues such as 'humans v. nature' and 'architecture v. nature.' One reason why our architecture gradually grew organic in shape and

became spaces that are a series of continuous components may be attributed to the aforementioned change and evolution in our design tool. Another reason would be that later projects involved contextually rich topography instead of urban areas paved with square buildings and square sites as was the case with Louvre-Lens (2012). Also, our understanding about function changed. But the most significant change in attitudes occurred as we came to challenge architectural issues of Mother Nature v. architecture, or environment v. architecture in a more direct manner. If I were to describe the imagery of an architecture in which programs are replaced by square rooms and arranged geometrically as being diagrammatic and mechanical, architecture with organic spaces and architecture in harmony with topography would be non-mechanical, organic and similar to life in imagery.

Curves

Teiji Ito refers to a spline ruler to illustrate the characteristics of curves seen in Japanese old architectures and the difference with curves in western architecture in his book Japanese Design Theory.(1) A spline ruler is used

by temple and shrine carpenters to draw curves. It is a thin piece of wood that is soft and flexible which is basically straight but can be bent to create any curvature one wishes to draw quick and easy. The tool proved to be handy in creating curves in roofs of temple and shrine architecture composed of various curves, as it made possible to connect several curves or copy roof inclinations of past buildings. Ito focuses on the fact that this ruler is basically a straight piece of wood that bends to create curves. The more it bends the greater is the curvature; the less it bends the larger the diameter of the curve. With zero bending, the curve becomes a straight line. What is interesting in this ruler is that the straight line is considered as one type of curve. Ito put the way curves are perceived and the situation in which straight line and curves were placed side by side in the same context in contraposition with those in western architecture. For example, an arc with extremely long diameter is infinitely close to a straight line, but it is still a huge curve, never a straight line. A curve and a straight line are two different things in principle, and a curve will never be a straight line in spite of its minimal curvature. On the other hand the spline ruler defines the straight line as an extension

のと捉えるようになってきたことと並行して，私たちの建築も徐々に流動的で連続的なものとなってきた。

私たちはまた，機能が変化してゆく空間だけでなく，機能が（使い方が）はっきりしない場をも考えるようになった。機能が何であっても，「場所づくり」は私たちの建築にとって最も重要なテーマの一つとなりつつある。建築は住宅であっても駅舎であっても，病院であっても，どんな機能であっても，居場所としての豊かさがあるかどうか，人間にふさわしい場所になっているかということは，大変重要なことだ。建築の形がいいとか，機能的によくできている，ということに加えて，場所としての豊かさを持った建築は，多くの人が求めるものではないだろうか。その意味でも，「その住宅は自分が帰属したい場所になっているか?」「その建築は居場所としての魅力があるか?」ということは，建築にとって大きな課題だ。機能を考えていくうちに，「場所としての力を持った建築」を目指すようになった。

生命的なもの

東日本大震災によって，日本の建築家はあらためて，「人間と自

然」「建築と自然」という問題に直面することになった。近年，私たちの建築が徐々に有機的な形状になり，部分部分が連続するような空間になってきたのは，一つには，先ほど述べたような設計ツールの変化，進化ということがあるし，またもう一つには，「ルーヴル・ランス」(2012年)のように敷地条件が，四角い建物と四角い敷地が並ぶ市街地とは違う，地形が豊かなコンテクストで建てるケースが出てきた，ということもある。また，機能に対する私たちの理解の変化もある。しかし特に，大自然と建築というテーマ，または環境と建築というテーマをよりダイレクトな建築の問題にするようになってきたということは，最も大きな意識の変化だと言える。プログラムを四角い部屋に置き換えてそれらを並べる建築を，ダイアグラム的なもの，機械的なもの，とイメージ的に言ってよければ，有機的な空間を持った建築，地形と調和するような建築などは，非機械的なもの，有機的なもの，生命的なもの，というイメージに近い。

曲線

伊藤ていじは著書『日本デザイン論』の中で，日本の古建築に見

られる曲線の特徴と，西洋建築の曲線の違いについて，たわみ尺を例にとって説明している(注1)。たわみ尺は，宮大工が寺社をつくるときに使う曲線用の定規で，木の薄い板状のもので，板は柔らかくたわむようになっている。基本はまっすぐだが，たわませることで自由に曲率を変えられる。色々な曲線を手早くつくることができたり，複数の曲線をつなぎ合わせたり，過去の建物の屋根勾配をコピーできるなどのメリットがあり，様々な曲線で構成された寺社建築の屋根の曲線をつくる際に重宝されてきた。このたわみ尺において伊藤が着目するのは，普段は直線である木が，たわむことで曲線になるという点である。たわめばたわむほど曲率が強くなっていき，逆にたわみが小さくなればなるほど，半径の大きな曲線になっていく。たわみがゼロになった段階で，曲線は直線となる。この定規が面白いのは，直線が，様々な曲線の一つに位置付けられていることだ。伊藤はこの曲線のありよう，直線と曲線が同じ文脈に並んでしまう状況を，西洋のそれと対置させた。例えば円弧は，半径が非常に大きくなれば，限りなく直線に近づくが，しかしそれは直線ではなく，大きな曲線である。曲線と直線は原理として別物であり，曲線はどれだけ直線に近づいて

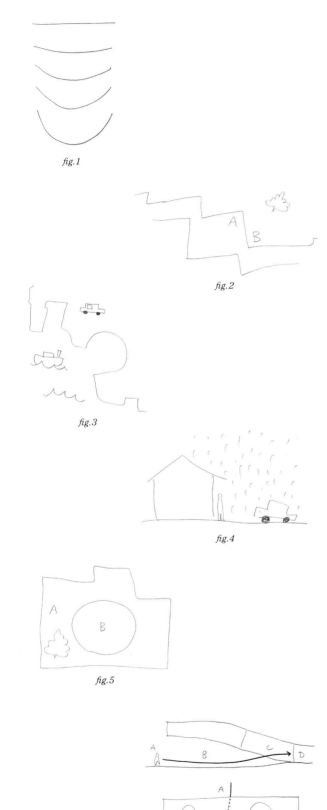

fig.1

fig.2

fig.3

fig.4

fig.5

fig.6

of the curve. The curve and the straight line share the same world (fig.1). Ito states that the idea of curve seen in the spline ruler is one of the greatest characteristics of curves in Japanese architecture.

It was in the mid-90s that we began tackling the curves. Back then, our design tool was two-dimensional CAD that only allowed us to draw curves that can be expressed with simple mathematical formulas such as arcs, elliptic arcs and hyperbolic curves. Although we wanted to draw curves that are closer to nature, mathematical formulas to produce them proved to be too complex to be handled by the CAD of that time. Following the progress in the calculation ability of computers, we are now able to freely draw more natural curves. Nowadays, one does not have to be a skilled temple and shrine carpenter to be able to draw curves that Ito tried to explain by referring to spline rulers, a world in which curves and straight lines are no different.

Like Flying Geese
I have come to take interest in the flying geese pattern (fig.2) since our first attempt in the configuration for Louvre-Lens. I find it especially intriguing in terms of relationship between landscape and architecture, harmony between inside and outside, and spatial experience. In an architecture that stretches in flying geese pattern is, in the case of Louvre-Lens, the inside does not physically blend with the outside: they are definitely two separate things. The buildings simply cross the site diagonally in a flying geese pattern. But this simple diagonal crossing creates an impression as if there were an inside-outside interaction. It is reminiscent of the relationship between the sea and land - as opposed to that in a reclaimed land where shorelines are straight, varied topography with convoluted coastlines around capes and coves offers a more diversified sea-land relationship (fig.3). For example, a place as depicted in fig.2-A gives a cape-like imagery of being amid a landscape while being inside a building, whereas a place like fig.2-B is closer to a cove, with an imagery of being enclosed in architecture. In other words, my fascination with the flying geese pattern comes firstly from the more diverse inside-outside relationship and secondly from the architectural experience that creates a feeling that expands both inward and outward.

も，直線になることはない。それに対してたわみ尺では，曲線の延長線上に直線がある。曲線と直線は同じ世界である——図1。このたわみ尺における曲線のありようは日本建築の曲線の最大の特徴の一つと，伊藤は述べている。

私たちが曲線に挑戦し始めたのは，90年代半ば頃であった。当時は設計ツールがCADだったこともあり，そこで描くことができる曲線は，円弧か楕円弧，双曲線といった，簡単な数式で表せるものに限定されていた。当時，もっと自然に近い曲線を描きたかったが，それは数式に置き換えればものすごく複雑なものであって，当時のCADでそれを描くことは可能ではなかった。しかしコンピュータの計算能力の発達によって，現在ではより自由で自然な曲線を描くことができるようになった。伊藤がたわみ尺を例に説明しようとした曲線，直線と曲線が同じものであるような世界を，熟練した宮大工でなくても誰でも今，描くことができる時代になった。

雁行する
「ルーヴル・ランス」で試みた雁行配置——図2というものに，このプロジェクト以降私は興味を持つようになった。特にランドスケープと建築の関係，中と外の調和，空間体験という意味で，面白く感じている。雁行して伸びてゆく建築は，「ルーヴル・ランス」の場合，中と外が物理的に混ざり合う訳ではなく，中と外はあくまでも別物で，単に建物が雁行しながら敷地を対角に（斜めに）横切ってゆくだけである。単に斜めに横切ってゆくというだけで，外と中の交流が生まれてくるような印象が出る。埋立地のような，直線の海岸線を持った陸地と海の関係に対して，海岸線が入り組んだ，岬や入江が多数あるような地形に富んだ陸と海の関係の方が，海と陸の関係が多様になることに似ている——図3。例えば図2-Aのような場所は，建物の中にいながらにして，ランドスケープの只中に飛び出るような，いわば岬のようなイメージとなり，図2-Bのような場所は，逆に外でありながら，建築に囲まれたイメージ，海岸線を例にとれば入江に近い場所が生まれる。つまり私が雁行形式に興味を持つのは，一つには中と外がより多様な関係を持つことで，もう一つは，建築の経験というものが，内外にわたって広がる感覚が生まれることだ。

Elevation

The major theme in Louvre-Lens was elevation. Elevation was no longer a result of a plan, as elevation itself became one of the greatest issues of architecture. As we imagine the process of approaching architecture from the city, the importance of elevation in architecture becomes clear: walking in the city and moving closer to an architecture, what we first see is its elevation. In most cases when people experience an architecture, they first experience its elevation, then its plan. Our experience of urban spaces such as streets and corners mostly starts with elevation. When we come to face the issue of harmony between environment and architecture, elevation proves to be one of the largest architectural components that have to be considered.

Memorial

An architecture on the street provides space to those who are inside while also providing space to those walking on the street in front of the building who are not directly involved with the architecture (fig.4). Architecture is not something one has to be inside to experience it; those who stand outside are perfectly capable of experiencing

it. Our architecture not being the only example, nearly every architecture creates space that is larger than the building itself. Therefore architecture has a great impact on the environment, powerful enough to exert changes on the surroundings. Environment and architecture have an inseparable relationship with each other.

Intermediate Region

Lately, I have been thinking about what can be called an intermediate region. An intermediate region is a third space created between the city and architecture, such as a garden around a building or a space under the eaves, most of them being exterior or semi-outdoor space. For example, with the 21st Century Museum of Contemporary Art in Kanazawa (2004, fig.5) by placing the building at the center of the site, the building came to be surrounded by a garden (fig.5-A), resulting in people passing through a garden to access the building instead of entering it directly from the street. Nothing exceptional about that, but I found some aspects to be interesting enough. One of which was that, because this garden space was directly connected to the city, people standing in this garden can feel both the atmo-

sphere of the city and that of the architecture. Another interesting aspect was that, in the process of approaching the architecture through this garden, people experience the spatial transition in which the atmospheres of the city and of the architecture change in a continuous manner.

Following the garden of the Museum in Kanazawa, we began tackling this intermediate region, the third space, in more architectural forms such as spaces under the eaves and porches, in addition to gardens. At the ROLEX Learning Center (2006, fig.6) people enter the building through a vast semi-outdoor space (fig.6-B) beneath the floating architecture rather than entering through the facade. Although this building can be approached from four sides, people still have to pass through this semi-outdoor space to get inside. In doing so, they experience the external space gradually turning into indoor space. Also, since this semi-outdoor space is found beneath the building and is connected to the inner courtyard, people can already have a feel of the inside and around the architecture while passing through this space.

立面

「ルーヴル・ランス」では，立面が大きなテーマになった。立面が平面の結果ではなくて，立面それ自体が建築の大きな問題の一つになってきた。私たちが街から建築にアプローチするその過程を想像してみると，建築の立面の重要さがよくわかる。街を歩いて，建築に近づいてゆくと，まず見えるのは立面だからだ。人々が建築を経験するその仕方というものは多くの場合，まず最初に立面を経験して，平面を経験するのはその後である。私たちが通りとか街角とかの都市空間を経験するやり方も，その多くはまず立面だ。環境と建築の調和という問題を考えるときに，立面は私たちにとって，考慮せねばならない最大の建築部位の一つということになる。

記念碑

街角に立つ建築は，その室内にいる人々に空間を提供するが，それと同時に，その建築とは直接関わり合いのない，建築の前の道を歩く人々にも空間を提供する──図4。建築はその中に入らない限り経験できない，というものではなくて，その外に佇む人も，十

分に経験できるものだ。私たちの建築だけに限らずほぼ全ての建築において，建築物がつくり出す空間は，建築物それ自身よりも大きい。そういうわけで，建築は環境的に大きなインパクトをもち，周辺の環境を変える威力を持つ。環境と建築は分離できない関係性を持っている。

中間領域

このことと関係して，最近私は中間領域というものをしばしば考えている。中間領域とは，例えば建物の周りの庭のような，または軒空間のような，街と建築の間につくられる第三の空間で，多くが外部空間か，半屋外空間である。例えば「金沢21世紀美術館」(2004年)──図5では，建物を敷地中央に置くことで，建物の周りに庭が生まれ──図5-A，それによって人々は道路からいきなり建物に入るのではなく，庭を通って建物に入る。大したことではなかったが，私は面白く感じた。一つは，この庭空間は街にダイレクトに繋がっているので，この庭に立っていると，街の雰囲気と建築の雰囲気の両方を感じることができる，ということで，もう一つ面白く感じたのは，この庭を通って建築に近づく過程で，街の

雰囲気と建築の雰囲気が連続的に変化していく空間的変化が感じられたことだ。

「金沢21世紀美術館」の庭の後，この中間領域，第三の空間は，庭という形だけでなく，たとえば軒下空間や縁側のような，もう少し建築的な形で試されるようになっていった。「ROLEXラーニングセンター」(2009年)──図6では，建物に入る際に，人々はファサードから入るのではなくて，大きく浮き上がった建築の下にできた大きな半屋外空間──図6-Bを通って，建物に入る。この建物は四方からアプローチできる建物だが，どこからアプローチしても，人々は必ずこの半屋外空間を通過して中に入る。そのことで，外部空間が段階的に室内空間になってゆくことを経験する。またこの半屋外空間は，建物の下であったり，中庭に繋がったりしているので，ここを通る過程ですでに建築の中や周りを感じることができる。

空間を纏う

「金沢21世紀美術館」のような「建築が庭で囲まれている」という関係性──図5を，もう少し建築的・空間的に発展させようとした例は，他にも「Junko Fukutake Hall」(2013年)や「Garden & House」

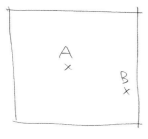

fig.7

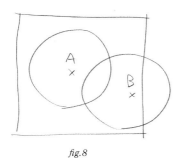

fig.8

Clad in Space

Besides the 21st Century Museum of Contemporary Art in Kanazawa, there are numerous examples of the relationship of 'architecture enclosed in garden' (**fig.5**) developed in more architectural/spatial manner, such as the Junko Fukutake Hall (2013) and the Garden & House (2011). We are challenging through various projects a situation in which architecture is clad in intermediate spaces, that is, standing surrounded by buffer zones such as space under eaves or garden, instead of architecture being thrown naked in the city. Architecture generates space not only inside but outside (**fig.4**). Garden & House is built in an extreme type of situation where it stands side by side with gigantic architectures 40 meters high, while trying to create an imagery of an architecture clad in space by being three-dimensionally surrounded by gardens within the gap.

Multicentric Architecture

From the 90s to this day we have long been fascinated by the idea of a 'multicentric world.' It is a space with multiple centers where several places serve as centers at the same time, rather than a pyramid-type hierarchical structure in which the center and the surroundings are permanently fixed. Projects such as the Stadstheater Almere (2006), Moriyama House (2005) and Shakujii Apartments (2011) for instance were designed as we imagined a place where all kinds of people would visit and do whatever they want in the building and where various places would become centers of activities. It may be described as a world where no one knows where the center is: it is a world with multiple centers but not one without a center.

There is this world 'neighborhood'—the city, for the sake of public administration, is divided into numbered districts in such a way that people can identify their location according to the division, such as "I am now at the center of the 1st district" or "I am living at the edge of the 1st district" (**fig.7**). In the city, in terms of administrative division, the edge of the 1st district and the center of the 1st district remain fixed, wherever a person might be at any given point in time. On the other hand, the spatial concept of 'neighborhood' is based on a person's community ties and activity range, so a person is always at the center of one's 'neighborhood.' If a person lives near the border between the 1st and 2nd

（2011年）など，多数ある。建築が裸で，街に投げ出されるのではなくて，建築がその周囲に中間領域的な空間をまとって，つまり軒下空間や庭といったバッファーゾーンをもちながら建つという状態を，いろんなケースでチャレンジしている。建築が，その中だけでなく，その外にも空間をつくり出す──図4。「Garden & House」は，高さ40メートルの巨大な建築に挟まれるという極端なシチュエーションに建つが，その隙間で庭に立体的に囲まれることで，空間をまといながら建築が建つイメージをつくろうとしている。

多中心的建築

「多中心の世界」への興味が私たちには長い間あり，それは90年代から今に至るまで，延々と続いている。それは例えばピラミッドのような，中心部と周辺部が不動であるような序列的構造ではなく，複数のいろいろな場所が中心になるような，中心を複数持った空間である。建築の例としては，「スタッドシアター・アルメラ」（2006年）や「森山邸」（2005年），「石神井アパートメント」（2011年）などのプロジェクトは，いろんな人々が建物に来て，皆が各々好き勝手に活動して，いろいろな場所が中心になるような，そういう場を想像しつつ設計した。中心がどこにあるのかよくわからない世界とも言えるが，それは中心がない世界ではなくて，複数の中心がある世界である。

「界隈」という言葉がある。街は行政上，1丁目，2丁目，3丁目，と分割されていて，それに従って考えれば，自分が1丁目の中心部に今にいるとか，1丁目の端っこに住んでいるとかという風に，自分の位置を確認できる──図7。行政上の街においては，自分が街のどの地点にいようが，1丁目の端と1丁目の中心は不動である。これに対して「界隈」という空間概念は，自分の近所付き合いや行動範囲をベースにしているので，自分はいつもだいたい「界隈」の中心にいる。1丁目と2丁目の境界近くに住んでいる場合，行政上の区画から見れば端に住んでいるが，「界隈」の観点から見れば，自分は中心にいる。この場合，界隈なるエリアは行政境界を超えている──図8。

「自分の居場所」なる空間には，「界隈」的なところが多分にある。例えば自分のプライバシー空間とか，動物のナワバリとかを考えてみると，そういったタイプの空間は，しばしば自分が中心になって，自分が境界に追いやられることはあまりない。私はこの

districts, the house is found at the edge of a district in terms of administrative division, but from the 'neighborhood' point of view the person is right at the center. In this case, the area called neighborhood transcends any administrative borders (fig.8).

A space recognized as a 'place for oneself' has much in common with 'neighborhood.' Taking a look at a person's own space of privacy or an animal's territory for instance, we find that such types of spaces are centered around the person or the animal and they are rarely chased off to the border. I have come to believe that this idea of 'neighborhood' and the multicentric structure have some kind of relationship between them (or find it fascinating if the two can be connected) , and looked for ways to somehow use this 'neighborhood'-type space when trying to create a place that is comfortable to many people—a type of architecture in which people will be everywhere and feel an extent of a place around each one of them, where each person will somehow feel being at the center. It appears to me as being one approach in creating a space of comfort in various types of architecture shared by many people such as residence, collective housing, community center or office.

Relationship Turns into Architecture

Architectures such as Nakamachi Terrace (2014) and Sumida Hokusai Museum (2016) are segmentalized into several elements; each part has a local centricity and independence that people can perceive. But at the same time they are also continuous and linked together, integrating and making up an entirety. This type of architecture may be seen as a result of the development of the idea of a 'multicentric architecture': a sort of architecture with a spatial composition in which people, when they are at any given spot inside the building — the kitchen for example — will experience the kitchen while they are in the kitchen, as well as experience the entire architecture.

The first thing that I find fascinating in this type of architecture is that architecture as a whole has a somewhat weaker integrity and constituent units of the architecture start to show on its exterior and shape, then show in the city; as the one-box, massive carton of architecture is broken, it becomes possible to grasp the relationship between each element that constitutes the city (things such as next door building, streets and topography) as well as the relationship between each element of architecture within the same context.

The second intriguing aspect in this type of architecture is that, those who visit the architecture and those who use the architecture can experience through its space how the architecture is made.Through the use of an architecture, people can understand how that architecture was formed. Architectural structure is not only for the safety of simply supporting the entire architecture, but also a tool for setting up an architectural experience.

To put these two points briefly: "relationship turns into architecture." Sejima calls such way an architecture is formed the 'shape of relationship'.(2) It is architecture as part of environment. Architecture is born where a sort of swirl of relationship is found. There are transparency, lucidity and democracy so that anyone can understand the dynamic whole-part relationship. For now, the way an architecture is formed is what we have been pursuing constantly through our projects.

(1) Japanese Design Theory (Kajima Publishing, 1966), pp.12-22.

(2) GA DOCUMENT 140, p.73; Shinkenchiku, November 2014 issue, p.91

「界隈」なる概念と，多中心構造とが，同じではないが関係しているように思えて（もしくは関係させると面白いと思い），多数の人間にとって居心地の良い場所をつくろうとするとき，この「界隈」的空間を利用できないかと考えた。いろんなところに人がいて，誰もがそれなりに自分を中心としたような広がり，自分を中心としたまとまりの場を感じるようなタイプの建築である。それは，住宅とか集合住宅とか，コミュニティセンターとか，オフィスとか，そういった複数の人間が同居するいろいろなタイプの建築において，心地良い空間をつくる一つのアプローチであるように思える。

関係が建築になる

「なかまちテラス」（2014年），「すみだ北斎美術館」（2016年）などの建築は，その全体がいくつかの要素に分節されていて，各部分はローカルな中心性を持って，各々の独立性を人々は感じることができる。しかし同時に，それらは連続し結合されてもいて，全体として一つというような一体化が起きてもいる。このようなタイプの建築は，「多中心的建築」のアイディアが発展していった一つの結果とも言える。建築の中のどこか，例えば台所であれば台所に滞在するときに，人々は台所を経験し，それと同時に建築全体を経験するというような建築の空間構成，つまり，部分の独立性と全体構造の両方を同時に経験できる建築，そういった建築のあり方である。

このタイプの建築が面白いと私が考えるのは，まず第一に，建築全体としての一体性が若干弱くなって，建築の構成単位が外観や形に現れ，それが街に現れる。ワンボックス的な，マッシブな建築の箱が壊れることで，街を構成する各要素（隣の建物とか道路とか地形とか）の関係と，建築内の各要素の関係とを，同一文脈上で把握することができるようになる。

また，私が感じる第二の面白さは，このようなタイプの建築は，建築を訪れる人，建築を使う人が，建築がどんな風につくられているかという建築のつくられ方を，空間を通して経験することができるという点だ。建築を使うことを通して，人々はその建築の成り立ちを理解することができる。建築構造が，単に建築全体を支える安全性のためのものであるだけでなく，建築の経験をつくり上げる道具になっている。

このような2点のことをまとめて一言で言うならば，「関係が建築になる」と言えるのではないだろうか。妹島はこのような建築のありようを「関係性のかたち」（注2）と呼んでいる。それは，環境の一部としての建築である。関係の渦のようなところに建築ができる。その建築では，全体と部分の動的関係性を誰もが理解できるような，透明性と明快性，民主性がある。これがいまのところ，様々なプロジェクトを通して私たちがずっと追い求めてきた建築のありようである。

注1：『日本デザイン論』（鹿島出版会，1966年）pp.12-22

注2：『GA DOCUMENT 140』p.73，『新建築』2014年11月号 p.91

Current Trial and Errors

現在の試行錯誤

Kazuyo Sejima

妹島和世

It has been some thirty years since I started creating architecture on my own. This collection of works covers my activities from the period between the twentieth and thirtieth years. Twenty-odd years have passed as SANAA, a design partnership with Nishizawa, and the latter half of that period is documented here. For the last five years we became a team of five, incorporating the trio of Tanase, Yamada and Yamamoto as partners.

I have been pursuing the same vision since the very beginning of my practice. Creating architecture involves creating borders and creating internal and external spaces. My vision was to connect those internal and external spaces; to create an internal space that would link any actions that take place inside; and make an external space that is in continuum with the environment that extends further outside. In another words, I wanted to create a place in which our actions and environment would link together. And I had a feeling that it would be a space like a park.

On each project I believe that I have always attempted to achieve this vision in some way or other through trial and error. As a matter of course as mentioned earlier I formed a design partnership with Nishizawa and came to work as a team of five over time, so I was not by myself in the development of these projects and would add that each member certainly works with slightly different images in mind. If Nishizawa or the other three members were to be asked for explanations, chances are they would all give different versions. And the way we create is always in a big collaborative work with our staffs.

On that basis, a quick summary from my point of view would be that, my focus was on the structure to start with, then on the spatial diagram, then on the program and then on the way they would be assembled. It was through ROLEX Learning Center (2009), a project that directly preceded the series of works presented in this volume, that I came to believe that I should think about programs and environment not only abstractly but also more specifically at the same time. Upon careful observation, it became obvious that prior to that, while I intended to think from both sides in order to connect internal and external spaces, in some projects it was the organization of interior programs that determined almost everything in architecture, or, to the contrary, urban density and proportions were the determining factors.

私が1人で建築をつくり始めてから，約30年が経つ。この作品集には，その20年目から30年目にかけての活動が収められている。西沢との共同設計SANAAから見てみれば，ほぼ20数年が経ち，その後ろ約半分が収められている。そしてこの5年は，棚瀬，ヤマダ，山本という3人がパートナーとなって5人で活動を始めた時である。

わたしはつくり始めた最初から，同じことを目指していた。建築をつくるというのは，境界をつくり内部空間と外部空間をつくり出すが，その内部空間と外部空間を繋げたい，さらに，つくり出す内部空間はその中で繰り広げられる行為を繋げるもので，外部空間は，そのさらに外に広がる環境に連続したものでありたいということである。つまり，私たちの行為と環境が繋がったものとなるような場所をつくりたいということであった。そしてそれは公園みたいな空間なのではないかと考えていた。

それぞれのプロジェクトで，試行錯誤しながらこのことをどうしたら実現できるか試みてきたつもりである。もちろん最初に書いたとおり，時間と共に西沢と共同設計を始め，その後5人で進めるようになったから，それらの展開は私1人ではなく，さらに言えば，人それぞれ少しずつ異なるイメージでつくっていることも考えられる。つまり西沢が，或いは他の3人が説明すれば，違った説明になるかもしれない。そして私たちのつくり方はいつも，スタッフの人たちとの大きな共同作業である。

その上で私の視点から簡単に整理すれば，はじめのうちは構造に，それから空間的なダイアグラムに，そしてプログラムに，組み立て方にと，注目してきたように思う。そして，この作品集の始まる一つ前のプロジェクト「ROLEXラーニングセンター」(2009年)を通して，プログラムや環境というものを，抽象的にだけでなく同時にもっと具体的に考えた方がいいのではないだろうかと思うに至った。それ以前は，内部空間と外部空間を繋ぐために，両方から考えると言っていながら，注意してみると，プロジェクトにより，インテリアのプログラムのオーガニゼーションからほとんど建築が決定されたり，あるいは逆に都市の密度やプロポーションから決められたりしていたこと

Looking at what surrounds architecture, diversity is everywhere. For example, the seemingly flat ground would move up and down; time flowing there would contribute in creating an invisible atmosphere of the land; being surrounded by lovely residential areas can mean anything from being adjacent to houses or adjacent to a small patch of green forest, to being right next to a kindergarten with children's voices echoing around. So I started to think about creating something that can specifically relate to such aspects. In other words, I began to look for ways to somehow create an architecture that would be composed of separate spaces that are each responsive to each place and are suited for each program as they form a weak integration as a whole. I wanted to create something bubbly where a variety of things overlaps with each other, as opposed to keeping things organized under a single index. In order for that to happen, a piece of architecture has to be composed of several parts; each part has to have a structure that is free from the overall structure; such parts have to be somehow gathered to make up one piece of architecture.

As a result, our architecture are becoming more complex. Some of the actual structural planning are not necessarily rational from a certain point of view. On certain occasions we have a hard time making studies, making drawings, and building for real. Sometimes they give me doubts that such orientation might be a little off the contemporary system and sense of values. The challenge is very demanding. But with the help of many others, some of the ideas came to be accomplished.

Today, I am probably not alone in perceiving the world is moving fast: occurrence of various phenomenons due to climate change; the current of the world that looked as though it were controlled by the western world being questioned if different movements were breaking out around the globe. In other words, there is a feeling that some of us are starting to move toward grasping once again what we humans are and wonder how we would do it. And our attempts for and thoughts about the future today is probably about finding what sort of architecture can be positioned in response to such movements within the cycle of nature.

に気づかされた。

　建築の周りを考えると多様である。例えば，平らなように見えても地盤は上下しているし，そこに流れていた時間が何かその土地の見えない雰囲気をつくり出していたりする。あるいは，周りは綺麗な住宅街だと言っても，住宅が隣にあるところと，緑が集まった小さな森が横にあるところ，子供の声が響きわたる幼稚園が隣接するところもある。そういうことに具体的に関係を持てるものをつくろうと考え始めた。つまり，全体性が弱い，それぞれの場所にそれぞれ反応しながら，それぞれのプログラムにふさわしいバラバラなスペースが集まってでき上がる建築をつくれないかと思い始めた。一つの指標でまとめられていくのでなく，色々なことが重なりあった，ぶくぶくしたものをつくりたいと思い始めた。そのためには，一つの建築はいくつかの部分からつくられる。部分はそれぞれ全体の構造から自由な構造でつくられる。それらがなんとか寄り集まって一つの建築になる。

　そうなって，つくる建築は複雑になってきた。構造計画も，ある視点から見れば，必ずしも合理的でないというものも生まれてきた。スタディするのも，図面化するのも，そしてそれを実際つくり上げるのもなかなか難しい時がある。こんな方向性は，現代のシステム，価値観からはちょっとずれているのではないかと思わされることもある。とても大変である。しかし，多くの人の力で，いくつかを実現することができた。

　今世界がどんどん動いているように感じるのは私だけではないだろう。気候の変動で様々な現象が起きたり，一見西欧がコントロールしていたような世界の流れが，色々なところで違う動きが生まれるのかと思わされたり，つまり自分たち人間というものを，あらためてどう捉え直すかという動きが始まっているような気がするのである。そしてそういう動きに，自然の循環の中にどのような建築であれば位置付けられるかというのが，私たちが今，そしてこれからに向けて，考え，試みようとしていることだと思う。

> Hitachi Station and
> Free-Corridor
> Hitachi, Ibaraki, Japan
> 2004–11
>
> Kazuyo Sejima & Associates

This is a project for the Hitachi Station and other connected buildings in the vicinity. The city of Hitachi lies nestled between the mountains and sea, a thin stretch of land running from north to south. This bridge-top station building will be a new gateway into this city, with an integrated design featuring a sprawling, horizontally expansive communal passageway that links the Hitachi Station Information Centers located in both the Central and Seaside Station Squares.

The building is a lightweight structure spanning a wide area, and is made from glass screens fixed at the top and base (alongside MJG metals) to provide a sense of openness. Although this is a sizable piece of architecture, the overall scale is controlled. Our aim was for this to become an everyday, familiar space which blends well into the surrounding landscape. The communal passageway and concourse have been finished with concrete flooring, glass screens, and a ceiling of perforated aluminum. Since these are all highly reflective materials, mirrored images of the ocean and townscape diffuse gently throughout the building. Interior connects smoothly with exterior in this open, transparent space.

From here, visitors can enjoy a 360° view of the Hitachi city. Our idea was to create a place where people are effortlessly exposed to the unique scenery of Hitachi, as they take in the ever-changing expressions of the ocean and city.

Aerial view from south toward Pacific Ocean

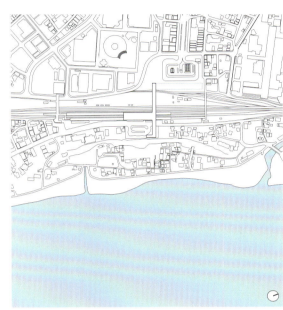

1 FREE CORRIDOR
2 CONCOURSE
3 OFFICE
4 TICKET GATE
5 TICKET RESERVATION OFFICE
6 SHOP
7 OBSERVATION DECK
8 CAFETERIA

Plan S=1:1200

Site plan S=1:10000

Free-corridor leading to observation deck and seaside exit

Observation deck

Free-corridor

日立駅自由通路及び橋上駅舎

日立駅および周辺施設全体の計画である。日立市は海と山に挟まれた，南北に細く延びる街である。その日立市の新しい玄関口となる橋上駅舎は，自由通路によって水平的に広がりながら，中央駅前広場と海岸口駅前広場，それぞれにある日立駅情報交流プラザへ繋がり，一体的なまとまりをつくり上げる。

建物全体は，大きなスパンの軽やかな構造体と，上下2辺支持(MJG金物併用)の開放的なガラススクリーンで構成されている。大構造建築物でありながらも，全体としてスケールを抑え，日常的で親しみやすい空間となり，周辺の風景の中に溶け込むことを目指した。自由通路とコンコースは，反射性の高いコンクリート床とガラススクリーン，アルミパンチングメタル天井で仕上げている。海やまちの景色が映り込んで，建物全体にやわらかく広がり，外部と内部が緩やかに繋がる開放的で透明な空間となる。

ここを訪れた人は，360度日立の風景を楽しむことができる。刻々と多様に表情を変える海とまちを眺めながら，日立らしさを自然に感じることができる場所になれば，と考えた。

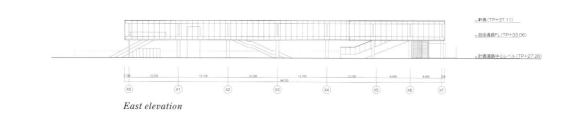
East elevation

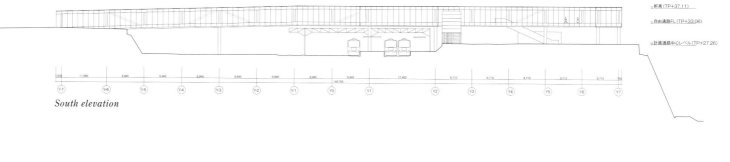
South elevation

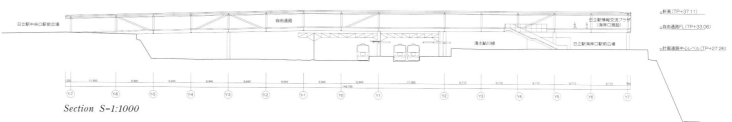
Section S=1:1000

Observation deck toward Pacific Ocean

View from concourse to cafeteria

Cafeteria

Louvre-Lens
Lens, France
2005–12

SANAA

View toward hall

In keeping with a desire to maintain the openness of the site and to reduce the ascendancy of this large project, the building was broken down into several spaces. Through their size and layout, which follow the gradual changes in terrain elevation, the buildings achieve balance with the scale of the site and the shape of the paths, landscape features evoking its mining history.

In order to visually and physically open up the site, the main glassed area features a hollow in the core of the building. This delicate glass box serves as an entry hall to the museum and is a genuine public space for the city of Lens. It is transparent and opens up to several directions of the site, and it can be crossed through to get to different quarters of the city.

The project avoids the strict, rectilinear shapes that would have conflicted with the subtle character of the site, as well as of free shapes that would have been overly restrictive from the perspective of the museum's internal operations. The slight inflection of the spaces is in tune with the long curved shape of the site and creates a subtle distortion of the inner areas while maintaining a graceful relationship with the artwork. The spaces are contained by a facade of anodized, polished aluminum that reverts a blurred and fuzzy image of the sites contours, reflections that change as one strolls by depending on the landscaping and available light. The main exhibition buildings flank the entry hall, the Gallery of Time on one side and the temporary exhibition hall on the other. The entrance hall leads to a lower level that contains storage space and artwork restoration areas. The museum thus opens its rear areas to the public.

In the park, two free standing buildings house the administration offices and the restaurant, linking the museum to the city. The entry to the museum is located at the center of the former pit and is the historical access to the site, rising gently from Paul Bert street. The transparent areas in the

Northeast view. From left to right, permanent exhibition wing, entrance hall wing, temporary exhibition wing and auditorium wing

building provide views of the surrounding wood and the city of Lens. This entry point provides a perspective of the entire building and of the panorama over the park reflected in the glass and aluminum surfaces. The entry area was designed as a void that is part of the landscape and visible from everywhere. It takes in visitors arriving at the museum from the main North entrance, as well as from the grassy areas to the East and the wood from the West. This large, transparent area of 68.5 x 58.5 m is an ample space within which diverse functional areas exist for the museum's visitors. There is a bookshop, a cafeteria for meeting friends, a place to obtain information about the exhibitions; or one can simply cross the hall to go from one side or the other of the park or the site. The glass "bubbles" are 3 m high and seem to float within the interior of the hall. They are primarily for publicrelated functions and provide areas for individual experiences.

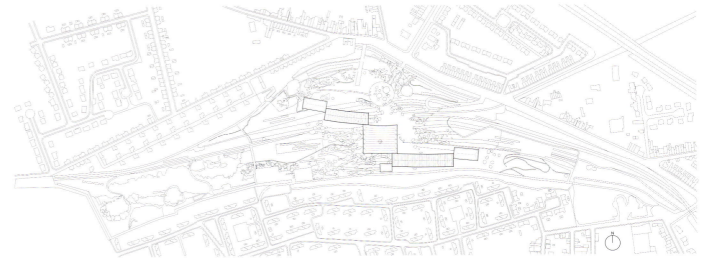

Site plan S=1:7500

ルーヴル・ランス

敷地の持つ開放性をそのまま残したいということと，この巨大プロジェクトの影響力を小さくしたいという気持ちから，建物ヴォリュームを小さく分割した。その大きさとカーブした配置が敷地のわずかな傾斜に従うことで，この建築は土地の持つスケール感やそこを走る道のかたち，かつて炭坑だった歴史を感じさせるランドスケープに呼応していく。

視覚的にも実際的にも，敷地に連続するために，建物の中心にヴォイド状のスペースとして，ガラス張りのメインエリアが置かれる。この繊細なガラス・ボックスは，美術館のエントランス・ホールであり，ランスの町のための本当の公共空間である。そこは透明で，敷地の幾つかの方向に開いているので，人々はここで交わり町の異なる部分に通り抜けることができる。

建物は，敷地の繊細さに合わない真っ直ぐな直方体形状ではないが，美術館の内部利用に過度の制約をもたらす自由形状というわけでもない。空間の微妙な湾曲が敷地の大きなカーブに合わさり，作品との優雅な関係性を保ちながら，内部空間に繊細な歪みを与えている。スペースは酸化皮膜処理され磨かれたアルミで覆われ，風景はあいまいでにじんだ像として再現される。その反射は，人が動くにつれ，その時の光と風景によって，変化していく。エントランス・ホールの両サイドが主展示室で，一方が「タイム・ギャラリー」で，もう一方が企画展示室である。エントランスの地下には，作品収蔵室と修復エリア。この美術館では，バックスペースも開かれている。

公園部分には，事務部門とレストランが入る，独立した棟が二つあり，美術館と町を結びつけている。美術館への入口は，敷地の中央にあり，それは以前と同じでポール・ヴェール通りから緩やかに上っていく。建物の透明な部分によって，周囲の森やランスの町が眺められる。このアプローチからは建物全体，そして外壁のアルミとガラスに映る公園全体のパノラマが目に入ってくる。エントランスは，ランドスケープの一部である隙間としてデザインされていて，どこからでも見られる。人々は，北側のメインの入口だけでなく，東の芝生側からも，西の森の側からも美術館に来ることができる。この 68.5×58.5m の大きな透明な空間には，来館者のための様々なファンクションが配される。ブックショップ，友だちと出会うカフェテリア，展示について知ることのできる場所，あるいは公園や敷地を反対側にただ通り抜けることもできる。エントランスには，高さ 3m のガラスの「バブル」が，幾つも浮かぶように配置されていて，基本的に社会的な活動や個別の経験のためのスペースとして使われる。

1 FOYER
2 AUDITORIUM
3 TEMPORARY EXHIBITION ROOM
4 LIBRARY / SHOP
5 RESOURCES CENTER
6 CAFETERIA
7 PIQUE-NIQUE AREA
8 SALON
9 MEMBER SPACE
10 ATELIER
11 GALLERY OF TIME
12 GLASS PAVILION
13 DISCOVERY SPACE
14 ART STORAGE
15 GROUP SPACE
16 STUFF SPACE
17 SMALL AUDITORIUM
18 TRAINING ROOM

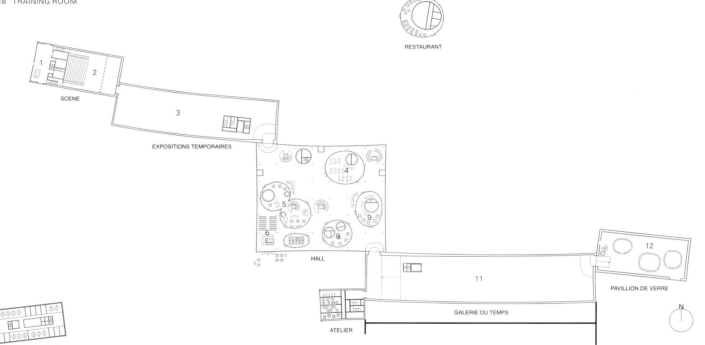

Ground floor S=1:2000

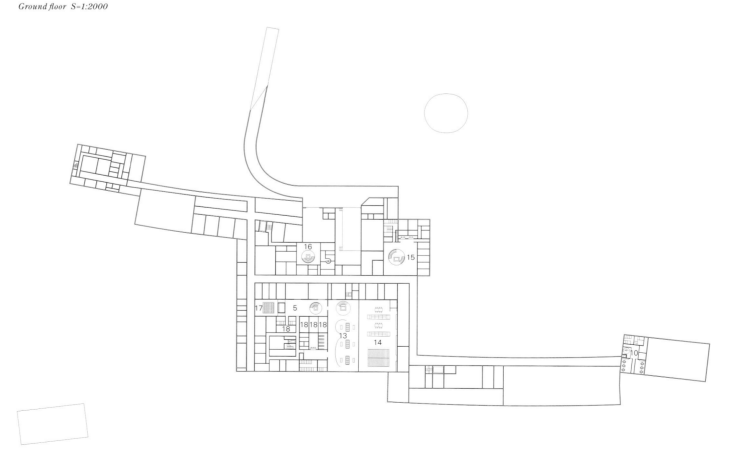

First basement

View from northwest. Temporary exhibition wing on right, entrance hall wing on center.

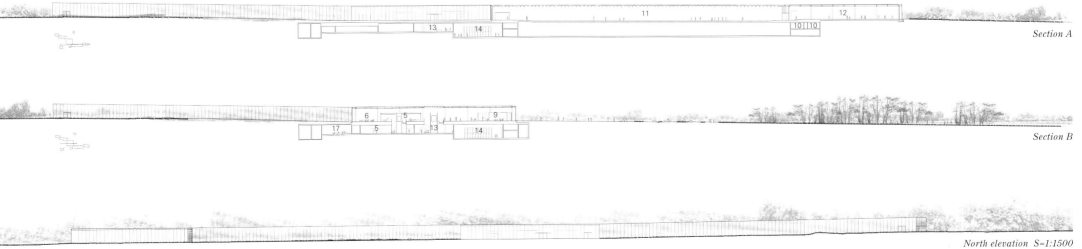

Section A

Section B

North elevation S=1:1500

View of entrance hall from north

Resources center on right

Entrance hall: view toward pique-nique area

Entrance hall

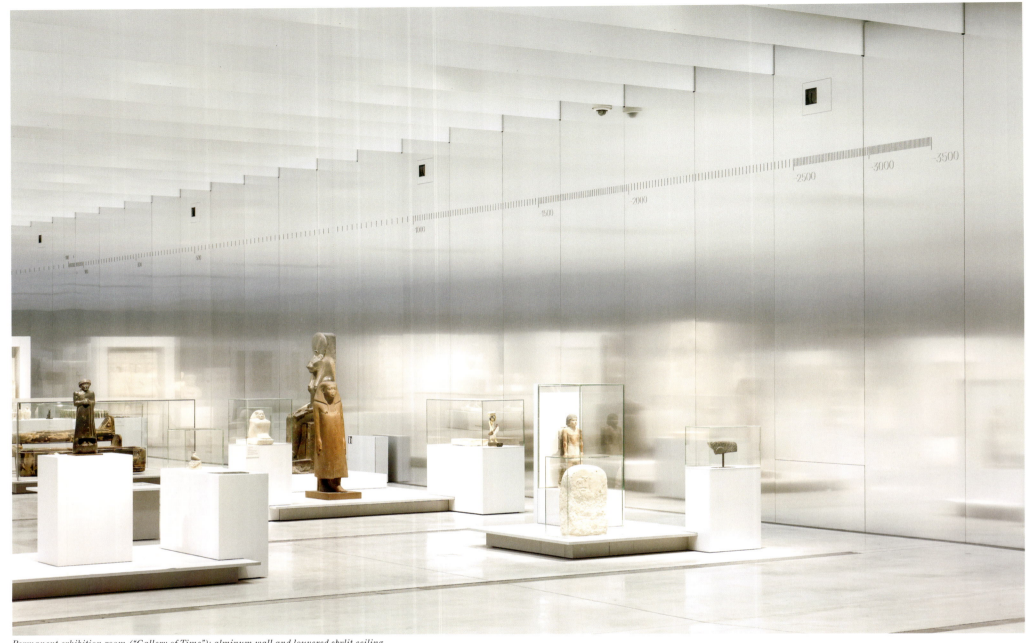
Permanent exhibition room ("Gallery of Time"): aluminum wall and louvered skylit ceiling

Discovery space on first basement

Glass pavilion

Permanent exhibition room ("Gallery of Time")

"Gallery of Time": wall and ceiling

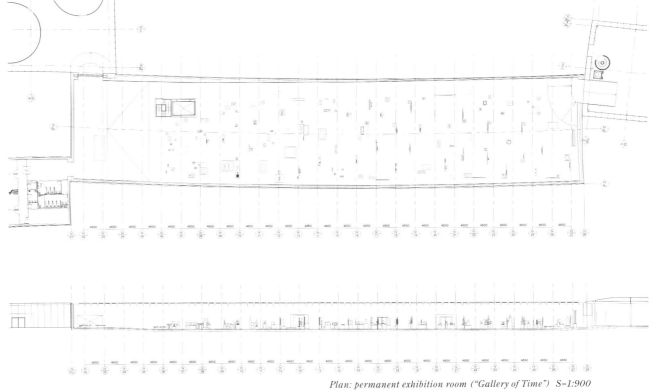

Plan: permanent exhibition room ("Gallery of Time")   S=1:900

Garden & House
Japan
2006–11

Office of Ryue Nishizawa

It is a residence/office that is planned in the high density area having high-rise residence and office buildings. Two women who works on an editorial job wanted to work and live in the historical city environment. Concrete demand condition was an office, shared living space, individual room, guest room, bathroom and so on. We felt that this is a program in the middle of the function such as an office, a residence or a dormitory. The site had 8 m x 4 m extremely small rectangular shape and three sides of the site were surrounded by over 30 m-high gigantic buildings without set back, which was a space like a bottom of the valley in between the gigantic buildings.

We wonder if we could design a building without walls because the width of the structure was subtract out of narrow site width if we built it by making structure walls as usual, and we felt the building would be very narrow. The final composition we selected is the plan that there are no walls, only horizontal slabs are vertically accumulated and a set of garden and room is arranged on each floor. We thought it makes open life that every room on each floor such as living room, private room, and bathroom has an exclusive garden to feel wind, to read or to enjoy the evening time. We can arrange rooms and gardens freely and distinctive relationship between rooms and gardens could be possible since rooms on each floor are smaller than slabs. We thought to design a transparent building without walls as a whole that we could feel maximally a bright environment in the dark site condition and happily and comfortably the special condition that we live in the center of the city as possible.

Downward view: stacked garden

West elevation facing street

Downward view of second floor

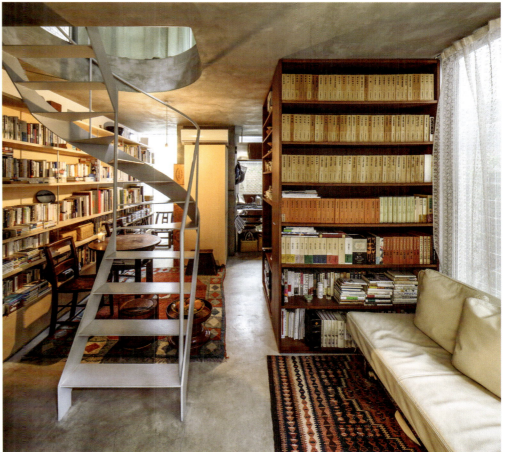

Space 1: view from entrance

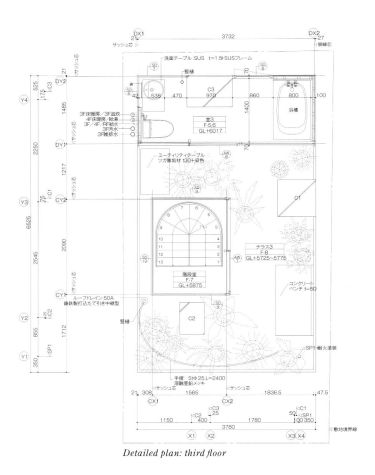

Detailed plan: third floor

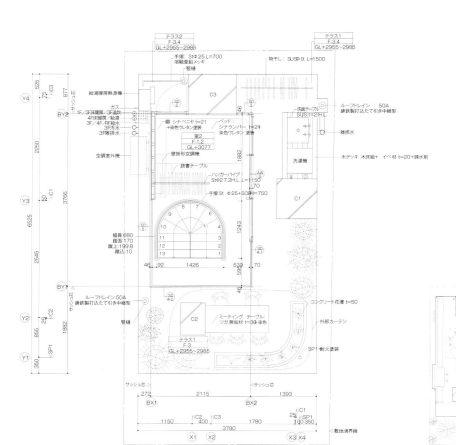

Detailed plan: second floor S=1:80

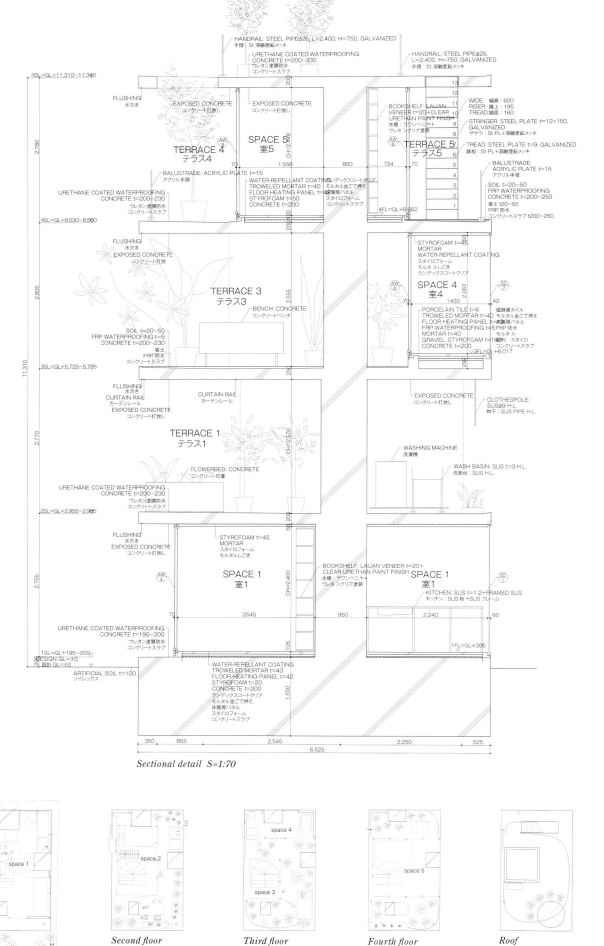

Sectional detail S=1:70

Second floor *Third floor* *Fourth floor* *Roof*

First floor S=1:200

Second floor: view toward terrace from space 2

Space 4 on third floor

East elevation

Space 5 on fourth floor

Garden & House

高層マンションやオフィスビルが多く建ち並ぶ高密度な街区に計画されている，住居兼オフィスである。住まい手は編集関係の仕事をしている女性2人で，歴史を持つ都市環境の中で仕事をしたり生活をしたりということを望まれた。具体的な要求条件としては，オフィス，共同リビングスペース，各個室，ゲストルーム，浴室などであった。オフィスのような，住居のような，もしくは寮のような，いろいろな用途の中間のようなプログラムであると感じた。敷地は8m×4mと極めて小さい長方形であり，左右と対面の敷地には高さ30mを越すたいへん巨大なビルがセットバックなしに建ち並んでいて，この敷地は巨大ビルに挟まれたまさに谷底のような空間であった。

普通に構造壁をつくって建物を考えると，狭い敷地幅員から構造の厚み分がさらに差し引かれて，室内がたいへん狭くなると感じたので，壁がない建物をつくれないかと考えた。最終的に選んだ構成は，各階壁なしのまま，水平スラブだけが垂直に積層されていき，各階に庭と個室がセットで配されるというものだ。各階の室はリビングだったり，各人のプライベートな室であったり，浴室であったりするが，そのどれもが専用の庭を持ち，屋外に出て風を感じたり，読書をしたり夕涼みをしたりといった，開放的な生活ができるように考えた。各階の室はどれもスラブの大きさよりも小さいために，部屋と庭を自由な形で取ることができ，階によって異なる部屋と庭の関係をつくることが可能となった。全体として壁のない透明な建物であり，暗い敷地条件の中でも最大限に明るい環境を感じられるように，また町の中心に住むという特別な状況をなるべく楽しく快適に感じることができるようにと考えて設計している。

Vitra Factory
Weil am Rhein, Germany
2006–12

SANAA

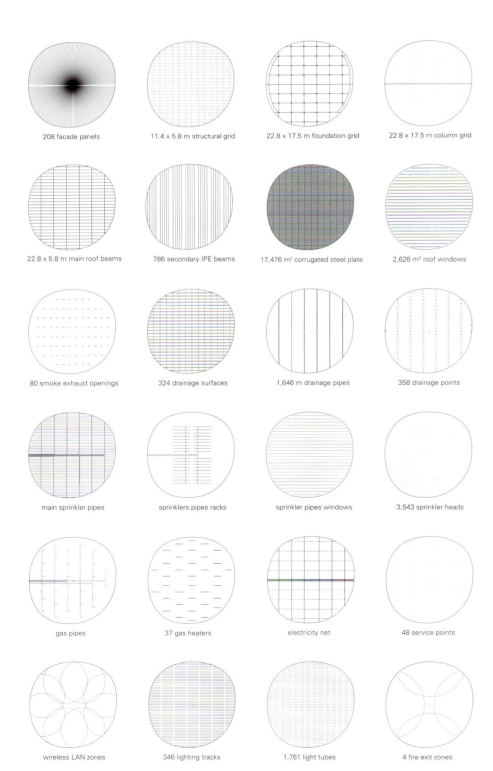

Diagrams

The Weil am Rhein, located in southern Germany facing the border with Switzerland, is the main campus of Vitra, a global manufacturer of designer furniture.

Frank O. Gehry, Zaha Hadid, Tadao Ando, Herzog & de Meuron, Álvaro Siza, Nicholas Grimshaw and other architects have previously been invited by Vitra to design the buildings on the campus grounds. SANAA was entrusted with the design for the furniture assembly and storage locations newly built on the Vitra Campus.

We proposed a rounded, but not quite circular, building as an alternative to a box-shaped factory for the Vitra Campus. This structure facilitates approaches from all directions without conceptualizing its front or back.

The shape and positioning of the building relates to the flow of transport that occurs on the site. This structure is more of an assembly facility, where components are gathered, assembled then brought to separate locations, rather than merely a production facility. It stands as a crossing point within the entire process, and a place where things are constantly moving in and out. We thought that a hub-like circular shape where vehicles would be circulating around the building was befitting based on that point as well.

Although it has a free-form exterior, the building interior has an extremely efficient systemized layout. Storage shelves and transported goods are placed in a variety of areas according to a rigorous logistics concept. The factory space has a wide 22.8 m x 17.5 m span through a delicate steel structure using columns that are 9 m high. This structure is optimized by using the stability provided by arc-shaped walls made from reinforced concrete. Natural light penetrates the space through linear skylights and openings cut into the exterior walls; light is further scattered throughout the space by the white surfaces of the structure. This creates the desired bright, relaxing working environment.

Random waveform panels are designed specifically to wrap around the structure like a curtain. This is to softly conceal indoor activities within the rooms, creating impressive views from their interstitial spaces. Random waves created by combining the front and back of three different corrugated panel types provide a vertical rhythm to the facade, while providing a special impression of the exterior view created using industrial products. The panel surfaces are made in brilliant white which reflect the surrounding trees and buildings so that the massive facility seems to dissolve into its surroundings.

The scale of the building for this project consisted of a total area of 30,535 m², with the desire that it be built only to a maximum two stories based on site regulations. Thus, half of the structure was built on vacant land, and the other half was constructed after tearing down the existing facility. The two divided buildings were wrapped in waveform panels, ultimately forming a single architecture.

South view

Plan S=1:1000

Site plan

1 Vitra Design Museum - Frank Gehry 1989
2 Conference Pavilion - Tadao Ando 1993
3 Dome - Buckminster Fuller 1975/2000
4 Factory Building - Frank Gehry 1989
5 Factory Building - Nicolas Grimshaw 1981/1983
6 Factory Building - Alvaro Siza 1994
7 Fire Station - Zaha Hadid 1993
8 Petrol Station - Jean Prouve 1953/2003
9 Factory Building - SANAA 2012
10 VitraHaus - Herzog & de Meuron 2009

1 HALL A
2 HALL B
3 HALL C
4 HALL D
5 WORKSHOP
6 OFFICE
7 DOCK
8 REST SPACE

ヴィトラ・ファクトリー

ドイツ南部，スイスとの国境に面するヴァイル・アム・ラインに，デザイン家具の世界的な生産者VITRAのメインキャンパスがある。これまでに，ヴィトラはキャンパス内の建物のデザインのために，フランク・O・ゲーリー，ザハ・ハディド，安藤忠雄，ヘルツォーク＆ド・ムーロン，アルヴァロ・シザ，ニコラス・グリムショウなどの建築家を招待した。SANAAは，このヴィトラ・キャンパスに新しく建つ，家具の組み立てと保管用の建物の設計を任された。

我々は，ヴィトラ・キャンパスでは一般的な四角い工場の代案として，丸い建物を提案した。この建物は表，裏という概念がなく，全ての方向からのアプローチをうながしている。

建物の形と位置は，敷地で行われる輸送の流れに関連している。この建物は，生産工場というより，アッセンブリー工場で，部品を集めてきてここで組み立て，また別の場所に持って行く。全体行程の中の通過地点であり，搬出入が激しい場所となる。その点からも，ハブ的に車が周りをぐるぐる回れるような円形がふさわしいと考えた。

建物の外形は自由でありながら，内部のレイアウトは効率よく組織化されている。様々なエリアに保管棚と輸送品が厳格な物流概念に基づいて設置されている。工場空間は，9mの高さの柱により，22.8m×17.5mのワイドスパンが，繊細な鉄骨構造で組み立てられた。この構造は，鉄筋コンクリートによる円弧状の外壁が持つ安定性を利用して，最適化されている。多数のライン状のルーフライトと外壁の開口を通して，空間に自然光が入り込み，白く塗られた構造体によって空間全体に放散される。それによって，求められていた，明るく心地よい作業環境をつくり出す。

特別にデザインされたランダムな波形パネルが，建物をカーテンのように包んでいる。それは，室内の活動をやわらかく隠したり，その隙間から印象的に見えるようにする。3種類のコルゲート・パネルの表裏を組み合わせてつくられるランダムな波長は，ファサードに垂直のリズムを与えると同時に，インダストリアル・プロダクツでつくられた外観に，特別な印象を与える。パネルの表面は，光沢のある白となっていて，周辺の木や建物を反射し，巨大な工場を周辺に溶け込むようにしている。

このプロジェクトの建物の規模は，延べ面積30,535m²であり，敷地の制約から二段階で建てることが求められた。そこで，まず半分を空地につくり，残り半分は既存工場を取り壊した後に建設した。分かれて建った2棟を，波形パネルが包んで，最終的に一つの建築とした。

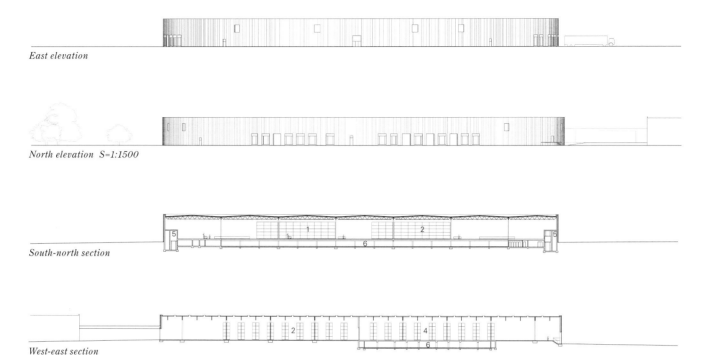

1 HALL A
2 HALL B
3 HALL C
4 HALL D
5 DOCK
6 PARKING

East elevation

North elevation S=1:1500

South-north section

West-east section

Corridor connecting to factory building designed by Nicolas Grimshaw

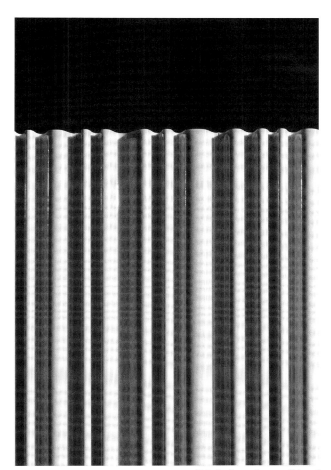

Detail of waveform wall panel

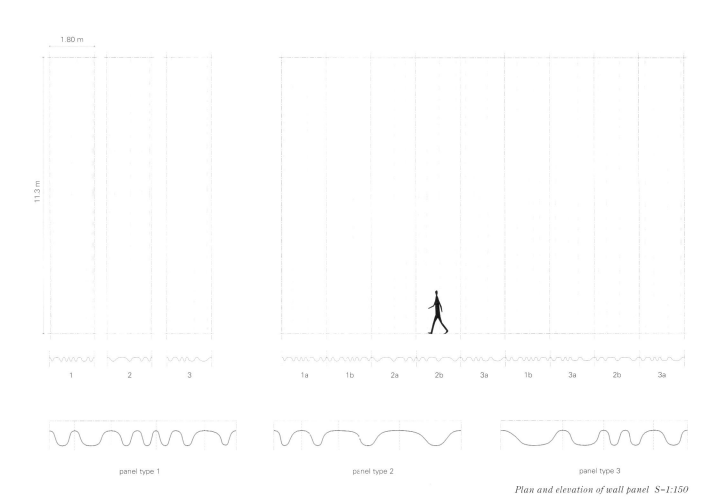

Plan and elevation of wall panel S=1:150

Office

Hall

*Hiroshi Senju Museum
Karuizawa
Karuizawa, Kitasaku-gun,
Nagano, Japan
2007–11*

Office of Ryue Nishizawa

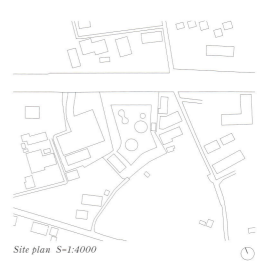

Site plan S=1:4000

When I was first approached by Mr. Senju, he asked me if it would be possible to think about a bright and open art museum unlike any other that has existed until now. It would be a bright and open space in which people would be able to experience Mr. Senju's world of artistic works, and at the same time be able to gather and leisurely relax in their own time.

The structure of the building is a singular space designed as a gently sloping landscape that conforms to the contours of the existing land. While regulating light with deeply extending the eaves, silver screens and UV cut glass, views of the local greenery, sunlight and scenery slowly fill the room, fusing and harmonizing Mr. Senju's art with the natural beauty of Karuizawa. Visitors can walk about as though strolling through the forest, engage with Mr. Senju's artworks, and appreciate the rich natural setting as they relax on the furniture placed throughout the space. The aim was to create an open space that feels simultaneously like a garden and a private living room.

◁ *View from southwest* *Glazed wall on west*

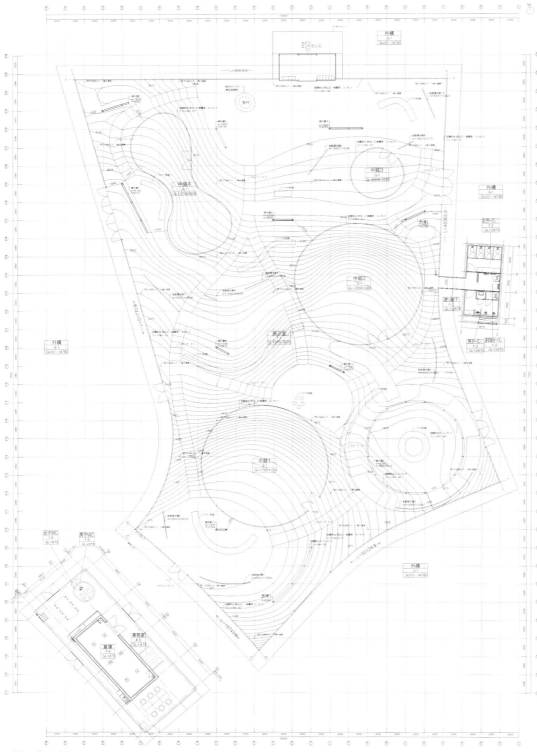

Plan S=1:400

Courtyard 4: wall for painting on left

軽井沢千住博美術館

最初に千住さんに声をかけていただいた時に，明るく開放的な，今までなかったような美術館を考えられないか，というお話を頂きました。明るい空間の中で，人々が千住さんの作品世界を体験でき，また同時に，集まってくつろいだり，自分の時間を過ごせたりできる空間です。

建物の構成は，既存の敷地地形にあわせて緩やかに傾斜していく，ランドスケープのような一室空間です。深く軒を出して，シルバースクリーンとUVカットガラスによって光を制御しながらも，軽井沢の風景や緑，光が室内に柔らかく入ってきて，軽井沢の自然と千住さんの芸術が，融合し調和します。人々は森の中を歩くようにいろいろな場をめぐり，各所に配された家具でくつろぎながら，千住さんの作品と対話したり，豊かな自然を感じたりすることができます。公園でもあり，同時にプライベートなリビングでもあるような，開かれた空間を目指しました。

Gallery: courtyard 1 on left

Garden view through translucent screen

The Fall Room in new wing added at 2013

Gallery with undulated floor and roof: view from main entrance

Courtyard 4

◁ *Gallery*

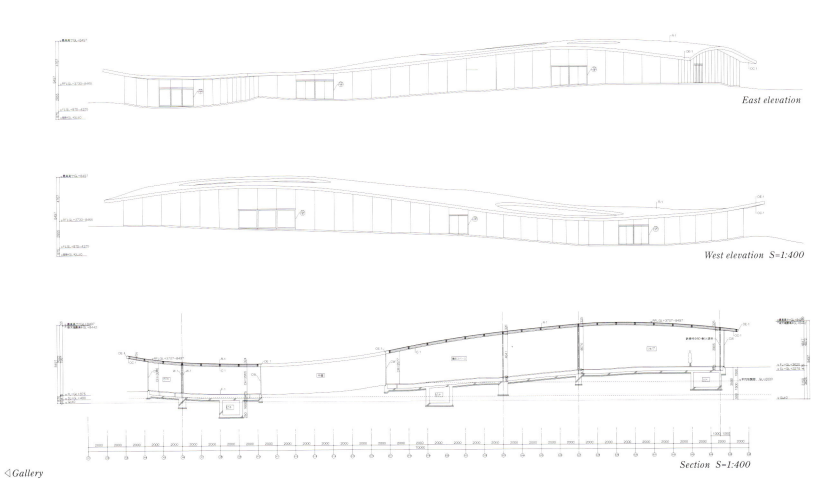

East elevation

West elevation S=1:400

Section S=1:400

Paris Apartments
Paris, France
2007–18

SANAA

It is a social housing complex that is now under costruction in Paris 16th district. The site is located in the place where filled with green between the city area and Bois de Boulogne, and four volumes that draws curves are arranged as if they are floating on the pilotis of the ground level. The ground is opened for residents, the outdoor space is created by upheaval topology, trees and shape of buildings. The exterior wall of buildings are made from the stucco and smooth curve is drawn there. A lots of windows are arranged and opened in various direction changing by the life of residents. Although the interior space is divided in simple grid system, each area changes direction and distance to the outside environment such as city, forest and courtyard by almost all the room facing curved circumference surface. By having a relationship with the circumference of the environment, transparency that softly connects the traditional town and calm forest is thought to be created in the entire building at the same time each interior space has a distinctive atmosphere.

Overall view

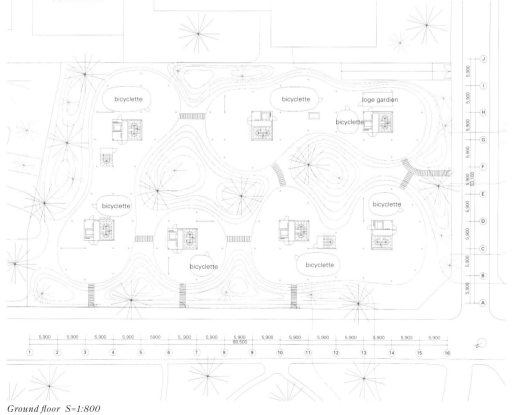
Ground floor S=1:800

Typical floor

Ground level: pilotis

Interior

Under construction

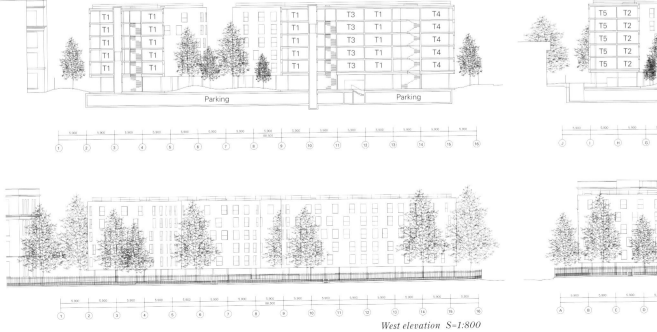

West elevation S=1:800

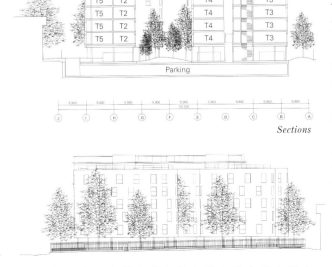

Sections

South elevation

パリ16区の公営集合住宅

パリ16区に建設中の公営集合住宅である。敷地は市街地とブローニュの森の間に位置する緑溢れた場所にあり，そこに曲線を描いたヴォリュームが四つ，1階のピロティを介して浮かぶように配置されている。地上は住民のために開放され，隆起した自然の地形と木々，建物の形状によって屋外空間がつくり出されている。建物の外壁はスタッコでつくられ，スムーズなカーブを描いている。そこに幾つもの窓が開き，居住者の生活でその表情を変えながら全方向に開かれる。内部はシンプルなグリッドで分割されるが，そのほぼ全ての部屋が曲面の外周壁に面することで，都市や森，中庭などの外部環境に対して場所ごとに向きや距離を変える。このように周辺環境と関係することで，それぞれの室内が特徴的な雰囲気を持つとともに，建物全体でも伝統的な街並みと穏やかな森とを緩やかに繋ぐような透明感が生まれればと考えている。

*Shibaura Office
(Shibaura House)
Tokyo, Japan
2008–11*

Kazuyo Sejima & Associates

This is a mid-rise building located in Tokyo's coastal areas on a large road. It will become the headquarters of a company involved in the business of printing, advertisement, and graphic design. The client requested for a space that joined together not just their own office, but also a shared office space for staff from other companies with whom they frequently collaborate, a hall for lectures and workshops, and a cafe that is open to the local community.

Rather than a simple office building that stacks together floors with identical floor plan, we aimed for a space with varied, three-dimensional relationships, with each floor having a distinct character and configuration while also maintaining a continuous line of sight and experience toward the proximate floors and city.

The streets surrounding the site are lined with moderately scaled buildings of various heights that for the most part fill the entirety of their plots. The site's condition was that the building can be five stories tall according to the floor area ratio. Considering the size of the surrounding buildings and the property's relationship to the street, a building that has a slightly set-back footprint and a height of around 30 m, which is slightly taller than the neighboring building, was thought to best fit the cityscape. Within these dimensions, plans with the same outline were divided according to function, with ceilings raised or lowered to create different heights. The space was constructed so that, while having this multitude of depths, it still had a sense of continuity and connection. Furthermore, by providing an semi-outdoor terrace covered in mesh, we tried to create a more open relationship with the surrounding environment.

A cafe that is like a park close to the city, a tall open-plan office, a shared office surrounded by the terrace, and a large top-floor foyer with views of the city… multiple spaces connect together in a smooth sequence. Beyond the spaces between the layers of slabs, one can catch glimpses of the town and sky. Inside, office workers, artists drawing in workshops, people taking breaks on the terrace, and locals in the cafe all carry out their various enterprises as they feel and experience the presence of each other and their surroundings. As an office building that opens up to the community, various interactions are born from this space, creating new city landscapes.

View from first floor mezzanine: second floor above and first floor below

◁ *South elevation* *Gallery/cafe open to public on first floor*

芝浦のオフィス (SHIBAURA HOUSE)
東京湾岸の大通り沿いに建つ, 印刷製版と広告のデザインや画像制作などを行う会社の拠点となるビルである. 自社のオフィスだけではなく, 共同作業を行うことの多い外部の企業の人やデザイナーの人たちが自由に使えるシェアオフィス, レクチャーやワークショップなどを行うことができるホール, 地域の人たちが気軽に立ち寄ることのできるカフェなどが求められ, それらの場所が全体でひと繋がりに感じられることが望まれた.

私たちは, 単に同一平面のフロアが積層されるオフィスビルではなく, フロアごとに異なる性格と形状を持ちつつ, 上下階や街に対して視線や体験が連続していくような, 多様で立体的な関係性を持つ空間を目指した.

敷地周辺には, 中規模のオフィスビルがほぼ敷地いっぱいの建築面積でいろいろな高さで建ち並んでいる. 5階まで建てることができる容積率の条件の中, 周囲の建物の大きさや通りとの関係から, 敷地の広さから少しだけセットバックしたフットプリントで隣よりも少し高い30m程度の高さの建物が街並みに合うように思われた. そのヴォリュームの中で, 同じ輪郭の平面をそれぞれの機能に合わせて分割し, それらを様々な天井高を持つように上下させ, 空間がいろいろな距離感を持ちながら連続していくような構成とした. さらにメッシュで覆われた半外部空間のテラスをつくることで, 周辺環境に対してより開放的な関係をつくり出そうとした.

街に近い公園のようなカフェ, 天井高の高い開放的なオフィス, テラスに囲まれたシェアオフィス, 街を一望できる最上階のホールなどの空間が緩やかに繋がっていく. スラブとスラブの重なりの間の向こうには, 街の風景や空が見えたりする. そのような中で, 働く人, ワークショップで絵を描く人, テラスで休憩する人, カフェでおしゃべりする地域の人など, それぞれがお互いのことや周辺の街を感じながら様々な活動が行われていく. 街に開かれたオフィスビルとしていろいろな展開が生まれ, 街の中での新しい風景となっていく.

Night view from east

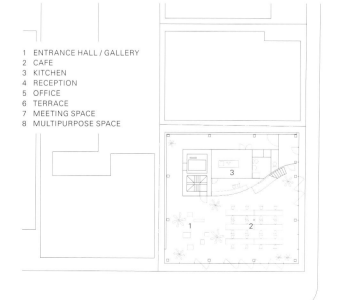
First floor S=1:400

1 ENTRANCE HALL / GALLERY
2 CAFE
3 KITCHEN
4 RECEPTION
5 OFFICE
6 TERRACE
7 MEETING SPACE
8 MULTIPURPOSE SPACE

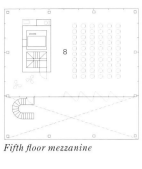
Fifth floor mezzanine

Fifth floor

Fourth floor

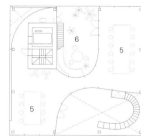
Third floor

Second floor

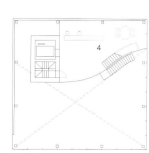
First floor mezzanine

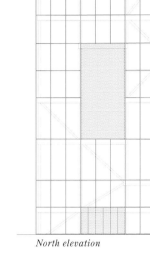
North elevation   *West elevation*

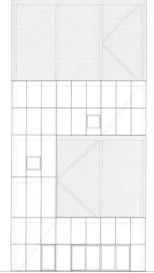
South elevation S=1:400   *East elevation*

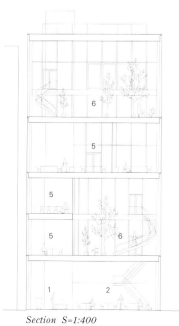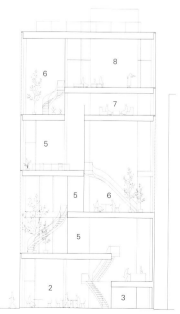
Section S=1:400

50

Office on fourth floor

Terrace on third floor: fourth and fifth floor above

Terrace on second floor

Office on third floor

Sumida Hokusai Museum
Tokyo, Japan
2009–16

Kazuyo Sejima & Associates

◁ Overall view from north facing park

South view over elevated train tracks

West elevation

The museum displays and stores a collection of Hokusai Katsushika who spent most of his life in Sumida-Ku and was born in the land of Sumida in the Edo era. The museum aims to be the center of civic life, and revitalize the region by also housing research and education facilities.

The site is located in a park that occupies a single city block close to Ryogoku station, and the museum can be approached from four different directions. Public programs such as the entrance hall, library, and lecture rooms occupy the first floor of the building. Offices and storage on the second floor, permanent and temporary exhibition rooms on the third and fourth floor and supportive spaces such as toilets and mechanical rooms underground.

We wanted to respect the scale of the surrounding streets where both large and small sized buildings stand. Rather than creating one large building, we decided to assemble several volumes of different sizes and gently gather them around each other in order to unify the surrounding landscape with the museum.

The Various 'slits' created between the volumes become an approach space to welcome people from all directions on the ground floor, and become an opening that becomes a viewing spot of the Tokyo Sky Tree far away on the upper floors. These slits offer a glimpse of internal activities creating a relationship with the surrounding environment, in a building where most of the building has opaque walls in order to protect the artwork and artefacts inside.

The exterior wall are slanted in order to connect the different sized plans on each floor, and is finished with aluminium panels in order to softly reflect the surrounding greenery and sky. Much like Hokusai's paintings which are said to have many perspectives in a single painting, we hope the surrounding landscape augmented in many angles on the walls become a reconstructed painting of its own.

Outside passage on east ▷

Outside passage: view toward entrance hall

View toward library from southwest

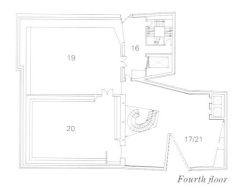
Fourth floor

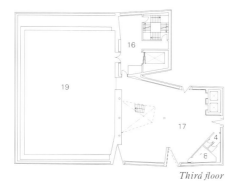
Third floor

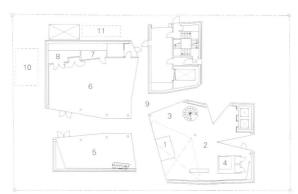
Second floor

First floor S=1:600

Basement

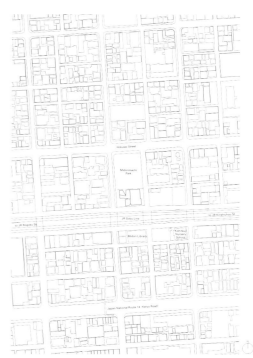
Site plan S=1:6000

1 WINDBREAK
2 ENTRANCE HALL
3 MUSEUM SHOP
4 WC
5 LIBRARY
6 LECTURE ROOM
7 ANTE ROOM
8 STORAGE
9 OUTSIDE PASSAGE
10 PARKING
11 BICYCLE PARKING
12 OFFICE
13 MUSEUM DIRECTOR'S OFFICE
14 RECEPTION ROOM
15 ARCHIVE SPACE
16 ELEVATOR HALL
17 FOYER
18 EXHIBITION SPARE ROOM
19 TEMPORARY EXHIBITION ROOM
20 PERMANENT EXHIBITION ROOM
21 VIEW LOUNGE
22 NURSING ROOM
23 MECHANICAL
24 DRY AREA
25 HEAT STORAGE TANK
26 ELEVATOR FOR LOADING

Office on second floor

Library on first floor

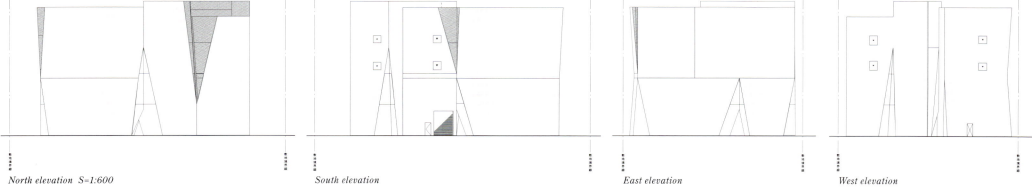

North elevation S=1:600   *South elevation*   *East elevation*   *West elevation*

Entrance hall: looking south

1 WINDBREAK
2 ENTRANCE HALL
3 MUSEUM SHOP
4 WC
5 LIBRARY
6 LECTURE ROOM
7 ANTE ROOM
8 STORAGE
9 OUTSIDE PASSAGE
10 PARKING
11 BICYCLE PARKING
12 OFFICE
13 MUSEUM DIRECTOR'S OFFICE
14 RECEPTION ROOM
15 ARCHIVE SPACE
16 ELEVATOR HALL
17 FOYER
18 EXHIBITION SPARE ROOM
19 TEMPORARY EXHIBITION ROOM
20 PERMANENT EXHIBITION ROOM
21 VIEW LOUNGE
22 NURSING ROOM
23 MECHANICAL
24 DRY AREA
25 HEAT STORAGE TANK
26 ELEVATOR FOR LOADING

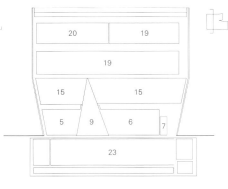
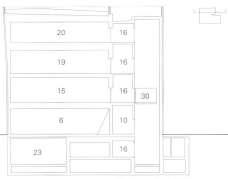

Sections S=1:600

Foyer on third floor. Exhibition "Sejima Kazuyo SANAA × HOKUSAI"

Foyer: view lounge on fourth floor. Exhibition "Sejima Kazuyo SANAA × HOKUSAI"

すみだ北斎美術館

江戸時代に墨田の地に生まれ，その生涯のほとんどを墨田区で過ごした葛飾北斎のコレクションを保存・展示すると同時に，研究や教育普及，さらに地域活性化の拠点として計画された美術館である。

敷地は両国駅からほど近い下町の中にある街区一つ分の小さな公園の中で，4方向どこからでもアプローチすることができる。階構成は，1階にエントランスホール，図書室，講座室といったパブリックなプログラム，2階に事務室や収蔵スペース，3・4階に常設・企画展示室，地下にトイレや機械室などの支援的なプログラムとなっている。

私たちはまず，大小様々な大きさの建物が建ち並ぶ周辺の街並とスケールを合わせるように，建物を大きな一棟ではなく，幾つかの大きさのヴォリュームが緩やかに集まって，周囲の街並と一体的に表れる美術館をつくろうと考えた。

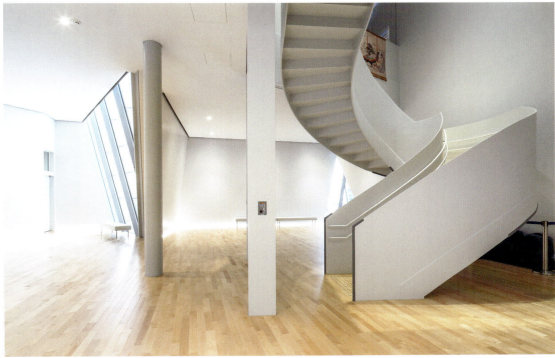

Foyer on third floor

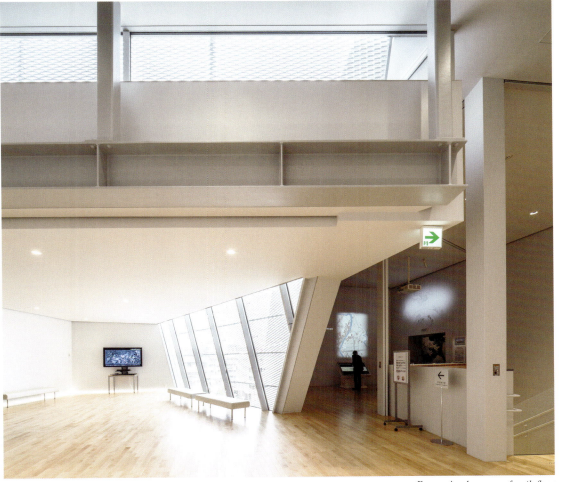

Foyer: view lounge on fourth floor

　そうして集まったヴォリュームの間に生まれる様々なスリットは，例えば地上では四方から人々を迎え入れるアプローチ空間となったり，また上階では遠く東京スカイツリーを望む開口部となったりする。内部の活動が垣間見えるこれらのスリットは，文化財の展示・保護という必要性能から大部分を不透明な外壁で囲われた建物に，周辺の環境との関係を生み出している。

　外壁は，階ごとに違う平面を繋ぐため斜めの壁となっており，公園の緑や周囲の建物や空など，周りの風景が淡く柔らかく映り込むアルミパネルで仕上げられている。北斎の絵の面白さの一つとして，一つの絵にいろいろなパースが同時に描かれているという点があると思われるが，この建物でも，色々な角度に傾けられた壁に映り込む様々な風景が，一つの立面として再構成されることで，そこに新しい絵が生まれたらと期待している。

Shakujii Apartments
Tokyo, Japan
2009–11

SANAA

Overall view from southeast

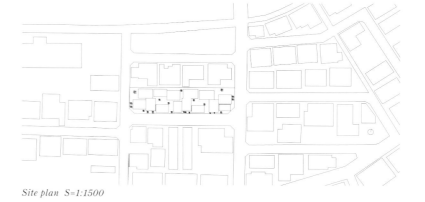
Site plan S=1:1500

Third floor

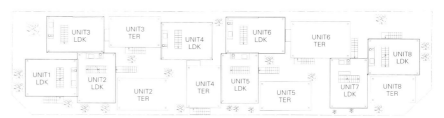
Second floor

First floor S=1:400

LDK LIVING/DINING/KITCHEN
BR   BEDROOM
BTH BATHROOM
TER TERRACE
GRG GARAGE

The project is an eight-unit, row house-style apartment complex located in a quiet residential district lined with low-rise homes. Instead of building an extensive volume within a neighborhood of single-family houses, the apartment is designed by slightly shifting room-sized volumes on the horizontal and vertical axis. Each volume is simply structured using columns and slabs of different levels. The apartment consists of roofed terraces and parking lots, and a host of uniquely designed units: some expand horizontally, some have rooms that continue vertically, and some are half underground with a relaxing ambience. By incorporating the gardens, terraces, and parking spaces into the arrangement of the apartment units, the entire complex becomes a highly concentrated building with varying depths. The spaces throughout the complex are characterized by a bright and airy ambience, as if the outdoors have been mixed into the indoors.

Shifts in small scales create variations in the relationships between not only the rooms themselves, but between outdoors and indoors, and among the inhabitants. An accumulation of these small, shifting relationships creates a building that is versatile and flexible as a whole. My goal was to create a versatile environment that loosely follows the surrounding scenery, while inspiring various relationships with the neighborhood.

石神井アパートメント

低層な家々が広がる閑静な住宅街に位置する全8世帯の長屋形式の集合住宅である。周囲は戸建てサイズのヴォリュームが建っている中、長大なヴォリュームを避け、部屋サイズのヴォリュームを平面、断面方向に小さくずらしながら配置した。各ヴォリュームは柱とスラブのシンプルな構造を持ち、様々なレベルのスラブを実現し、住戸は平面的に広がった部屋や、断面方向に続く居室、半地下の落ち着いた部屋の他に、屋根付きのテラスや駐車場で構成されている。庭やテラス、駐車場も部屋と一緒に並べることで、高密度だけれども明るく風通しがよく様々な奥行きを持つ建物となり、屋外と屋内が混ざり合ったような空間が建物全体に広がっている。

小さなスケールでのずれが部屋と部屋との関係性だけではなく屋外や屋内との関係性、住む人々の関係性を多様なものとし、それらが集まることによってできる全体としての一つの柔らかな建物のかたちが表れた。周辺の街に様々な関係性をつくり出しながら、街に緩やかに連続しつつ、柔らかな環境がつくり出されることを目指した。

Unit 6

Unit 7: bedroom on basement

Terrace of unit 3

Section a-a' S=1:400   *Section b-b'*

East view from entrance of unit 5

LDK LIVING/DINING/KITCHEN
BR   BEDROOM
BTH BATHROOM
TER TERRACE
GRG GARAGE

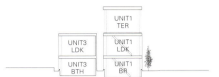

Section c-c'

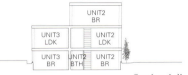

Section d-d'

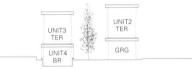

Section e-e'

Section f-f'

Section g-g'

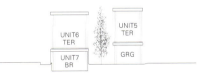

Section h-h'

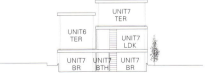

Section i-i'

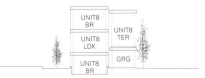

Section j-j'

Soneiji Cemetery Pavilion "Muyuju-rin"
Ichikawa, Chiba, Japan
2009–14

Kazuyo Sejima & Associates

Overall view from west

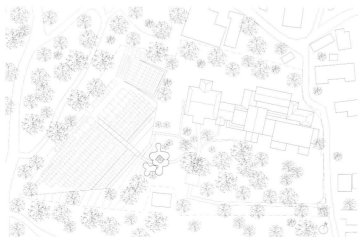

Site plan S=1:2000

The project is an attached facility and *eitai kuyo* (eternal service) grave on the premises of Soneiji, a Buddhist temple located in the city of Ichikawa, Chiba. The chief priest of the temple wished for an *eitai kuyo* grave as a form of a contemporary cemetery, and requested a new landscape design that aligns with the temple's future outlook. We envisioned a rich green environment that continues from the adjacent park into the temple, and a horizontal aluminum canopy that extends along the hill that rises towards the graves. Underneath the canopy is a hall for the *eitai kuyo* grave, as well as a foyer, purification fountain, and terrace. The space also serves as the entrance into the cemetery.

Aluminum alloy is used in the roof, columns and reinforcement braces. The roof, made of 12 mm-thick plates that were welded on-site, is randomly supported by solid 60 and 70 mm-diameter columns. The structure is finished with polished aluminum material, and the walls are 3 mm-thick anodized aluminum.

Since the project also involved creating both an indoor and a half-outdoor resting place in the garden area, we aimed to design a space that naturally blends into the surrounding landscape.

Sunlight and fragments of the surrounding scenery are gently reflected in the surface of the aluminum. We hope that the structure will continue to emanate a bright and transparent ambience into the landscape.

View from north: purification area on right

Hall for cemetery with aluminum walls on left. Path to graves on west

1 ENTRANCE
2 FOYER
3 TERRACE
4 PURIFICATION AREA
5 HALL FOR CEMETERY

Plan S=1:250

Section S=1:200

Hall for cemetery

總寧寺永代供養施設「無憂樹林」

千葉県市川市の總寧寺の境内にある永代供養墓とお寺の付属施設の計画である。ご住職は、現代の新しい墓地の形として永代供養墓を望まれ、また、お寺の将来像を見据えた境内のランドスケープ計画を依頼された。私たちは、隣接する公園から境内へと続く緑豊かな周辺環境と、水平に広がり、墓地へと登っていく起伏に合わせて、アルミの庇を掛ける計画を考えた。庇の下には、永代供養墓を祀るお堂と、ホワイエ、水場、テラスがあり、墓地へと入っていくゲートとしての意味も持っている。

屋根・柱・ブレースにアルミを用いたアルミニウム合金造で、現場溶接した厚さ12mmの屋根プレートを、φ60又はφ70の無垢柱でランダムに支える構造としている。構造の仕上げはアルミ素地の研磨仕上げで、外壁は厚さ3mmのアルミプレートのアルマイト仕上げとしている。

それほど大きくないとはいえ、インテリアのスペースと休憩等の半屋外スペースを庭の中に計画するため、まわりの風景になるだけ自然に溶け込むようなものをつくりたいと考えた。

アルミは柔らかく周りの風景と光を反射する。いつ訪れても明るく、透明な風景をつくり出す建築であってほしいと願っている。

*United Church of Christ in
Japan, Ikuta Church
Kawasaki, Kanagawa,
Japan
2009–14*

Office of Ryue Nishizawa

◁ *Overall view from northeast* *Night view of entrance*

This project was for the reconstruction of an old Protestant church in a residential area in Ikuta, Kanagawa Prefecture.

In our plans we were requested to provide room for a chapel, large assembly hall, office space, pastor's room, garden and parking lot. Later on, it became clear that the parking lot would need to be maximized as much as possible; with this, the requirement then was to make sure that multiple functions were included inside a two-story building.

The new church contains an assembly hall, entrance area and office on the first floor, and a chapel, pastor's room and conference room on the second floor. In terms of arrangement, we decided to build the church on the southern half of the site, on what used to be the garden. This caused the locations of the church and garden to be completely reversed, with the northern side that contained the old church now acting as the garden area, entrance and parking lot.

Due to the structure of the building, the very large spaces of the assembly hall and chapel needed to be positioned one above another, which would cause the building to become far too large if we stacked them normally. Instead, we pitched the roof to create low hanging eaves, and faintly divided the entire building into three segments to curb the overall scale. In this way, we hoped to create an exterior that did not overwhelm the surrounding residential area. The three segmented areas have mismatched shapes due to differences in their spatial scales, indoor functions, and relations to their surroundings. The chapel, for example, has a symmetrical pitched gable roof over its central altar. We had the gable of this room face east towards the rising sun so that sunlight filters through the opening at the central upper area of the roof. To provide a smooth approach from the road through the garden and into the church interior, we angled the roof of the entrance so that it faces the road, and installed a large sliding door that can remain open at all times. The open space of the assembly hall merges seamlessly into the neighborhood grounds; it was designed so that the goings-on of people inside the church could be seen and appreciated from outside as well. Thus we devised various ways to create a sense of continuity between the interior and exterior of the architecture, as well as a sense of harmony with the surrounding residential area. We expect that both the building and garden will be used by various people as an open place much like a public park, as befitting of a place of worship.

Site plan S=1:2500

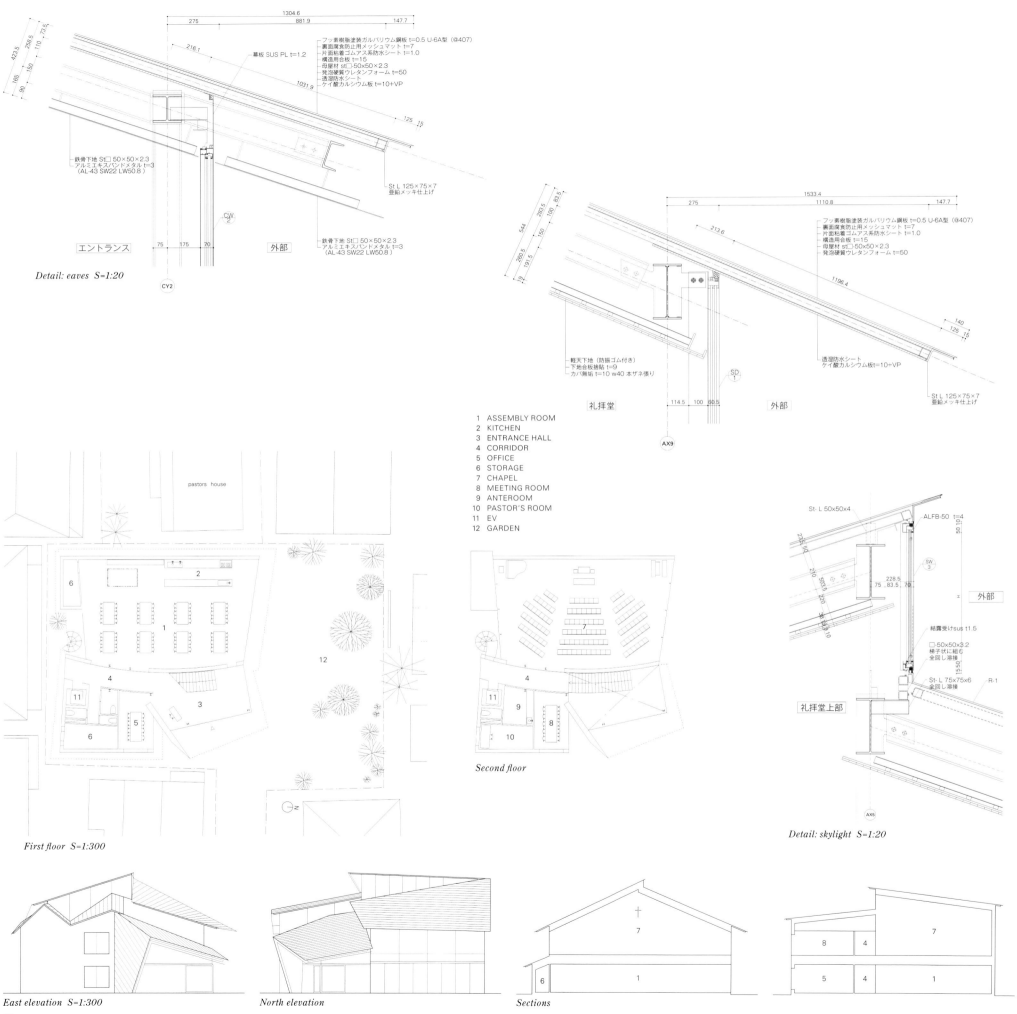

Detail: eaves S=1:20

1 ASSEMBLY ROOM
2 KITCHEN
3 ENTRANCE HALL
4 CORRIDOR
5 OFFICE
6 STORAGE
7 CHAPEL
8 MEETING ROOM
9 ANTEROOM
10 PASTOR'S ROOM
11 EV
12 GARDEN

First floor S=1:300

Second floor

Detail: skylight S=1:20

East elevation S=1:300

North elevation

Sections

Night view of north elevation

Meeting room on first floor

日本キリスト教団 生田教会
神奈川県生田の住宅地に建つ，プロテスタント教会のプロジェクトである。

この計画は，旧会堂の建て替え計画で，要望として，礼拝堂のほか，大きな集会室，事務室，牧師室，庭，駐車場用地などが求められた。その後，駐車場の用地を最大限確保したいという要望から，諸機能を2階建てに納めることが与件となった。新しい会堂は，1階に集会室とエントランス，事務室，2階に礼拝堂と牧師室，会議室を持つ。配置としては，かつて庭であった南半分の場所に建つこととなった。その結果，旧会堂が建っていた北側がアプローチと駐車場を兼ねた庭となって，会堂と庭の関係が反転する配置となった。

建物の構成上，集会室と礼拝堂という二つの大空間を積層する必要があり，それらを普通に積むとたいへん大きくなるので，ここでは屋根傾斜をつけて軒高を低くして，また建物全体を柔らかく三つの棟屋に分けてスケールを抑えて，住宅地を圧倒しない佇まいを目指した。分節された三つの棟屋は，その空間規模や室内機能，周囲との関係などから，各々違う形となった。例えば礼拝堂は，聖壇を中心とした対称的切妻勾配屋根の室であり，妻側を東に向けて朝日を取り込むとともに，屋根中央を切り開いて上方から光を取り入れる形とした。エントランスは，道路，庭，室内というアプローチをスムーズなものにするために，エントランス棟屋全体の角度を振って，道路へ正面する形とし，常に開かれうるような大きな引き戸を設けた。集会室は，外と地続きの開かれた空間で，人々の活動や交流が外からも感じられる空間とした。そのように様々なやり方で建築内外の連続感，住宅地との調和を考えた。建物も庭も，これからいろいろな人に使われて教会の活動に合った開放的で公園のような場所になっていくことを期待している。

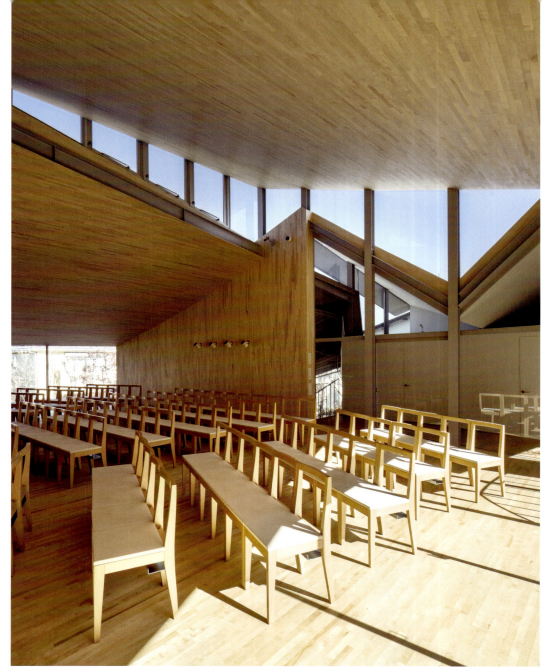
Chapel: looking toward entrance

Entrance

Chapel: looking south

*Tsuchihashi House
Tokyo, Japan
2009–11*

Kazuyo Sejima & Associates

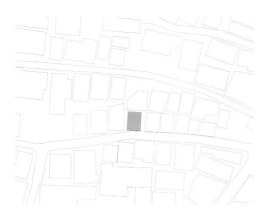

The project is a residence for a couple and two children, built in a crowded residential district where old blocks of land are left. The client desired a house that is fun to live and brings many discoveries. Although the site was a small plot of land surrounded by neighboring houses, it had peaceful atmosphere. Therefore, we thought of a shape that takes in the calmness to interior and extends itself to the limit of the site.

We made big openings at shifting locations in many floors and stacked them in the same height that gives unifying sense without a break. On each floor we placed from bottom a living room, a dining room, wet area with a terrace, a bedroom and a room-like rooftop on top. While every room owns independent place, the openings of floors blur the outline and create a string of space. It makes various relationships in the residence.

We intended the terrace on the bathroom floor to give stretch to the floor, but also, aiming at continuing to the lower dining room, a part of the terrace can be seen from the bedroom and the rooftop and is connected to the adjoining road through interior space. Every place has diverse connections to others. No matter where you are, you will feel the extent toward the whole. The space is open and is unimaginable from the smallness of the plot of land.

In order to compose the uncluttered space, we selected 50 mm x 100 mm section columns, 12 mm thick flat bar braces and floors made of 3.2 mm thick steel plates and 25 mm thick keystone plate. Structural elements emerge in a furniture scale and we targeted that the whole is united in light impression.

There is a time when things afar and things in close coexist. Sometimes they exist separately and other times they are continuous. We hope that the patterns are produced numerously and the space always offers new discoveries.

Evening view

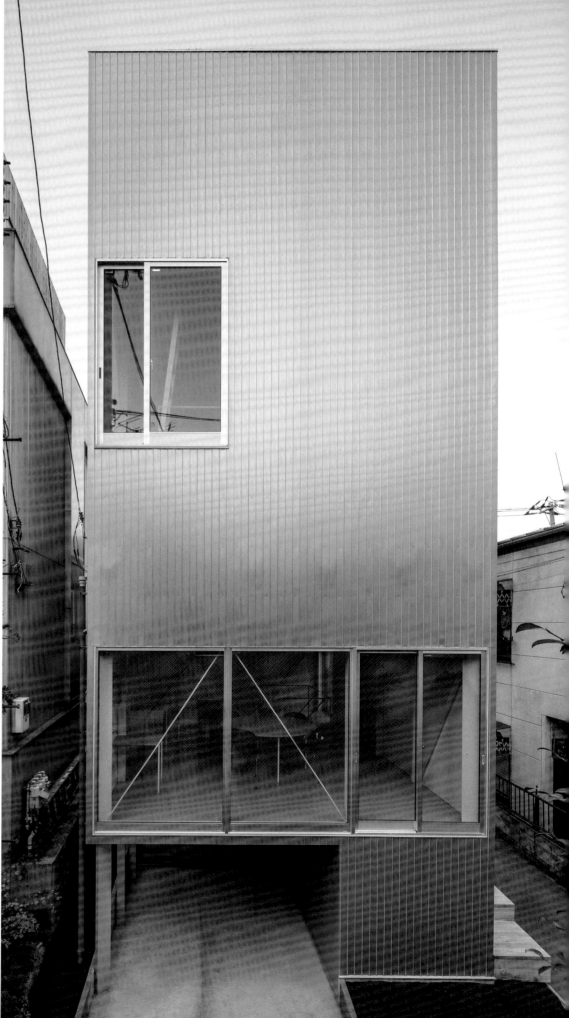

South elevation

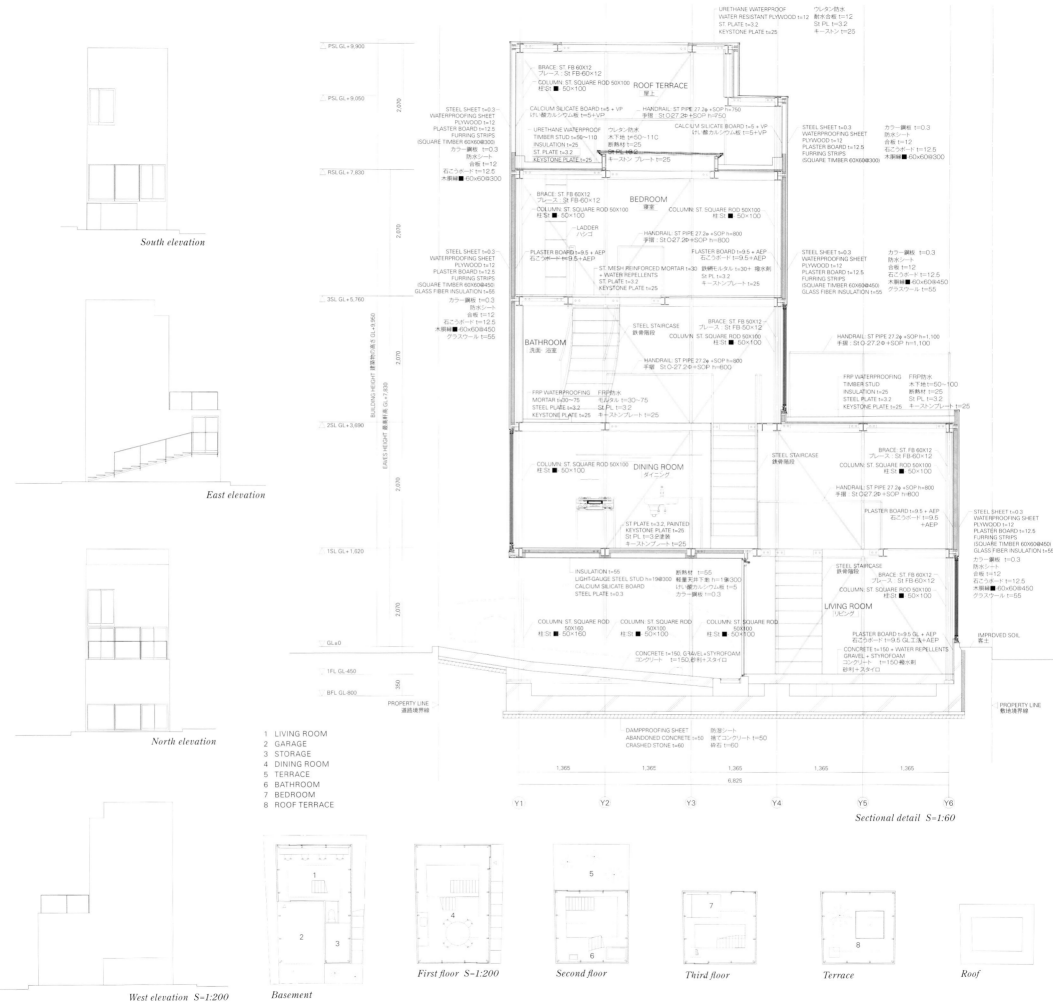

Downward view toward terrace and dining room

土橋邸

古くからの街区を残した住宅密集地に建つ，夫婦と子供2人のための住宅である。クライアントは住んでいて楽しくなるような，色々と発見のある住宅を望んでいた。敷地は隣家に囲まれ小さな土地ではあったが，どこかのどかな雰囲気があり，そののどかさを内部に取り込みながら，敷地いっぱいに伸びていく形はどうかと考えた。

私たちはたくさんの床に大きな開口を各階ずらしながら開け，それらを上下途切れることなく一体感を感じられる高さで積み重ねた。各床には下からリビング，ダイニング，テラス付きの水回り，寝室とその上に部屋のような屋上を置いた。それぞれに独立した場所を持ちながらも，床の開口がそれらの輪郭を曖昧にし，ひと繋がりの空間となって，住宅の中に様々な関係性を生み出している。

浴室階のテラスはその階に広がりを与えつつも，下のダイニングと連続するように考え，また寝室からの眺めや，屋上からもテラスの一部が覗け，そして前面道路とも室内を挟んで繋がっている。それぞれの場所は多様な繋がりを持ち，またどこにいても全体への広がりを感じられ，小さな土地からは想像もできない程，開放感のある空間となっている。

私たちはこの開放的な空間を構成するために，50mm×100mmの柱と，厚み12mmのFBブレース，そして3.2mmの鋼板と25mmのキーストーンプレートからなる床を選択し，構造体が家具のようなスケールで建ち現れ，全体が軽やかな印象でまとまることを目指した。

遠くにあるものと近くにあるものが同時にあって，それらが別々にある時もあれば，連続する時もある。そのパターンが幾つも生まれていき，いつも何か新しい発見のある空間になっていけばと思っている。

Living room

Bedroom

Dining room

View toward bathroom; dining room below

*Kyoto Apartments
(Nishinoyama House)
Kyoto, Japan
2010-13*

Kazuyo Sejima & Associates

L   LIVING
D   DINING ROOM
K   KITCHEN
BR   BEDROOM
BTH   BATHROOM
TAT   TATAMI ROOM
GDN   GARDEN

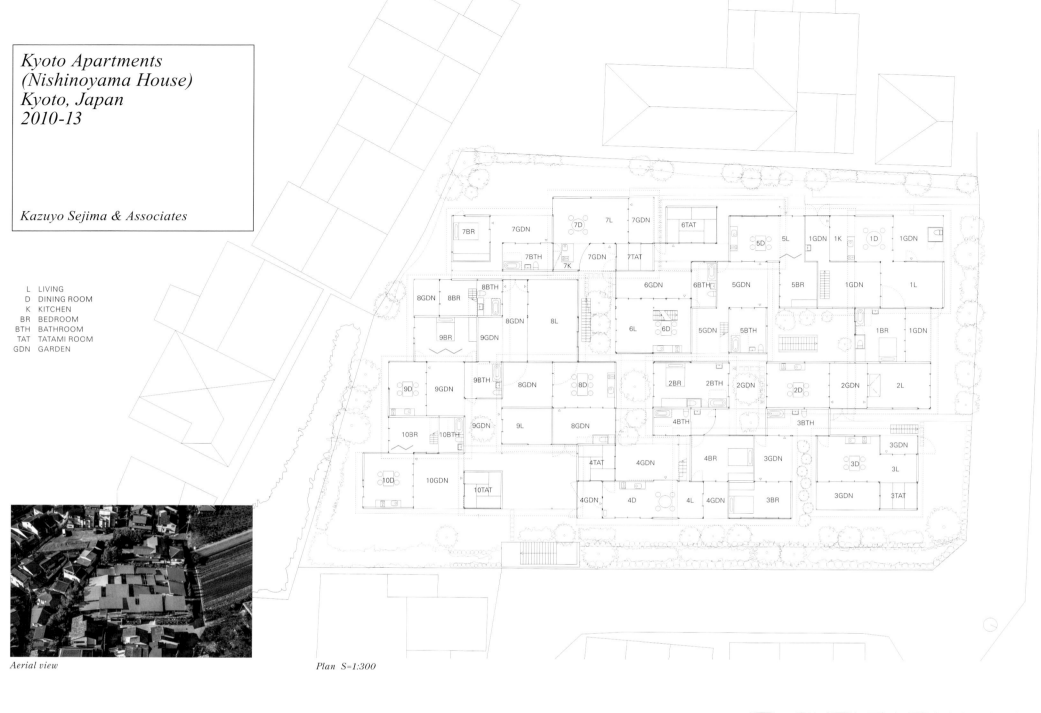

Aerial view

Plan S=1:300

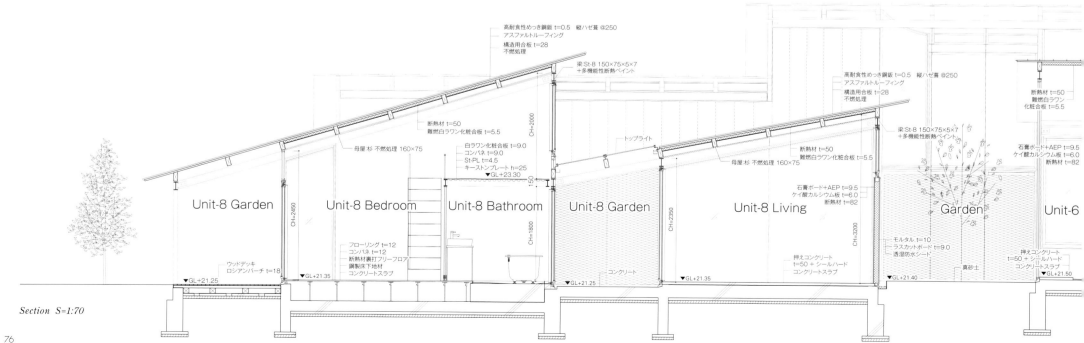

Section S=1:70

View from street on east

The project is a 10-unit rental housing complex in a quiet residential area in Kyoto. The complex is built on a gently sloping site with a distant view of the Kyoto city and Mount Hiei. According to the city's regulations, projects of this area are required to follow the local landscape, including roof design, colors and materials used.

Instead of enveloping the entire complex with one large roof, we chose to design 21 separate roofs with similar sizes as those of the surrounding buildings. We took each room, as opposed to each unit, and covered them with different roofs to create a mixed cluster that amount to a large connective roof of the entire complex.

Each unit is sized around 55 to a 100 m^2, consisting of three to four rooms with either a loft or a basement. These units contain three different roofs, one of which is connected to another unit. This results in an assortment of unique floor-plans that are connected by a large roof, a concept that is distinctly different from a community of single-family homes. Spaces are positioned on different levels according to the site elevation, and the gradient, direction, and height of the roofs are also diversified to generate vertical changes in the expansion and illumination of the spaces.

As if one is pushing through an entangled space, the complex stands as an ambiguous and unpredictable amalgamation of public/private, and indoors/outdoors, where a living room might be standing in one corner, a sun-drenched bathroom in another; a shady deck and an alleyway lead to the neighboring inner gardens and backyards, and a common courtyard appears between the roofs.

The variance in the design's spatial composition promotes a sense of excitement and the fun of living in this complex. We hope that this vibrant spirit will emanate towards the surrounding environment to create a uniquely fertile environment and a harmonious panorama.

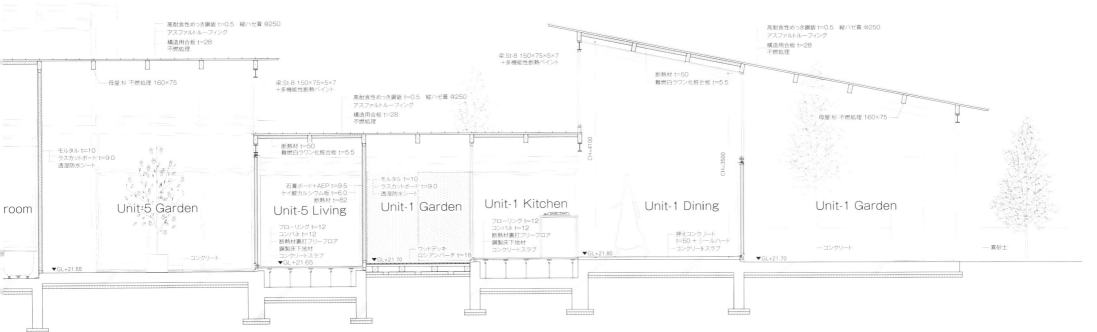

◁ *Overall view from north*

View toward unit 5 and 6 from path on north

Common terrace

京都の集合住宅（NISHINOYAMA HOUSE）

京都の閑静な住宅地に建つ，10戸からなる賃貸の集合住宅である。敷地は遠くに比叡山や京都の町並みを一望できるなだらかな丘陵地にある。京都市の規制により，屋根形状や色彩，素材への配慮と，町並みとの調和がとれた計画がこの地域一帯の建物には求められる。

私たちは，1棟の建物にそのまま大きな屋根を架けるのではなく，周りの建物に近い大きさの21枚の屋根を，住戸単位というよりは部屋単位に架けていき，バラバラな屋根の集まりによって一つの大屋根が感じられるような集合住宅をつくろうと考えた。

各住戸は 55～100m^2 程度で，三つから四つの部屋とロフトまたは地下で組み合わされるが，1住戸には3枚の屋根があり，そのうちの1枚の屋根が他の住戸にまたがっているため，戸建て住宅が単に集合するのとは異なる様々なプランが一つ屋根の下に広がっている。また，敷地の高低差に合わせて少しずつ段差をつけて全体を配置し，さらに屋根の勾配や方向，高さも変えているため，光の入り方や空間の広がりなど，断面的にも変化が生まれている。

分け入っていくような空間の繋がり方の中で，たまたまそこにリビングがあって，サンルームのお風呂があり，木陰の縁側，お隣の坪庭や裏庭へと続く路地，屋根の切れ間にあらわれるみんなの中庭など，屋内と屋外，パブリックとプライベートが偶然混ざり合ったような割り切れない関係で全体が成り立っている。

どこをとっても違う展開を見せる空間構成は，ここに住んだら楽しいという気持ちを湧き立たせてくれる。そのいきいきとした感じが，屋内外だけでなく周辺とも繋がって，集まるからこそ生まれる豊かな環境と良好な景観を築き上げられたらと思っている。

Court of unit 2: looking east

Unit 5

Unit 3

Unit 2: court connecting bathroom and dining / kitchen

◁△*Various spatial composition promotes the fun of living*

Treform, W Wing
Tokyo, Japan
2010–12

Office of Ryue Nishizawa

Overall view of W wing from southeast

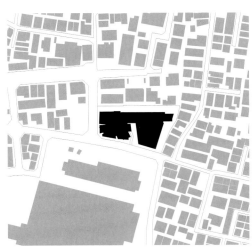

Site plan S=1:3000

The W wing is a five-story concrete box frame construction, and shares the first-floor entrance lobby and building manager's office with the N and E wings. Its exterior is not a simple rectangular volume, but undulates in diverse patterns–bulging, collapsing, and having notches in some areas of the outer wall. Because of this, each apartment unit has two to as many as three exterior-facing walls, giving the room interiors access to windows that open directly into the outside air on the south, as well as east and west sides. Thanks to this, light and ventilation conditions have markedly improved, creating airy interior spaces filled with light. Furthermore, the setback of the building exterior has allowed room for terraces to be attached to each unit, creating spacious residences in which both indoors and outdoors can be enjoyed. The building's irregular, three-dimensional outline also serves to counter exterior regulations such as sloping surfaces and shade. One could say that this incredibly efficient formation has enabled us to procure the maximum building volume within the specified site conditions. With this design we have provided residents with a richly varied floor plan, in which each of the airy living spaces have their own unique contour, room layout and terrace.

トレフォルム, W棟

W棟は，コンクリート壁式構造による5階建ての建物で，N棟，E棟，W棟の3棟全体のエントランスロビーと管理人室を1階に併設しています。外観は，ただの四角いヴォリュームではなく，外壁が出っ張ったりへっこんだり，または切れ込みが入ったりと，多様で起伏に富んだ外観となっています。そのことによって，すべての住戸タイプが2面ないし3面外部に面する状態となります。室内側から考えると，南面だけでなく東面や西面などあちこちの面に，外気に直接面した窓をとることができるようになります。そのことによって，採光条件や通風条件が格段に向上し，明るく光に満ちた，風通しのよい室内空間が生まれます。また，外観がセットバックすることで各住戸にはテラスが付き，中と外の両方を楽しむことのできる開放的な住空間となります。イレギュラーかつ立体的に変化してゆく外形は，斜線制限や日影などの外形規制をかわす役割をも持ち，与えられた敷地条件内で最大限の容積を確保することができる，効率的な造形とも言うことができます。各住戸は異なる外形と間取りとテラスを持って，全体として多種多様な住戸プランのヴァリエーションと，開放的な住空間を提供します。

Room 505 with V shape plan

Room 302

Room 403: looking to bathroom

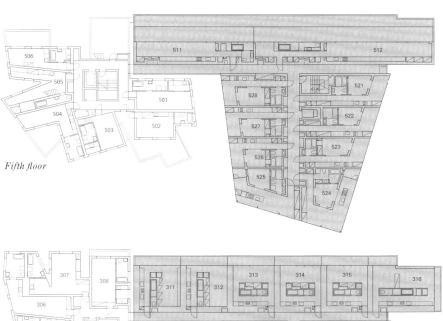
Fifth floor

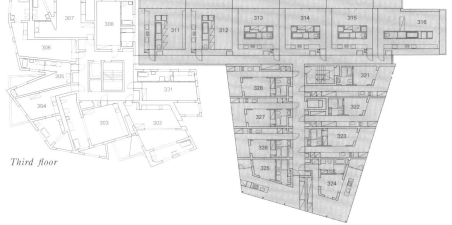
Third floor

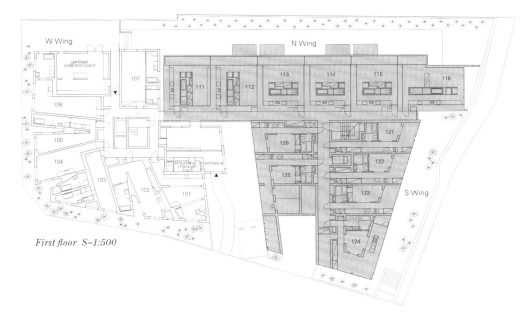
First floor S=1:500

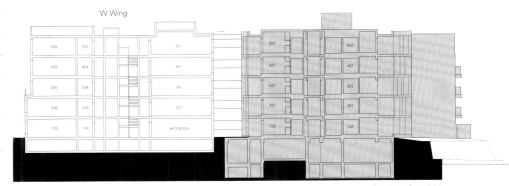
Section S=1:500

Junko Fukutake Hall
Okayama, Okayama, Japan
2010–13

SANAA

◁ Overall view from south

South view of commons space. Covered plaza on left

1 ENTRANCE
2 COMMONS SPACE
3 FOYER
4 HALL 1
5 HALL 2
6 HALL 3
7 WAITING SPACE
8 MEETING SPACE
9 COURTYARD
10 COVERED PLAZA

Plan S=1:500

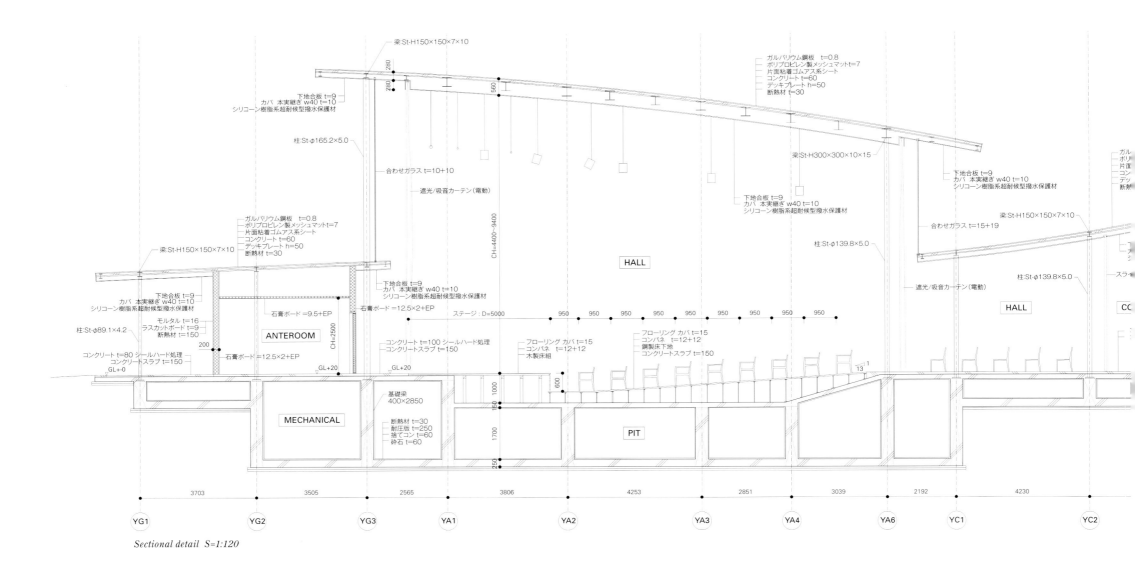

Sectional detail S=1:120

South elevation

North elevation

West elevation S=1:500

East elevation

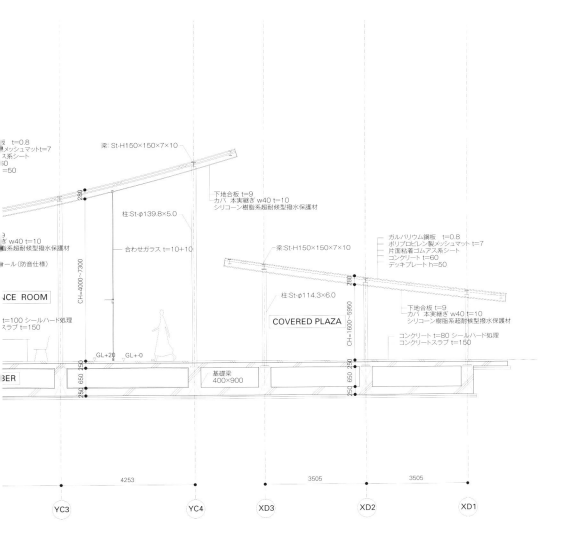

View toward hall 1. Hall 3 on right

This is a multipurpose hall built on the Shikata campus of Okayama University.

With a goal to create "a beautiful university town" that is also an international research and educational hub, Okayama University is currently undergoing the process of constructing an open campus that is also rooted to its local area.

The project demanded a building that will provide a place for free and easy communication: a monumental and symbolic building that embodies the university's openness, that also bridges between the school and its local community.

For the campus and the plaza overlooking the town, we proposed an open, arbor-like building that can be entered from any point, by placing roofs of various sizes directed towards multiple directions. The entrance hall, called the "commons space," the foyer, and the 3 small, medium, and large auditoriums are gently connected, yet also softly intercepted by the delicately covered roofs.

The auditoriums can be converted with curtains for a variety of uses, from lectures, meetings and music events; they can be sectioned as a small hall, or opened as a large venue that contains a maximum of 450 people.

The spaces under the eaves and the covered plaza invite people to enter from different directions, providing a place for interaction open not only to the campus, but to the town as well.

Ms. Junko Fukutake, who donated the building to the school, mentioned that she hopes it will be "a rational, generous, and borderless place of new encounters; a place that invites free and delightful communication; a place that produces serendipity." Our hope is that this building will live up to her words, by being used and cared for by those both inside and outside the school.

Entrance: view from east

South view

Hall 1

Looking toward south from commons space

Foyer

Junko Fukutake Hall（岡山大学 J-Hall）
岡山大学の鹿田キャンパスに建つ，多目的ホールである。

岡山大学は，国際的な研究・教育拠点としての「美しい学都」を目指し，地域に根ざしたオープンなキャンパスづくりを進めている。

開かれた大学というメッセージを象徴し，モニュメンタルでありながらも地域と大学を繋ぐ架け橋となるような，人々が気軽に関わりあえる交流の場としての建物が求められた。

私たちは，キャンパスや街が見える広場に，いろいろな大きさの屋根を様々な方向に向けて，どこからでも出入りができるような，内外に開かれた東屋のような建物を提案している。コモンズスペースと呼ばれるエントランスホール，ホワイエ，大中小の三つのホールは緩やかに繋がり，ひらりと架けられた屋根が，それぞれを柔らかく分節している。

ホールは，レクチャーや会議，音楽イベントなど用途や規模によってカーテンで変化をつけられるようになっていて，部分的に小ホールとして使ったり，最大で約450人を収容する一体的なホールとして使えたりと，多目的に利用できる。

ふらっと立ち寄れる軒下空間や屋根下広場は，いろいろな方向から人々を迎え入れ，キャンパスのみならず街に向かって開かれた，市民のための交流の場となる。

建物を寄付された福武純子さんは，この建物に対して「合理的で寛容でボーダレスな出会いの場，自由で愉快なコミュニケーションを誘発する場，セレンディピティを生み出す場」という思いを述べられている。この建物が，学内外の人々に親しみをもって使われることにより，その言葉に相応しい建物となることを期待している。

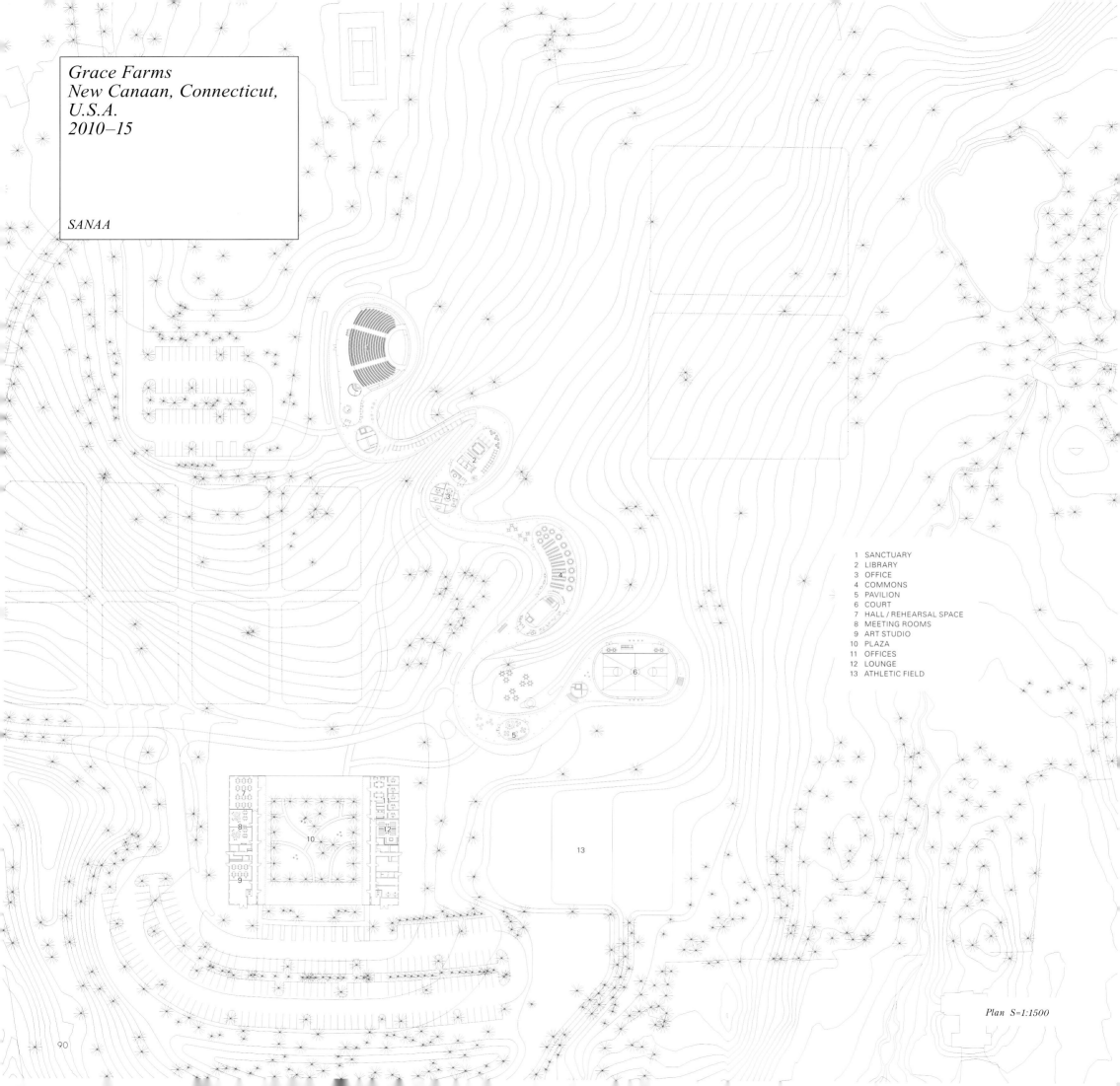

Grace Farms
New Canaan, Connecticut,
U.S.A.
2010–15

SANAA

1 SANCTUARY
2 LIBRARY
3 OFFICE
4 COMMONS
5 PAVILION
6 COURT
7 HALL / REHEARSAL SPACE
8 MEETING ROOMS
9 ART STUDIO
10 PLAZA
11 OFFICES
12 LOUNGE
13 ATHLETIC FIELD

Plan S=1:1500

Evening view from west. Library on left, Office on center, Commons on center ahead

This is a project in New Canaan, Connecticut, USA that was completed in October 2015. The site is located about one hour drive from New York, and is within a quiet neighborhood lined with houses surrounded by spacious backyards. The land is a large property on a slope filled with trees, lakes, wetlands, and grazing paddock. The program is diverse, including a multi-purpose hall, dining room, gymnasium, and library, as well as an athletic field and BBQ courtyard in the landscape. Once the doors are open, the building will continue to be available to the public.

We proposed a building covered with a long large roof, and floats in the center of the site. Winding and crossing the hills freely, this wood-frame structure follows the landscape and creates many covered outdoor spaces across the expansive property, while also forming courtyards. The large roof itself is made of anodized aluminum panels. The entire roof structure softly reflects the scenery, allowing the building to become part of the landscape as it ceaselessly shifts its expression from moment to moment.

The interior programs are found under the large roof, organized and wrapped in glass volumes according to their character and use—one space may be quiet and more secluded, while another may be a community space where many guests could gather. In both plan and elevation, these glass volumes are at times located close to one another, while others are placed further apart, creating different views and atmospheres. From one room, one may see the large lake in the distance and from another, one can overlook the wetlands in the gently descending landscape below. This large roof also gives way to a variety of ambiences such as a lively room facing an active plaza, or a calm space with sunlight trickling through the foliage of the trees.

The outdoor programs are dispersed throughout the expansive site. Some are situated in the courtyard and under the large roof and integrated with the indoor programs, while others are placed farther away from the roofed areas to be enjoyed together with the beautiful surrounding nature.

In this rich and natural environment, we sought to make a piece of architecture that becomes a part of the landscape. We hope the visitors will enjoy the beautiful changing nature through the spaces and experience created by the facility.

Overall elevation S=1:1000

◁ View from lower part of roof

Partrial west view. Stairs to Sanctuary on left, Library and Office on right

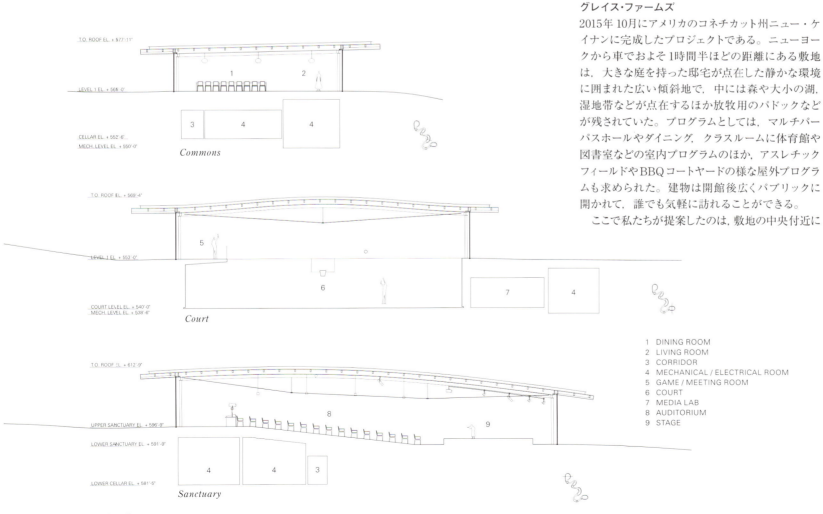

1 DINING ROOM
2 LIVING ROOM
3 CORRIDOR
4 MECHANICAL / ELECTRICAL ROOM
5 GAME / MEETING ROOM
6 COURT
7 MEDIA LAB
8 AUDITORIUM
9 STAGE

Section S=1:300

グレイス・ファームズ

2015年10月にアメリカのコネチカット州ニュー・ケイナンに完成したプロジェクトである。ニューヨークから車でおよそ1時間半ほどの距離にある敷地は，大きな庭を持った邸宅が点在した静かな環境に囲まれた広い傾斜地で，中には森や大小の湖，湿地帯などが点在するほか放牧用のパドックなどが残されていた。プログラムとしては，マルチパーパスホールやダイニング，クラスルームに体育館や図書室などの室内プログラムのほか，アスレチックフィールドやBBQコートヤードの様な屋外プログラムも求められた。建物は開館後広くパブリックに開かれて，誰でも気軽に訪れることができる。

ここで私たちが提案したのは，敷地の中央付近に浮かんだ長く大きな屋根に覆われた建物である。木梁で架構したその大屋根は，地形に沿って伸びやかに湾曲しながら自由に敷地をまたぎ，広い敷地にたくさんの庇空間をつくると同時に囲われた中庭スペースをつくり出している。また大屋根の上はアルマイト処理されたアルミのパネルで仕上げられている。穏やかに反射する屋根全体が周りの風景を写し込み，建物自体が周りの景色と馴染んでいくとともに，日ごと時間ごとにその表情と印象を変えていく。

室内プログラムは，静かに過ごす場所，大勢で集まる公共性の強い場所というような，その性格と用途によってガラスのヴォリュームに分け，大屋根の下に置いた。それぞれが平面上でも断面上でも互いに近づいたり離れたりしながら置かれていることで，ある部屋からは遠くに大きな湖が見え，別の部屋からは前方へなだらかに下る斜面とその先に広がる湿地帯が見渡せるというように，部屋ごとで眺めが異なっている。また賑やかな広場に面した部屋があったり，木漏れ陽の落ちる静かな場所があったりと，一つの大屋根が覆う部屋の全てに，眺めだけでなく雰囲気も異なるスペースが生まれている。

また屋外プログラムは，大きな敷地のあちこちに点在させてある。その一部は中庭や大屋根の下に置かれて室内プログラムと混じり合い，残りは大屋根から離れて周りの美しい自然とともに楽しめるようになっている。

恵まれた環境が広がるこの場所では，建築がランドスケープの一部のような物になればと考えた。そんな建築がつくり出すスペースや体験を通して，来館者が変化に富んだ美しい自然を身近に感じながら楽しい時間をすごしてくれたらと思っている。

Commons (dining room)

Sanctuary (auditorium)

Court (gymnasium)

Perimeter of Court

Library

◁ View from Sanctuary

Perimeter with curved glass walls

97

*La Samaritaine
Paris, France
2010–*

SANAA

This is a plan for renovating La Samaritaine, a well-established department store in Paris. The site is located on the right bank of the Pont Neuf in Paris's First Ward, facing the Seine River. The existing program is an urban complex with a department store, offices, public housing, kindergarten and hotel. Although the plan has two major elements: the preservation and renovation of the historic architectural components, and new construction facing the famous Rue de Rivoli, the new La Samaritaine holds out the promise of contributing to the city as a whole.

We worked to create an innovative flow of pedestrian traffic within the structure by adding a passage at the center of the old and new buildings that stretches from the Rue de Rivoli to the Seine River side. There are three courtyard spaces (one existing and two newly planned), connected by this passage, each with its own personality. People can enjoy the views of the sky from indoors since the courtyards have open ceiling spaces up to the top floor, making it a place for a variety of interactions. The new facade facing the Rue de Rivoli is made of glass that curves gently, consistent with the rhythm and scale of the adjacent Ottoman-style French windows. The goal was to create a new harmony between the historic streetscape and the modern buildings by mirroring the surrounding environment to the highly reflective glass facade in depth. The intent is that the renovated older portions and newly planned ones become a single unified facade, resulting in a new identity for La Samaritaine.

Aerial view *View of Rue de la Monnale* ▷

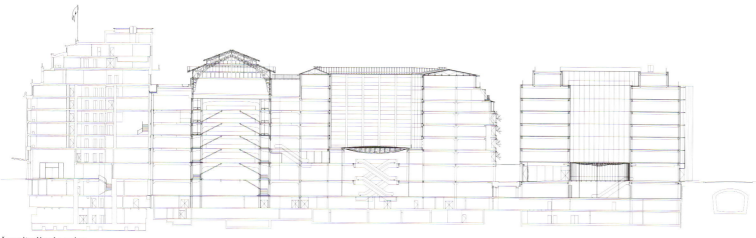
Longitudinal section

Elevation: Rue de la Monnale

Ground floor

Atrium of Verriere

Facade model

Atrium of Rivoli

ラ・サマリテーヌ

パリの老舗百貨店ラ・サマリテーヌの改修計画である。敷地はパリ1区、ポンヌフ橋の右岸に位置し、セーヌ川に面している。百貨店、オフィス、公営住宅、幼稚園、ホテルという都市的複合プログラムを持つ。計画には歴史的建築部分を保存改修しながら現代に見合う性能にすることと、リボリ通りに面する新規建築という二つの大きな要素があるが、それらが一体として新しいラ・サマリテーヌとして都市に貢献することが期待されている。

私たちはリボリ通りからセーヌ川へと至る"パッサージュ"を新旧建物の中央に設けることで、新たな人々の流れを建物内に生み出そうとした。このパッサージュによって接続される三つの中庭空間(既存のものが一つと新たに計画したものが二つ)があり、それぞれが異なる個性を持っている。これらの中庭は最上階まで吹抜けの空間であるため、屋内にいながら空の景色を楽しんだり、様々な交流が行われる場所となっている。リボリ通りに面した新たなファサードは、隣接するオスマン様式のフランス窓のリズムやスケールに合わせて緩やかにカーブしたガラスファサードとした。反射性の高いガラスファサードに周囲の環境が奥行きを持って映り込むことで、歴史的な街並みと現代的な建物との新しい調和を目指した。改修される歴史的な部分と新しく計画される現代的な部分とが、一つの一体的なファサードとなり、ラ・サマリテーヌの新しいアイデンティティとなることを目指している。

*Nakamachi Terrace
Kodaira, Tokyo, Japan
2010–14*

Kazuyo Sejima & Associates

The Nakamachi Terrace stands facing the Oume Road. The old landscape and nature remain strong despite the bustle of traffic along the road. There are trees around this site with a canal running behind, and farmland spreads out across the area interspersed with residential houses. The Nakamachi Terrace was built here, combining the existing community center and the library.

We wanted to create a building that blends with the environment that retains its unique feel. Although it faces the street, the location not only depends on the road it faces, but it also spreads out in all four directions. We also envisioned that the local residents would gather together at this building from scattered directions. We wanted to think about a building that is perfect for this type of landscape and use.

Further, in the two different existing buildings, there were originally a variety of places that were created over time to accommodate necessary uses. Since we would be combining these two buildings, it didn't make sense to simply recreate the old. We wanted to create a variety of these spaces inside the new Nakamachi Terrace in novel, innovative ways.

As a result, we came up with the idea for a structure that connects a variety of spaces, as opposed to a single clustered building. Air flows around multiple clusters which house the different spaces, and the building begins to blend into the surrounding area. It opens up in many directions and invites people to enter, with not only a single front but many. The numerous clusters create interior spaces that have their own unique aspects. It gradually results in one body by connecting these elements together. Although a larger interior space is created in this process, it is segmented to avoid becoming excessively large by lowering the floor level and raising the ceiling height in various places.

Since the building itself is not so large, this became a fairly complex structure. Without a large central location, we think it became a building that houses various spaces on top of one another in a large bunch. The glass and wall surfaces are wrapped in expanded aluminum metal which gently reflects light, and stands out in all directions. We hope that this building will become a new communal space for the residents of this area.

◁ *Overall view from south* *Night view from east*

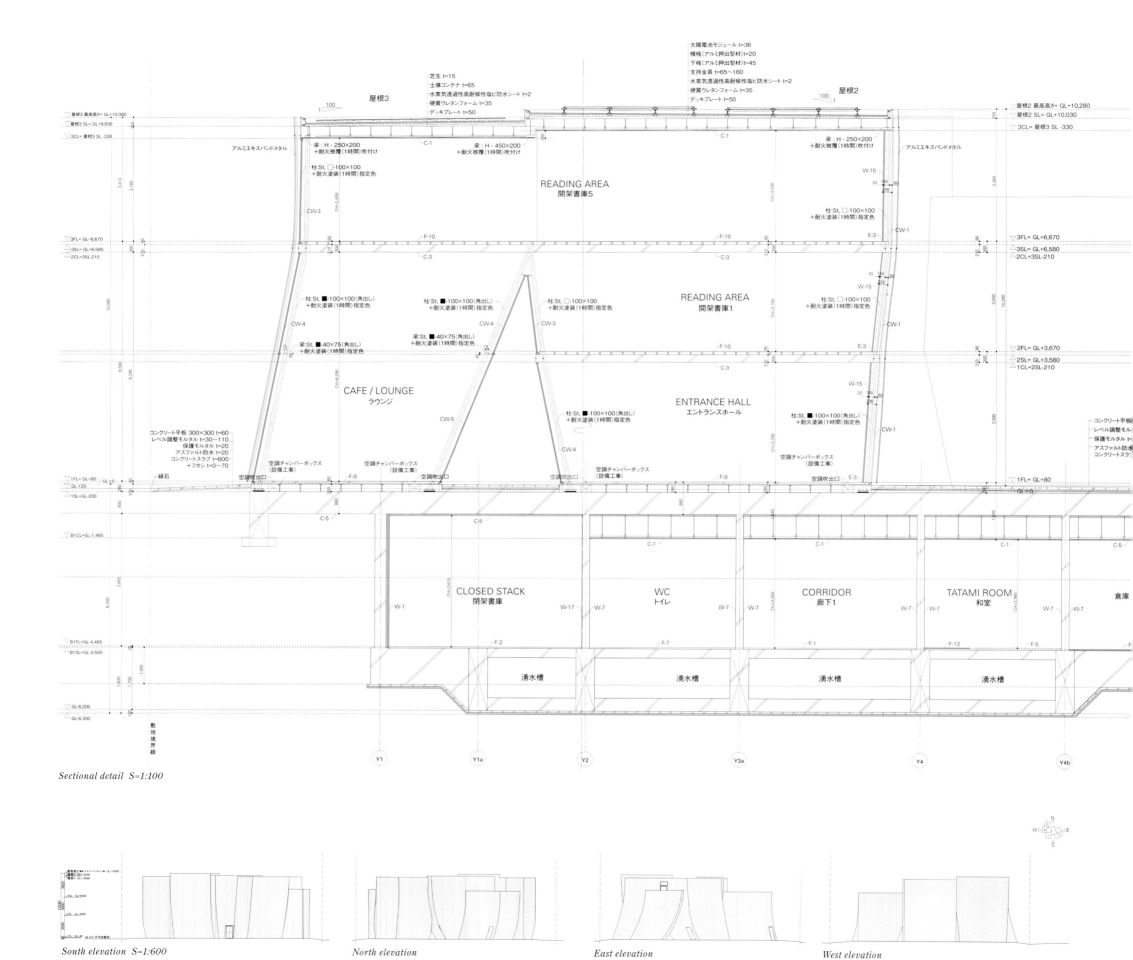

Sectional detail S=1:100

South elevation S=1:600

North elevation

East elevation

West elevation

1	ENTRANCE
2	RECEPTION
3	CAFE
4	COOKING STUDIO
5	WORKSHOP
6	READING AREA
7	LECTURE ROOM
8	NURSING ROOM
9	TERRACE
10	HALL
11	TATAMI ROOM
12	STUDY ROOM
13	READING TO CHILDREN
14	OFFICE
15	CLOSED STACK
16	LIGHT COURT
17	STORAGE
18	MECHANICAL

Third floor

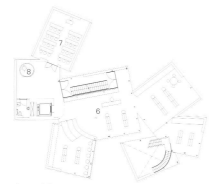

Second floor

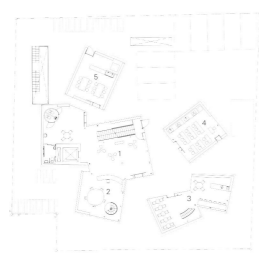

First floor S=1:500

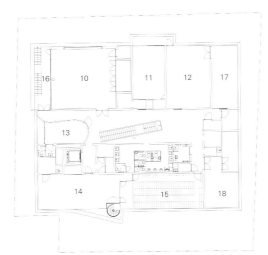

Basement

View toward cafe from outdoor corridor

Cafe

103

Outdoor corridor: looking to entrance

なかまちテラス（小平市立仲町公民館・仲町図書館）
なかまちテラスは青梅街道に面して建つ。街道沿いには，交通量が多いながらも，昔ながらの風景や自然が色濃く残されている。この敷地の周りにも木々があり，後ろ側には用水路が流れ，さらに住宅に混じって田畑が広がっている。ここに，もともとあった図書館と近くにあった公民館を合体して，なかまちテラスを建てることになった。

独特の雰囲気を残す環境に混じり合った建物をつくりたいと思った。街道に面しているとはいえ，前面道路だけに依存する場所ではなく，四方全体に広がりを持った場所である。そして地区の人が四方からバラバラとこの建物に集まってくることが想像される。そのような風景，使い方にふさわしい建ち方を考えたいと思った。

また，もともと異なる二つの建物には，時間とともに必要に応じてつくり出されたいろいろな場所があった。もちろん，二つを合わせて新しい組み立てをするのであるから，同じものを並べても仕方が無いが，そのいろいろなスペースをこのなかまちテラスにもできるだけ多く新しい形でつくりたいと思った。

その結果，一つの塊の建物でなく，いろいろな場所が繋がってでき上がる建物を考え出した。いろいろな場所のための複数の塊の間には空気が流れ，建物と周りが混じり合い始める。いろいろな方向に開いて人々を迎え入れ，いろいろな方向に正面を持つ。複数の塊は内部ではそれぞれ個性を持つ室内空間を生む。それらが繋がって段々一つの塊になる過程で，より大きな室内空間をつくり上げるが，大きくなり過ぎないように，断面的にも注意を払い，床を一段下げたり，あるいは天井を一段高くしたりして，分節している。

それほど大きくない建物であるから，複雑な建物になった。どこかに大きな中心的な場所がある建物でなく，いろいろな場所が団子みたいに重なり合った建物になったと思う。ガラスの面も壁の面も光を柔らかく反射するアルミのエキスパンドメタルで包まれ，全方向に向かって立っている。これが，この地区の人のための，そして，この環境の中の，新しい公共空間になれたらと思う。

104

Second floor: looking south

Second floor: reading area

Terrace on third floor

Inujima "Art House Project" phase II
A-Art House, C-Art House
Inujima, Okayama, Japan
2011–13

Kazuyo Sejima & Associates

The Inujima Art House Project is an exhibition of modern artworks in tandem with the living conditions of the island residents, predicated on the exhibit being updated every three years. The exhibit spaces disbursed within the village are built by leasing unoccupied homes, warehouses and vacant land, and are carefully created over time. The works themselves are based on the surrounding environment and built on these exhibit spaces, including the exterior areas.

The history of modernization that forms the backdrop to Inujima has remained strong up to now, with transformation brought about by quarrying and copper refining industries which, as a result, created a terrain and landscape according to the lifestyles of its people that have persisted for generations. The island is also abundant in its gentle contours and overflows with nature. The exhibit spaces were planned to utilize the unique aspects of each of the sites. Phase 1 consisted of four art houses (House F, House S, the Gazebo at Nakanotani, and House I) completed in 2010. Three years later, House A and House C were built as Phase 2.

House A was combined with House S which preceded it, located in a plaza-like space surrounded by houses and rolling hills. House A, like House S, is an acrylic structure, with a ring-like shape using 30 mm-thick acrylic panels. Since the area is surrounded by private houses, fields and plants, visitors will simultaneously experience the artwork together with the environment when walking through the tunnel and looking out from the courtyard.

House C is an exhibit space where a portion of an old, abandoned house from over 200 years ago was reused. Although the results of a survey of the existing structure revealed that some of the trusses were suffering from rain erosion, many of the remaining building members were still usable. Furthermore, the bases of the columns were simply eroded

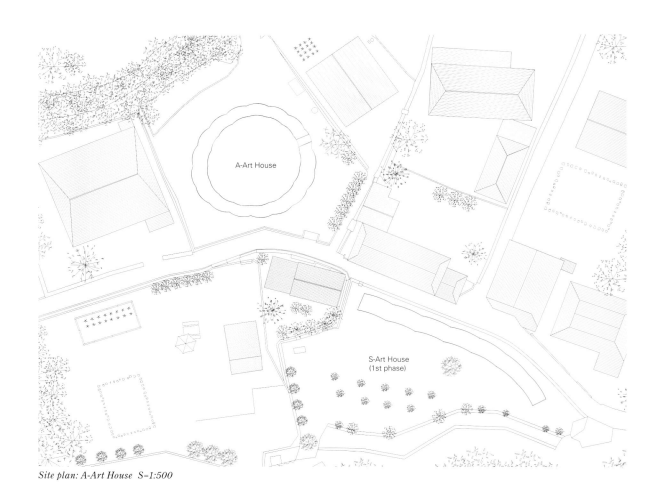

Site plan: A-Art House S=1:500

Section: A-Art House S=1:150

away. We reused as much of the structure from the existing members and made new additions where necessary, reinforcing here and there as needed, adding new elements and fully reassembling the structure in order to create the exhibition space. There are removable storm shutters across much of the exterior which are kept open based on the specifics of the exhibit, creating a space that spreads out across the entire site.

This artwork was created utilizing the surrounding area and the uniqueness of the exhibit space under the direction of Yuko Hasegawa. Artworks in the Phase 2 exhibit are made by Kohei Nawa for House F, Yusuke Asai for a site inside the village, Haruka Kojin for House S and A, Jun Ngen Hatsushiba for House C, and Masanori Maeda for House I.

We feel that the relationship between daily life on the island and this project have come closer together thanks to the addition of House A and House C exhibit spaces. The architecture and art are established by the landscape created through layers of history and daily life on the island, which offer and renew the values added to the island's landscape. Through this project, we hope to create a new synergistic relationship between the daily life, scenery and nature of the island.

犬島「家プロジェクト」A邸, C邸

「犬島〈家プロジェクト〉」は、3年ごとに展示変えをすることを前提とし、島の人々の生活環境とともに、現代アート作品を展示するものである。集落内に点在する展示スペースは、人が住まなくなった家屋や倉庫、空地を貸してもらい、ゆっくりと時間をかけながらつくられる。作品は、周辺の環境を前提としながら、外も含めた展示スペースにつくられる。

犬島の風景はこれまでの近代化の歴史が色濃く残り、採石や銅の精錬が行われてきた産業の変遷、そこで代々続く人々の生活により地形や風景がつくり出される。また島は緩やかな起伏に富み、自然にあふれる。展示スペースは、各敷地がもつそうした個性的な特徴を活かしながら計画していった。2010年に第1フェーズとして完成した4軒(「F邸」、「S邸」、「中の谷の東屋」、「I邸」)に続き、3年後の今回、第2フェーズとして「A邸」と「C邸」が加えられた。

「A邸」は、先にできた「S邸」と組み合わせたもので、家々と緩やかな丘に囲まれた広場的な場所に位置する。「S邸」と同様にアクリル造であり、30mm厚の透明アクリル・パネルを使ったリング状の形をもつ。周囲を民家や畑、植物といったものに囲まれており、トンネルを通って中庭から見渡すと、それらの周辺環境とともにあるアート作品を体験することになる。

「C邸」は、もともとあった200年以上前の倒壊寸前だった空き家の一部を再利用した展示スペースである。既存家屋の調査をした結果、小屋組の一部は雨で腐食していたものの、当時の部材の多くが使える状態で残っており、また柱については、柱脚が腐食している状態であった。それらの部材の中から使えるものはできるだけ構造体として利用し、足りないものを新しく加えながら展示スペースとなるように、必要に応じて少し補強したり、新しい部材を足したりしながら全体を組み直していった。建物外周部の多くは取り外し可能な雨戸であり、展示内容によってはそれらを開け放し、敷地全体に広がるような展示スペースとなる。

アート作品については、長谷川祐子さんのディレクションのもと、それぞれ周辺環境と展示スペースの個性を活かした作品がつくられる。第2期展示として「F邸」に名和晃平、集落内に淺井裕介、「S邸」、「A邸」に荒神明香、「C邸」にジュン・グエン・ハツシバ、「I邸」に前田征紀による作品がつくられた。

今回、「A邸」と「C邸」の二つの展示スペースが付け足されたことにより、島の日常生活とプロジェクトの関係は、より近いものとなってきたように感じている。島の歴史、日常の積み重ねによってつくられた風景により建築・アートは成立し、またそれらにより島の風景に新しい価値が与えられ、更新されていく。このプロジェクトを通して、島での日常と風景や自然との新しい相乗的な関係をつくることができればと考えている。

Site plan: C-Art House S=1:500

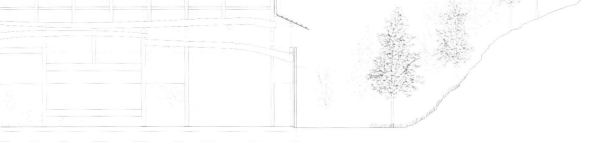

Section: C-Art House S=1:150

A-Art House: view from northwest

A-Art House

A-Art House: view from inside

C-Art House

C-Art House: view from southeast

C-Art House

*Dangozaka House
Tokyo, Japan
2011–14*

Kazuyo Sejima & Associates

The site is located almost in the center of a fairly wide dead end street lined with 6 houses. None of the lots are large, and the houses themselves are built right to the edge of their plots. However, in such a densely populated city, this dead end is creating a certain generous atmosphere that feels like a private garden for these 6 houses.

When I started to think about how to design a home for a couple and their two children, I came up with the concept of the "shape of relationships." This is not about implementing their relationship into the design. If we try to create a house by "connecting this and this together" and "separating this from this," the house would become a mere diagram. Rather, I wanted to think about the idea of the relationship and how to translate it into a physical space. I thought about how to implement a design that inspires different relationships and enable the family of four to live freely in a house that, as mentioned before, stands so close to the neighboring houses on both sides, inside a blind alley that feels like a garden. When I thought about what this would look like, I realized that perhaps it should remain loosely defined and ambiguous. Structure became important as I tried to include the relationships between neighbours and family members, and to create a place that inspires various kinds of interactivity. From here, I started to design a wooden structure. Strong yet light and flexible, which naturally led to the use of wood.

From the street, one enters a small earth floor, or the kitchen when entering from the backdoor, then stepping up onto the dining room, down again into the library, a study in the back, a small backyard, half-step up onto the children's room, a few steps back to the bathroom areas, 5 steps up to the family room, 4 steps up to the bedroom, and a terrace further up. Each room is connected while also retaining a sense of independence, and the entire house is also a single room. Various spaces expand and contract depending on the situation. There is only the "shape of the relationship" and a structure that made such things possible.

South elevation

Southwest view: snowy day

Downward view: family room on left

団子坂の家

割合幅広い，袋小路に面して，6軒ほどの住宅が並んで建っている。その真ん中あたりが敷地である。どの家の敷地も決して大きくなく，周りのどの家もパンパンに建っている。ただし袋小路は高密度な都市の中で，6軒のためのプライベートな庭のようにも感じられるゆとりの空間を生み出している。

夫婦と子ども2人が住むこの住宅について考え始めた時，関係性の形というのを思い付いた。それは，関係を形にしていくというのではない。つまり，こことここをこんな風に繋ぐとか，こことここを離すとか，それをそのまま形にすると，それはすごくダイアグラム的な建築になってしまう。そうではなく，関係性という概念を形にしたいと思った。最初に書いたとおり，両隣にピッタリくっつきながら，袋小路を庭のように捉え，家族4人がのびのび生活を送れる場所，そのためにいろいろな関係性が生み続けられる形について考えた。それはどんな形なのかなあと考えた時，ふわふわした形ではないだろうかと思った。隣の人や，家族間でつくられる関係性を内包しようとした時，いろいろな関係性が生まれる場所をつくろうとした時，ストラクチャーが重要だと思った。そこから，木造の構造に進んだ。ストラクチャーが強く，でも，軽くて，柔らかい。それで木造になった。

通りから小さな土間，そして，勝手口からキッチン，そこから1段上がってダイニング，また1段下りて図書コーナー，裏側に書斎，小さな裏庭，半階上がって子ども室，数歩上がって水回り，5歩上がって家族室，さらに4歩上がって寝室，その先にテラスがある。どれも独立しながら，同時に隣と繋がっており，全体はワンルームでもある。いろいろな場所が，その時の状況で膨らんだり押し込められたりする。そういうことを可能にしてくれたらと思う関係性の形，ストラクチャーだけがある。

View from dining room

View from street

Second floor_2

Second floor_3

First floor S=1:200

Second floor_1

1 EARTH FLOOR
2 DINING ROOM
3 KITCHEN
4 STUDY
5 CHILDREN'S ROOM
6 BATHROOM
7 FAMILY ROOM
8 BEDROOM
9 TERRACE

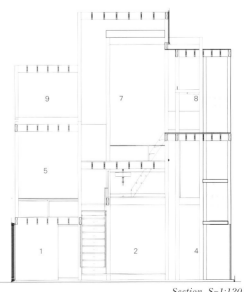
Section S=1:120

Competition for MECA
(Maison de l'Économie
Créative et de la Culture en
Aquitaine)
Bordeaux, France
2011

SANAA

View over river from northeast

Aerial view. Site located on behind station and facing river

View toward main entrance

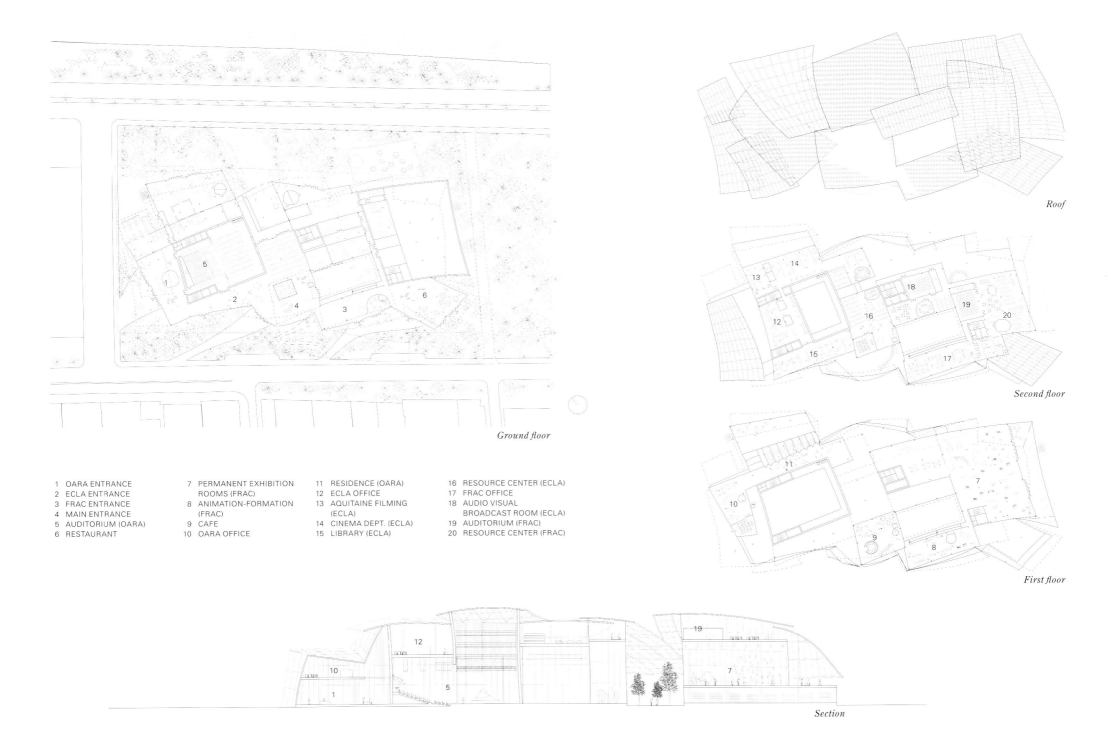

Ground floor / *Roof* / *Second floor* / *First floor* / *Section*

1 OARA ENTRANCE	7 PERMANENT EXHIBITION ROOMS (FRAC)	11 RESIDENCE (OARA)	16 RESOURCE CENTER (ECLA)
2 ECLA ENTRANCE		12 ECLA OFFICE	17 FRAC OFFICE
3 FRAC ENTRANCE	8 ANIMATION-FORMATION (FRAC)	13 AQUITAINE FILMING (ECLA)	18 AUDIO VISUAL BROADCAST ROOM (ECLA)
4 MAIN ENTRANCE	9 CAFE	14 CINEMA DEPT. (ECLA)	19 AUDITORIUM (FRAC)
5 AUDITORIUM (OARA)	10 OARA OFFICE	15 LIBRARY (ECLA)	20 RESOURCE CENTER (FRAC)
6 RESTAURANT			

The plan called for an innovative cultural facility complex that would group together three art organizations of Ecrit, Cinéma, Livre, Audiovisuel (ECLA, literature and movie organization), Fonds Régional d'Art Contemporain (FRAC, visual arts organization) and l'Office Artistique de la Région Aquitaine (OARA, performing arts center).

The site is located in the commercial district along the Garonne River, behind Bordeaux Station. It was important for the building to have a landmark exterior since it is the first architecture people would see when they enter the city by TGV train.

This new cultural facility is an experimental place that not only allows visitors to gain an appreciation of the area, but to study and be creative. We proposed a grid plan in consideration of future expandability, flexibility and adaptability. We created a large grid distorted based on the visible relationship with the shape of the site and the train station, envisioning an innovative and freeform platform system that could be used freely.

The three organizations are linked and merged spatially within this 3D platform. Expressing this relationship on the building exterior, the roof and walls partially envelop the space, and in other areas move apart from the structure and connect to the city landscape. Our goal was to create a building that would inspire a flurry of new, experimental cultural activity that would spread out across the city, becoming a symbol of the city of Bordeaux.

創造経済文化センター

FRAC (visual arts organisation) と ECLA (literature/movie organisation), OARA (performing arts centre) という三つのアート・オーガニゼーションを, それぞれが独立しながらも一体的に融合する新しい文化施設のコンプレックスの計画である。

敷地は, ボルドー駅の裏手, ガロンヌ川沿いの商業地区に位置している。TGVで街を訪れると最初に見える建物となるため, ランドマークとなる外観が求められた。

この新しい文化施設は, 訪問者が何かを鑑賞するだけでなく, 勉強をしたり, ものづくりを行うような実験的な施設として考えられており, 私たちは, 将来的な拡張可能性やフレキシビリティ, アダプタビリティを考え, グリッドプランを提案した。敷地形状や駅との視覚的な関係をもとに歪ませた大きなグリッドをつくり, どこでも好きに使えるような新しく自由なプラットフォームのシステムを考えた。

この立体的なプラットフォームの中で, 三つの機関が空間的に連続し, 融合していく。それらの関係性が外観にもそのまま現れるように, 屋根・壁が部分的に空間を包み込み, あるところでは離れて街と連続していく。新しく実験的な文化活動の賑わいが生まれ, 市街地へと広がり, ボルドーの街のシンボルとなる建築を目指した。

*Yoshida Printing Inc.
Tokyo HQ
Tokyo, Japan
2011–14*

Kazuyo Sejima & Associates

This is a rebuilding project of a printing company specialized in high quality printing, located along the Hokusai-dori Street in Sumida, Tokyo. The old office building, which formerly stood on the same location, had been afected by the 2011 Great East Japan earthquake. There was a need for a new building that houses both office and printing facilities, and serve as the company's Tokyo base.

The site is located on a corner lot surrounded by streets on three sides. A mixture of high- and mid-rise office buildings, cultural facilities, stores and apartments, as well as some old houses and factories line the neighborhood. While retaining a reasonable amount of open space around the building, we positioned the structure so that its facade would stand along similar lines of the exterior walls of the surrounding architecture. We envisioned a building that simultaneously takes part in, yet stands independently from, the local community. The facade is enveloped in expanded metal screens on all four surfaces. The view is gently filtered from both outside and inside, letting the ambience of the busy street scenery and the office space to seep through in both directions. Our goal was to create an office that lives among the local community.

Instead of a departmentalized composition of the former office, a new kind of space that fosters the development of fresh collaborations was called for. We envisioned a flexible space that can be easily altered to match the ever-changing number and scale of departments within an office environment. Unlike in a conventional arrangement where the floors remain entirely flat, we divided and vertically alternated the floors, gradually connecting various spaces that emerge between the four floors. Although physically distanced apart, the spaces on the floors above and below feel as if they are connected.

The expanded metal screens and glass curtain walls create a double-skin facade, where the metal is slightly angled to defect direct sunlight and allow ventilation. While the building is air-conditioned, the facade also features numerous hopper windows and large sliding windows, creating an office space that can take in the pleasant breezes of Japan's spring and autumn air.

Evening view of west elevation

Overall view from southwest

1 ENTRANCE HALL
2 UNLOADING ROOM
3 PARKING
4 MECHANICAL
5 EV
6 WC
7 LOCKER ROOM
8 MULTI-PURPOSE TOILET
9 RETAIL
10 OFFICE 1
11 OFFICE 2
12 OFFICE 3
13 OFFICE 4
14 OFFICE 5
15 OFFICE 6
16 OFFICE 7
17 LUNCH ROOM
18 FOYER
19 VISITOR'S ROOM
20 SMALL MEETING ROOM
21 LOUNGE
22 LARGE MEETING ROOM
23 TERRACE 1
24 TERRACE 2

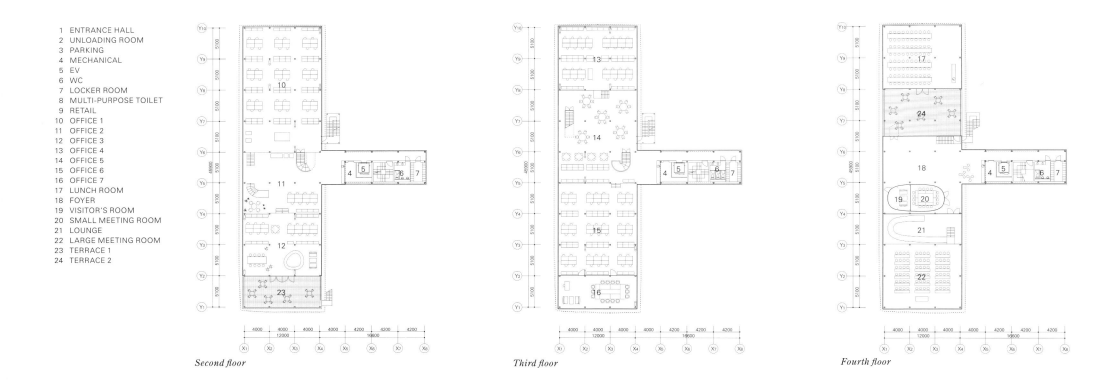

Second floor   *Third floor*   *Fourth floor*

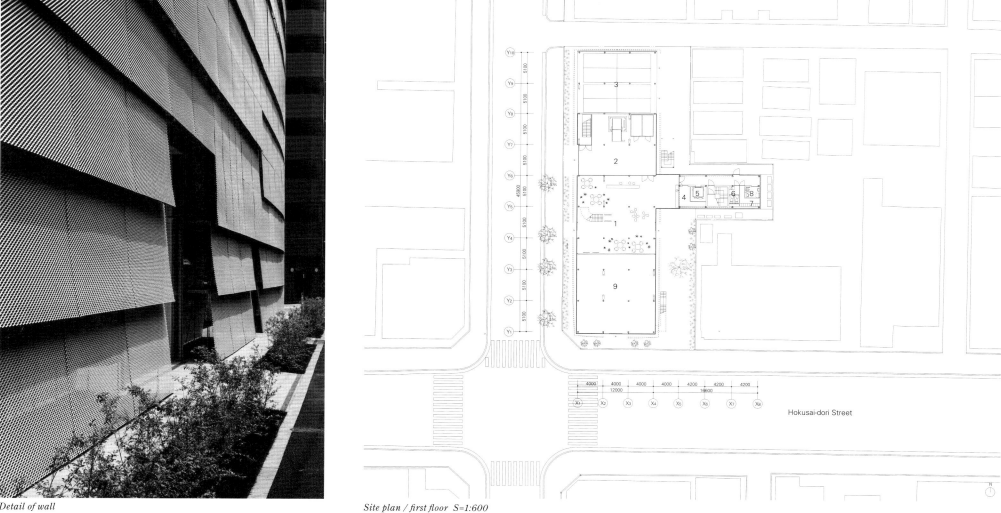

Detail of wall

Site plan / first floor S=1:600

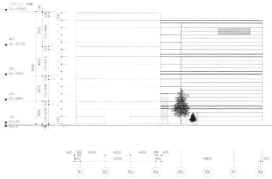
South elevation with expanded metal screen

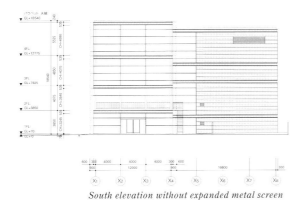
South elevation without expanded metal screen

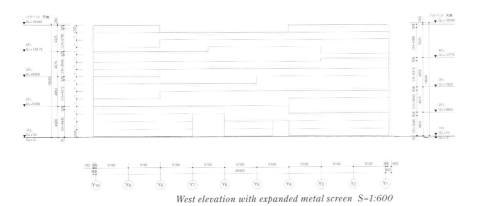
West elevation with expanded metal screen S=1:600

West elevation without expanded metal screen

Downward view from southwest

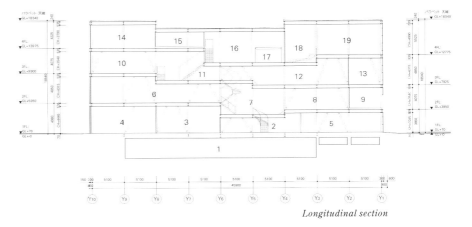
Longitudinal section

View toward small meeting room from terrace 2

Third floor: View toward office 6 from office 5. Foyer above

Office 2 on second floor. Office 1 on right above

Entrance hall

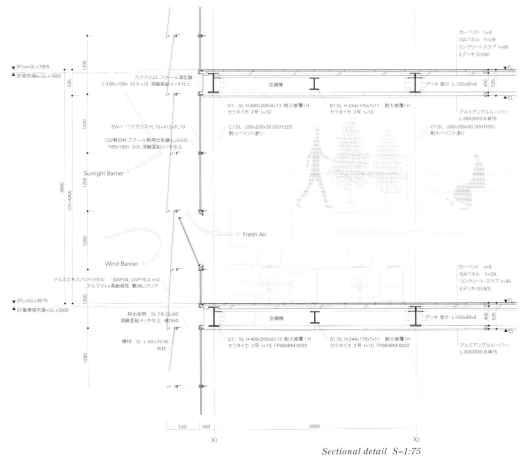
Sectional detail S=1:75

ヨシダ印刷東京本社

東京都墨田区の北斎通りに面する，美術印刷を中心とする印刷会社のオフィスビルの建替えである。もともと同じ敷地に旧社屋が建っていたが，東日本大震災で被害を受けてしまったことで，オフィスと印刷機械室を併せ持つ新たな東京の拠点となる建物が求められた。

敷地は3方向を道路で囲われた角地で，周辺には文化施設やオフィスビル，マンションやショップといった中高層のビルが近い距離で建ち並ぶ一方，古くからの住宅や工場も混在する。地域との繋がりが密接に感じられる土地の中で，周囲の建物と壁面線をある程度そろえながら適度な空きを保ち配置することで，一緒にまち並みをつくっていきながら，一方でインディペンデントな存在としてもあり得るような建ち方をイメージした。四周をエキスパンドメタルのスクリーンで覆われた外観は，うっすらと内部の様子を見通すことができ，逆に内部からは通りを行き交う人々の様子や，まちの雰囲気を身近に感じることができる。お互いを感じ合いながら関係性を持つことができる，まちとともにあるオフィスを目指した。

オフィスとしては，これまでの部署ごとに分かれる使い方ではなく，コラボレーションして新しいことにも取り組んでいけるような空間が望まれた。使っていくうちに新しい部署ができたり，その規模が変化していったりするオフィス特有のイベントに対し，どのようにでも使っていけるフレキシブルな空間をイメージし，同一平面のフラットな床が積層されていく一般的な構成ではなく，ここではその床を切って断面的にちょっとづつずらし互い違いにすることで，1階から4階までの様々な場所を緩やかに繋ぎながら最終的に一つの全体像となるようにした。上と下の空間は距離としては離れているが，感覚的にはすぐ近くに感じられる距離感となっている。

外壁はエキスパンドメタルのスクリーンとガラスカーテンウォールからなるダブルスキンの構成で，日射をカットしつつワンクッション置いた採光と通風が行えるよう，エキスパンドメタルは少し傾斜させ開いた感じにして張っている。機械による空調・換気で環境制御もするが，日本の春や秋はやはり気持ちの良い季節なので，外壁には外倒しの窓や大きな引き違いの窓を多く設け，より自然が感じられるオフィスとしている。

View of lounge from small meeting room

*Skolkovo Innovation Center
Guest Zone
Moscow, Russia
2011*

SANAA

The Central District defines the arrival to Skolkovo Innovation Center and provides a vibrant public heart of the overall master plan. The Skolkovo Dome is in central district of the city and portrays our vision as the entrance hall of Skolkovo. The sequence into the city from this entrance hall reflects the new city's philosophy of espousing Nature with Innovative Technology.

An huge iconic and transparent structure that connects the arrival flows to the main districts of the city through a new microclimate; an unconventional and exceptional gathering space for visitors and inhabitants animated by public programs. This symbolic environment contains an Art Center and Sciences Museum while having train station facilities, an observatory tower and a transportation hub. These programs can extend out to the open space within this dome making the entire space a synergetic space with constant interaction between new technology, artwork, people and nature. The favourable semi-indoor conditions inside the dome offer an immense platform where the programs extend their activities to this exceptional space according to the seasons, needs, and events. We believe this combination between activities and an extraordinary space will attract researchers and visitors a field of unlimited experimentations.

The Skolkovo Dome is the symbol of the new Skolkovo Innovation Center, which is not represented by an object like other historical cities, but is represented by the atmospheric quality of the space which all visitors can experience upon arrival to Skolkovo Innovation Center.

スコルコボ・イノベーションセンター・ゲストゾーン

スコルコボ・イノベーション・センターという新都市の玄関となる中央地区には，新都市全体計画に活気をもたらす公共的な機能が集まっている。スコルコボ・ドームは，その中央地区にあって，この都市のエントランスホールとなる。私たちはこのエントランスホールから新都市へと至るシークエンス自体が，自然と最新科学の新しい融合を探求するこの新しい都市のあり方を感じさせるようなものにしたいと考えた。

透明感のある構造によってつくられる巨大で象徴的な新しい環境は，この街を訪れるすべての人々を歓迎すると同時に，公共的なプログラムで新都市に住む人々のための憩いの場となる。この特殊な環境の中には，駅機能や交通ハブといった交通機能と展望台の他に，アートセンターと科学博物館とがある。それらがこのドーム内のオープンスペースにその活動を広げていくことで，ドーム全体が，新しい科学技術と芸術，自然，および人との間の絶え間ない交流を促す場所となることを意図した。ドーム内部の環境は通年にわたって心地よい半外部空間となるように計画されており，ドーム内のアクティビティは，季節や企画に応じて，自ずと広がってゆくだろう。この特別な空間が研究者や訪問者にとって限りない創造の場となればと考えた。

スコルコボ・ドームは歴史的な都市のいわゆるシンボルではなく，ここを訪れる人々に全く新しい空間と環境の質を与えることで，その経験自体がこの新しい街のシンボルとなることを目指した。

Overall view of plaza

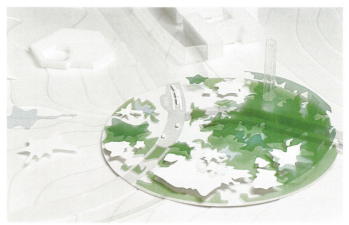
Model

Interior

Site plan

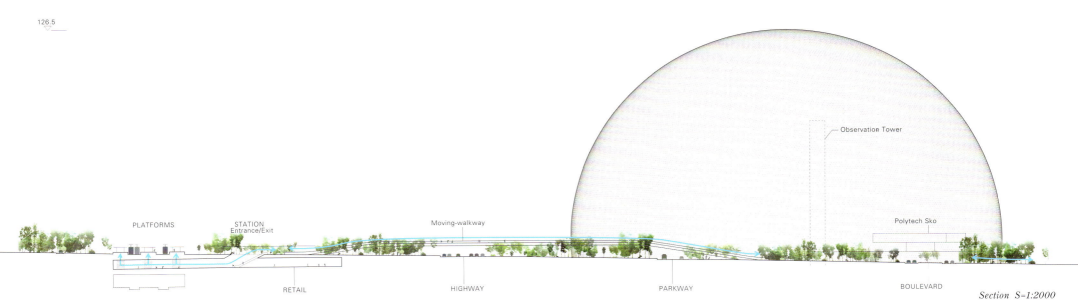
Section S=1:2000

Overall view from southwest

Terasaki House
Kanagawa, Japan
2011–14

Office of Ryue Nishizawa

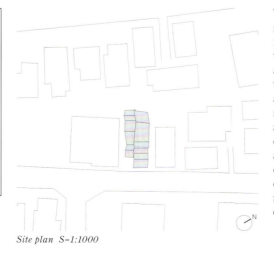

Site plan S=1:1000

The house sits on top of a valley on the outskirts of Tokyo. Surrounded by numerous farms and a large public park, the area is teeming with ample greenery. Within such an environment, we found this site to be particularly appealing. Located on the edges of a valley, it is close to a large park, with unobstructed views and spatial openness. To take advantage of the site's unique and favorable conditions, including its light, great views, and richly green surroundings, we developed a plan for a single-story house with a courtyard. We placed a large roof over the rooms and the courtyard, and created an open space where the indoors extend to the courtyard and beyond. The roof is shaped in an elongated strip along the narrow site that stretches to the north and south. However, instead of placing a single large roof, we designed it so that it curves and bends into a shape that is different from a single gabled or sloping roof, and gently envelops the indoors with a warm atmosphere. Also, the design integrates both shadow and light in the indoor spaces, by capturing light through the openings of the roof.

Our goal is to create a comfortable living space protected by its framework, with a sense of transparency that continues into the surrounding environment's fertile.

Courtyard: looking south

Courtyard: view toward street

Courtyard: looking north

1	LIVING ROOM	7 STORAGE
2	DINING ROOM	8 TERRACE
3	KITCHEN	9 UTILITY SPACE
4	COURTYARD	10 BEDROOM
5	BATHROOM	11 STUDY
6	WC	12 CARPORT

First floor S=1:200

Basement

寺崎邸

東京近郊の，丘の上に建つ住宅である。周辺には大きな公園や農園などがあり，豊かな緑に恵まれている。その中でもこの敷地は，丘の端に位置していて，大きな公園をすぐ近くに持ち，開かれた眺望の良さと空間的な開放感を持つ，特別な魅力があった。そのような恵まれた条件，明るい光，眺めの良さ，緑豊かな周辺環境といった，土地がもつ諸条件をよく取り込みたいと考えて，いろいろスタディした結果，中庭形式の平屋建ての平面構成を考えた。部屋と中庭を一つにまとめるような大きな屋根を架けて，室内と中庭，外が連続してゆくような，開放的な空間を考えた。敷地が南北に細長いので，屋根は敷地形状に沿って長く伸びていく形状となるが，単に長い大屋根を1枚架けるというのではなく，それを割ったり曲げたりして，切妻や片流れといった単一勾配屋根とは違う断面形状とし，室内をつつみこむような雰囲気をつくり出した。また同時に，屋根を割ったその裂け目から光を取り込んで，影と光が同居する屋根下空間を考えた。

架構によって包まれた，落ち着いた居住空間でありながら，周辺環境の豊かさに繋がってゆく透明感を併せ持つ空間を目指している。

Entrance approach

Bathroom

Kitchen: view toward living room

Living room: view toward kitchen and dining room

Living room: bathroom / closet behind wall

Bedroom

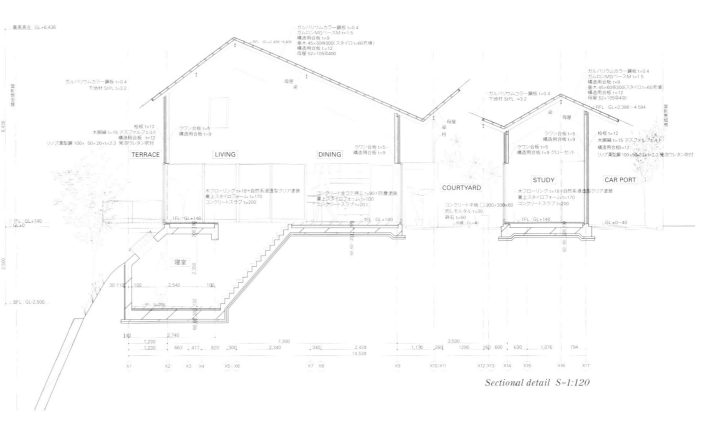
Sectional detail S=1:120

*Miyatojima Project
Higashimatsushima,
Miyagi, Japan
2011–14*

SANAA

Miyatojima is part of Matsushima, a nationally designated special scenic spot, surrounded by a beautiful terrain of hills interwoven by the sea. Even during a short walk, scenes of the rich terrain covered in various vegetation appear one after the other, providing views of deeply inset coves and sudden expanses of the ocean. In this richly endowed environment of the island are four beaches, each having communities of about 50 households. Of these, the three communities of Ohama, Tsukihama, and Murohama suffered major damage during the 2011 Great East Japan Earthquake.

Talking with the island's residents, we gave thought to the new lives of the people of these communities and the scenery they would create, including their move to a higher ground as well as plans for reconstructing the former locations. At each of the beaches, we designed the communities so that they are carefully tailored to the unique and beautiful terrain, while each home having a sense of the sea. As for reconstructing the former community locations, we gave thought to plans which highlighted the unique qualities of each beach: a natural park at Ohama, a camp site and fishing experience facility at Tsukihama, and a fisheries co-op, a work area, and rest area spread throughout Murohama.

宮戸島の計画

宮戸島は，国が指定する特別名勝松島の一部を担っており，丘と海が入り組んだ美しい地形が広がっている。少し散策する間にも，入江が深く入り組んでいたり，海が突然広がったりと，様々な植生とともに豊かな地形が次々と展開する。その恵まれた環境の中で，島には四つの浜にそれぞれ約50戸の集落があり，2011年の東日本大震災により，大浜，月浜，室浜の三つの集落が大きな被害を受けた。

私たちは島の人たちと話し合いながら，集落の高台移転とその跡地利用計画を含めた，震災後の新しい集落の生活と風景を考えることとなった。それぞれの浜ごとに，特徴ある美しい地形に寄り添いながら，そして各住戸から海が感じ取れるように集落を配置することとした。また，元々集落があった跡地利用についても，大浜は自然公園，月浜はキャンプ場や漁業体験施設，室浜は漁協と作業場と休憩所が広がり，各浜の特色を生かした計画を考えた。

Drawing: vegetation of existing landscape

Drawing: inundation area by seismic sea wave (tsunami) on 3.11. 2011

Drawing: reconstruction and relocation plan of 3 villages at Miyatojima

Drawing: transition plan of area damaged by salt through flower fields

Home for All Tsukihama in Miyatojima: view toward sea

Undulating structure consisting of simple purlins over waving beam

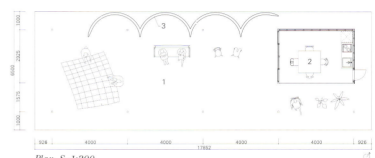

1 WORK SPACE
2 REST SPACE
3 WINDBREAK FITTING

Plan S=1:200

*Home for All Tsukihama
Higashimatsushima,
Miyagi, Japan
2013–14*

SANAA

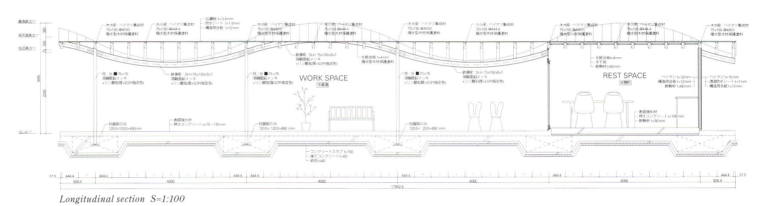

Longitudinal section S=1:100

Tsukihama is a community surrounded by intricate terrain. Fronted by a beautiful small sandy beach, Tsukihama had many small inns, tourist businesses such as nature tours, as well as fishery operations that had historically harvested seaweed and abalone. After the Great East Japan Earthquake, while it resumed operations as the only swimming beach on Miyatojima, there were far less number of inns, and businesses could not resume to the numbers before the disaster. For this reason the community decided to make fishery the main pillar and solution for reconstruction. There were many inquiries from all over Tsukihama to create a central place that would host fishery operations and morning markets as a step towards reconstruction, as well as a place for relaxation and entertainment for the local residents. In response, we decided to build a Home for All in the location of the former public center.

We decided to build a dynamic and light roof, and a space that could be used for both work and rest. The structure was built as an open rigid frame to enable fishermen to enter with vehicles and spread out their fishnets. The undulating simple frame, with the purlins spanning over the unidirectionally flowing beams, produces a shell effect and maintains the horizontal force. By keeping the roof low to conform to the surrounding environment, we thought about allowing cool southerly breezes in the summer, and using fittings to prevent cold northern winds during the winter.

In the early mornings, the space becomes lively with fishermen spreading out their catches; in the afternoon, elderly residents come to enjoy and relax on the sandy beach. In the evenings, fishermen return from the sea and gather around for their nightly feasts. The goal of this Home for All was to once again recreate the lively beach atmosphere that had existed before.

宮戸島月浜のみんなの家

月浜は入り組んだ地形に囲まれた集落である。美しい小さな砂浜が目の前に広がる月浜には多くの民宿があり，自然を生かした体験ツアーなどの観光業と，また昔からノリやアワビを始めとする漁業が営まれていた。東日本大震災被災後，宮戸島唯一の海水浴場として再開したが民宿は少なくなり，本来の集客を見込むことは難しいため，漁業が復興の柱となり，活路を見出すことになった。月浜の方々から，復興の起点となるような，漁業の作業や朝市を行ったり，訪れた人の休憩所や月浜区民の憩いの場所になる場をつくれないかと持ちかけられ，「みんなの家」を公民館跡地につくることになった。

私たちは，動きのある軽やかな屋根といろいろなことに使える作業場と休憩所をつくることにした。漁師が車を乗り入れたり網を広げたり大きく使えるように，開放的なラーメン構造とした。また，片方向に流れる梁の上に母屋が架かった波打つシンプルな架構はシェル効果を生み水平力を保っている。周辺環境に合わせて屋根を低く抑えることで，夏は涼しい南風を通し，冬は建具と共に冷たい北風を防ぐことを考えた。

早朝は漁師が採れた物を並べて賑わい，昼にはおじいさんたちが砂浜を眺めてゆったりしている。夕暮れ時には仕事を終えた漁師が海から戻ってきてワイワイ酒盛りが始まり，夜が更けていく。かつてこの場所にあったいきいきとした浜の風景がこの「みんなの家」をきっかけに再び広がっていくことを目指した。

*Home for All Miyatojima
Higashimatsushima,
Miyagi, Japan
2011–12*

SANAA

Site plan S=1:8000

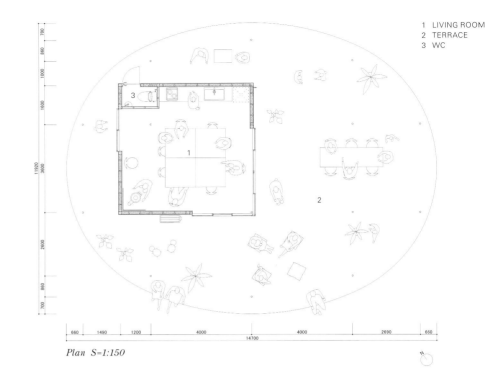
Plan S=1:150

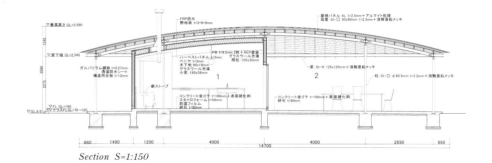
Section S=1:150

After the Great East Japan Earthquake, many temporary housing units were erected on the school grounds of the Miyatojima elementary school located in the center of Miyatojima. Due to the number of residences within the temporary housing complex, there was no space for a communal gathering place, making it difficult for the residences to meet or entertain visitors.

It was therefore decided with the local residents to build a House for All, where everyone could leisurely gather at a place centrally located on the island. We thought it would be a good idea to create a building which could accommodate many residents under a large roof.

The curved purlins were arranged on a steel framework, with a large, round, lightweight roof covered in thin 2.5 mm-thick aluminum sheets. Beneath the roof is a living room and a semi-outdoor terrace with a view of the sea. The living room can be opened to connect with the terrace as one large space.

The place was designed to provide a warm and welcoming space for anyone who should happen to stop by, with tea parties in the living room, fishermen's get-togethers on the terrace, and children playing in all corners.

東松島市宮戸島のみんなの家

東日本大震災のあと，宮戸島のほぼ中心に位置する宮戸島小学校の校庭に多くの仮設住宅が建てられた。その仮設住宅地内には世帯数の関係から唯一集会所が併設されなかったこともあり，お客さんを招き入れるような場所や住民同士の憩いの場所がなかった。

そこで，島の中央に位置するこの場所に，気軽に立ち寄ることのできるみんなの家を住民の方たちとつくることとなった。私たちは，包み込むような大きな屋根の下に住民の皆さんが集まれるような建物が良いのではないかと考えた。

鉄骨の骨組みにカーブした母屋をかけ，厚さ2.5mmの薄いアルミの板を葺き，軽くて丸い大きな屋根をつくった。その屋根の下はリビングルームと海を望むことができる半屋外のテラスとなっている。リビングは大きく開けてテラスと一体となって使うことができる。

リビングではお茶会が開かれ，テラスでは漁師たちの宴が始まり，その横で子どもたちが遊んだりする。ふらっと立ち寄ると誰かがいて，居間のように暖く迎えてくれるような場所を目指した。

Home for All Miyatojima

Home for All Miyatojima: large open space under roof

*Matsushima Nature Retreat
Miyagi, Japan
2014-*

SANAA

Elevation

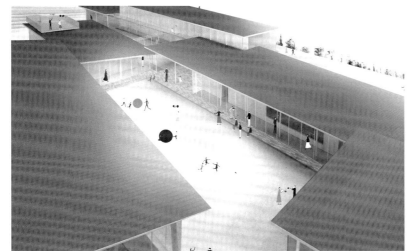
Courtyard

Aerial view

1 ENTRANCE	5 MULTI-PURPOSE HALL	9 BATHROOM
2 DINING ROOM	6 MEMORIAL SPACE	10 MACHINE ROOM
3 KITCHEN	7 BEDROOM	11 STORAGE
4 OFFICE	8 EVENT SPACE	12 GYMNASIUM

This is the reconstruction project for Matsushima Nature Retreat, a facility in Miyagi Prefecture that was destroyed by the tsunami during the Great East Japan Earthquake. Matsushima Nature Retreat used to stand in the Nobiru district of Higashi-Matsushima City, and was used by the locals as a lodging site for elementary and middle school trips, as well as an outdoors facility for group camping.

For reconstruction, the site was relocated to the school grounds of the former Miyato Elementary School, which was also on schedule to closing down. We divided the project into five different buildings: lodging, gymnasium, cafeteria, offices, and baths. These were staggered on top of an artificially created plateau. The idea was to create multiple plazas of various characteristics at the same time.

Each building is connected via the corridors, allowing visitors to circulate throughout the buildings. Walking down these corridors, one encounters various rooms and activities taking place in the plazas. While each building has a single sloping lean-to roof, their size and direction are set to match the background landscape that runs from the top of the mountains down to the site. In this way, we aimed to design a building that is involved with nature and becomes part of the surrounding scenery.

松島自然の家

東日本大震災の津波で全壊した宮城県松島自然の家の復旧計画である。松島自然の家はかつて東松島市野蒜地区にあり、県内の小中学校の宿泊研修やグループでのキャンプなどの野外活動施設として親しまれてきた。

再建するにあたり、廃校が決まっていた宮戸小学校の跡地に移転することとなった。私たちは建物を宿泊棟、体育館棟、食堂棟、事務室棟、浴室棟の5棟に分け、それらを人工的な台地上の敷地にずらしながら配置した。そうすることで同時に敷地内に性格の異なるいろいろな広場をつくり出そうと考えた。

各棟は回廊によって繋がっており、利用者は建物内を回遊することができる。回廊を歩いていくと、いろいろな部屋や広場での活動に出会うことができる。各棟はそれぞれ片流れの屋根となっているが、敷地の背後の山から麓へと繋がる地形に沿うように大きさや方向を計画することで、自然と触れ合い、周囲に溶け込む建物となることを目指した。

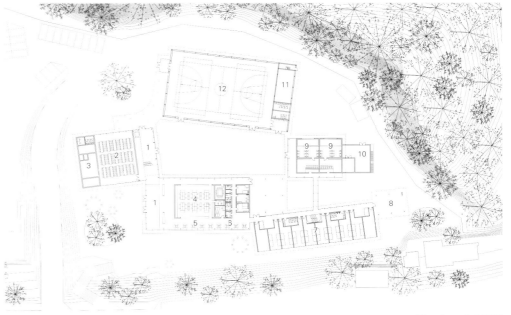
First floor S=1:1200

Junko Fukutake Terrace
Okayama, Okayama, Japan
2012–14

SANAA

This is a cafe located inside the Tsushima campus of Okayama University.

The university has been working on their improvement plan for a few years towards building a campus that is open to the local community. The Junko Fukutake Hall, completed two years ago at the Shikada campus, was born from the benefactor Junko Fukutake's desire to create a place where different people could meet and communicate. This time, the project has involved building a cafe called the Junko Fukutake Terrace at the Tsushima campus.

The site is located on the main entryway, facing a beautiful road lined with ginkgo trees that runs centrally north-south through the campus. Around the site are university facilities including research labs, lodges, sports gym as well as facilities used by local residents such as housing and restaurants. These facilities coexist alongside each other in a neighborhood where university staff, students, and local residents regularly come and go. We planned for the cafe to become an open space that can be peacefully enjoyed by everyone.

While the building is a university facility, we designed it with a single large roof that runs adjacently to the road to make it inviting to the local people as well. Avoiding existing trees, the roof is shaped with a soft curve to create a place where people can gather and enter effortlessly from the road. The cafe is nestled beneath a slightly overhanging roof, and through the windows, customers can enjoy watching the scenery of students riding their bicycles to school. Towards the back of the building, there is a lawn area with a gradual slope that blends into the adjacent grounds, designed to create a feeling of greenery that stretches into the distance.

The Junko Fukutake Terrace is not only limited to its role as a cafe; it is a place where university activities like seminars and festivals can take place, and also serve the community as a gallery and a venue for hosting other local events. We hope that it becomes a place where a wide variety of interactions are born between the people both within and around the university.

◁ *Overall view from south. Roof weaves through roadside trees* *View from street on east*

View toward cafe space from place under roof

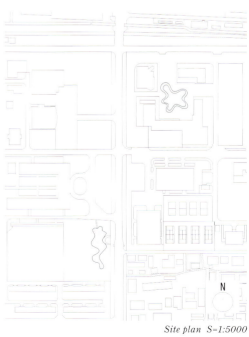

Site plan S=1:5000

131

Junko Fukutake Terrace

岡山大学の津島キャンパス内に佇むカフェである。

　岡山大学は数年前から地域に開かれたキャンパスづくりを目指し，キャンパス整備計画を進めている。建物を寄贈された福武純子さんの，様々な人が出会い，コミュニケーションを誘発する場になって欲しいという思いから，2年前鹿田キャンパスに多目的ホールの「Junko Fukutake Hall」を完成した。そして今回津島キャンパスにつくられたのがカフェの「Junko Fukutake Terrace」である。

　キャンパスの正門入口にあたる敷地は，キャンパス中央を南北に貫く，銀杏並木の美しい道に面している。敷地周辺には研究所や宿舎，体育館などの大学施設と，住居や飲食店などの地域住民が利用する施設が並存し，大学の関係者と地域住民が常に行き来する場所である。私たちはカフェが開放的で誰もが居心地よく過ごせる場となるように計画した。

　大学の施設でありながら地域の人たちも気軽に立ち寄ることができるよう，道に沿って1枚の大きな屋根を配置した。既存の樹木を避けながら，人が集まれるような場所をつくったり，道から自然に人が入れるように考えて，柔らかいカーブで形をつくっている。少し広がりのある屋根の下にはカフェがあり，カフェの中からガラス越しに，通学する学生たちが自転車でまちなかを走る風景が見えてくる。建物の奥には緩やかな高低差のある芝生の広場をつくり，それが隣のグラウンドと繋がっていて，緑がずっと奥に広がっていくような場所となるように考えた。

　「Junko Fukutake Terrace」がカフェという用途に限らず，ゼミや収穫祭などの大学の活動の場として，またギャラリーや地域のイベントなどの市民にも活用され，多様なコミュニケーションの生まれる場所になって欲しいと願っている。

Cafe space

Table installed around pillar at place under roof

Seats for cafe space

Plan S=1:500

View toward lawn field through curved glass wall

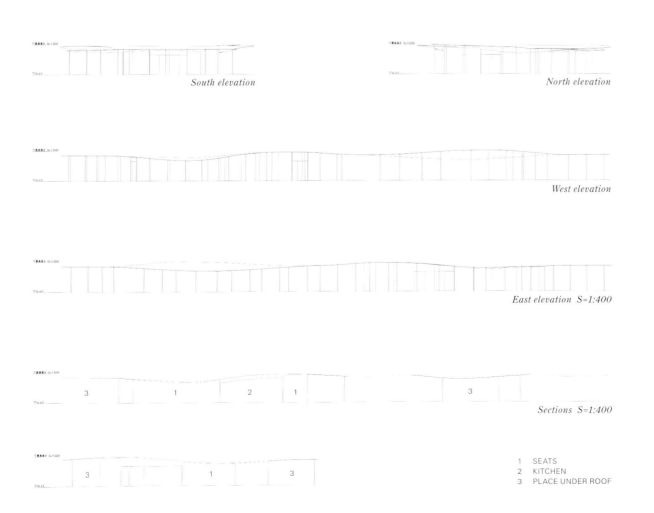

South elevation

North elevation

West elevation

East elevation S=1:400

Sections S=1:400

1 SEATS
2 KITCHEN
3 PLACE UNDER ROOF

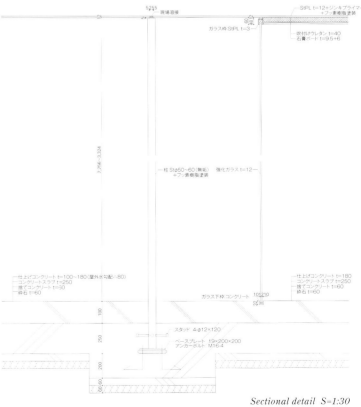

Sectional detail S=1:30

Competition for New National Stadium Tokyo, Japan 2012

SANAA
in collaboration with Nikken Sekkei

Aerial view from southeast

We submitted a proposal for the international design competition for the new National Stadium which was held in 2012. The plan called for transforming the aging National Stadium into one that holds 80,000 spectators for soccer, rugby, track and field, and other sporting competitions, as well as a variety of non-sporting events. The proposal also demanded that the construction symbolize a new age.

We thought that a stadium being not only closed like a completed object, but open like a knot within the flow of the city, nature and people, was perfectly suited for the area.

The roof, with its gentle changes according to the wind flow, streetscape and other features of the surrounding environment, and the concourse which connects directly from around the area continuously to the stands, creates a majestic 3D park which ties the stadium to nature and the city. The single sloped deck connected by the concourse has soft fold-like shapes with numerous overlaps that create a variety of boundaries so one can really feel the surrounding environment while having a sense of unity and presence. This stadium, which connects to the surrounding park, opens up to the street as a place to relax, even when there is no event being held.

The spectators gather together from various locations on the street flowing into the stadium where the players themselves compete while feeling the landscape of Tokyo along with the assembled fans. We hoped that through these multiple and continuously dynamic experiences, the excitement of the people prompted by the stadium will spread out across the shrine grove and the neighboring streets, promising to become a novel landscape for Tokyo itself.

Translucent model *Diagram: mobility and circulation*

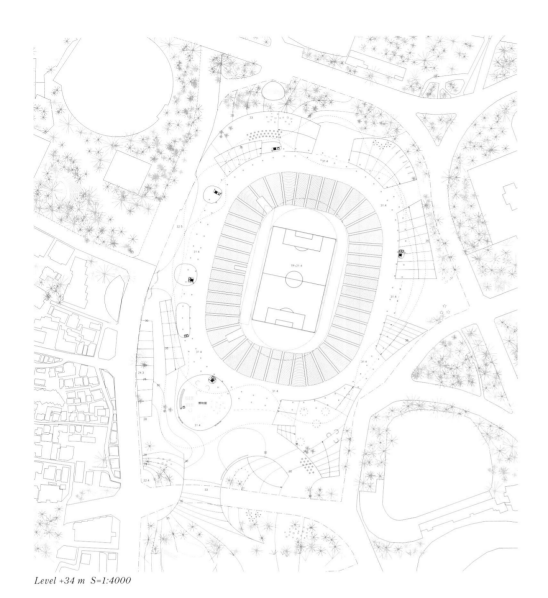

Level +34 m S=1:4000

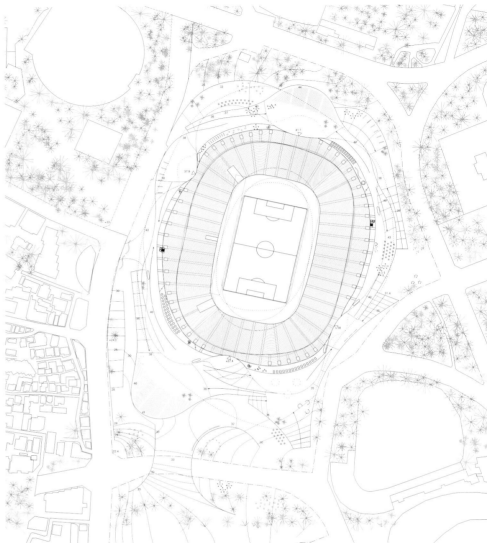

Level +37 m

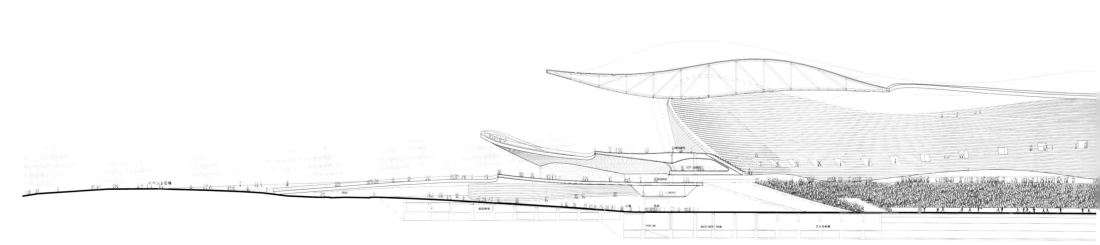

Section S=1:1200

新国立競技場

2012年に行われた新国立競技場の国際デザインコンクールの応募案である。国立競技場の老朽化による建替えで、サッカーやラグビー、陸上競技などを行える8万人収容のスタジアムであり、かつ様々なイベントなどにも対応できるような計画である。また、それと同時に、新しい時代を象徴するような建築の提案を求められた。

私たちは、新しい未来のスタジアムのあり方として、完結したオブジェのような閉じた形のスタジアムではなく、有機的に周囲と繋がりを持つことで、都市や自然や人々の流れの結び目のような、開かれたスタジアムがふさわしいと考えた。

風の流れや街並みなど周囲の環境に応じて穏やかに変化している屋根と、周辺から連続してスタンドへと直接繋がっていくコンコースによって、自然や都市とスタジアムが連続する雄大な立体公園のような場をつくり出す。コンコースから繋がるワンスロープのスタンドは、ヒダのような柔らかい形が幾層にも重なるようにしてできており、一体感と臨場感を持ちながらも、周辺の環境を感じることができるように、多様な境界を生み出している。周辺の公園と連続するこのスタジアムは、イベントのない時でも憩いの場所として街に開かれる。

街のいろいろなところから観衆がスタンドに流れ込むように集まり、プレイヤーたちは観衆とともに東京の風景を感じながら競技を行う。このような多様でダイナミックな連続した体験により、スタジアムで生まれる人々の興奮が、神宮の杜や街へと広がり、東京の新しい風景となることを期待した。

Level +43 m

Concourse

View from seat

*Fukita Pavilion
in Shodoshima
Shodoshima, Kagawa,
Japan
2012–13*

Office of Ryue Nishizawa

Site plan S=1:1000

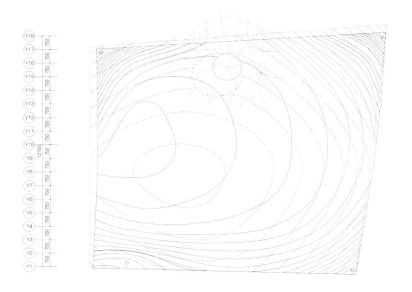
Plan S=1:200

The Fukita Pavilion with its cafe and restaurant was built within the grounds of a shrine near the Fukuda Harbor in Shodoshima. The adjacent former Fukuda Elementary School was reborn in 2013 as the Fukutake House, along with the Setouchi Triennale. The original plan for the cafe was placed within the school building, but after visiting the site we felt that enclosing all activities indoors was a waste of opportunity, and began to think of taking the cafe out of the school grounds to take advantage of the beauty and serenity of the local Fukuda environment.

There was a gym in the schoolyard of the Fukutake House, and a shrine and its grounds right next to it. The grounds of the shrine, the schoolyard and the gym were put to loving use by the local residents. We therefore considered a plan to separate the cafe into a kitchen and seating area, placing the exterior seating within the grounds of the shrine, and the interior seating and kitchen area in the gym to create flow from the shrine to the elementary school. The outdoor seating area inside the shrine grounds is the gazebo called the Fukita Pavilion, a semi-outdoor space made of two steel plates that look as if the decomposed granite surface of the shrine premises had peeled and lifted upward.

The goal of building within the shrine premises was to create a structure without a foundation that is light and low to the ground, and feels as if it can be easily moved. Its structure involves curved steel plates like the bottom of a ship placed on the ground, covered by a steel plate roof which sags with its own weight. The two curved steel plates are welded together at the edge of the overlap to form a shape where one plate supports the other. The steel floor plate is kept in place by the steel roof; the steel roof, with a large span that sags in the middle, is in turn supported by the steel floor plate.

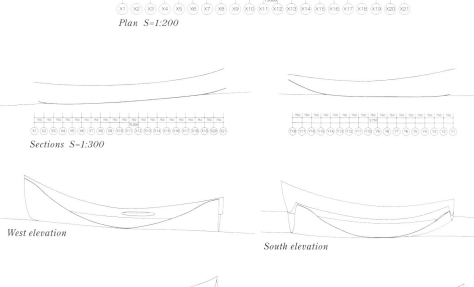
Sections S=1:300

West elevation

South elevation

East elevation S=1:300

North elevation

View from north. Gymnasium of elementary school on right

The interior and exterior spaces made from the two steel plates become an extension of the shrine grounds, playground equipment, seating and resting area, and children's playground. The goal was to create an open structure where not only the children, but also the wind and wildlife can pass through. Although the pavilion is a permanent structure, our goal was to make it look like it was simply dropped and installed, so that it is light and playful like a playground equipment or a landscaping element. We chose a beige color for its tone to keep in line with the decomposed granite of the ground and the palette of the surrounding environment.

小豆島の葺田パヴィリオン
小豆島・福田港近くの神社境内に建つ，カフェ・レストランのパヴィリオンである。隣の旧福田小学校は，2013年，瀬戸内芸術祭の開催にあわせて福武ハウスとして再生した。このカフェは当初の計画では，校舎内に計画されていたが，現地を訪れて，美しく静かな福田の地区の環境の中で，すべての活動が校舎内に収まってしまうのがもったいなく感じ，カフェを校舎の外に考えるようになった。

福武ハウスの校庭には体育館があり，そのすぐ隣に神社と境内があった。境内も校庭も体育館も，地元の人々に愛され使われていた。そこで，カフェを厨房部分と客席部分の二つにわけて，屋外客席部分を境内側に，屋内客席と厨房部分を体育館に置く計画を考え，それによって，境内と小学校側を動線的に繋げようと考えた。屋外客席部分が「葺田パヴィリオン」と呼ばれる，境内に建つ東屋で，境内の真砂土の地面がそのままめくり上がったような，鉄板2枚による半屋外空間である。

境内に建つということで，基礎がない建築，動かせそうなくらい軽く低いものを目指した。構成としては，船舶の底のようにカーブした鉄板が地面に置かれ，その上に鉄板屋根をかけて，自重によってたわむ，というものだ。カーブした2枚の鋼板が重なりあって，端部が互いに溶接されることで，お互いにお互いを支え合って形が成り立つ。床の鋼板は屋根鋼板の存在によって開いてゆくのが抑えられ，屋根鋼板の方は床鋼板によって支えられつつ，大スパンなので真ん中でたわむ。

2枚の鋼板でつくられた内外の空間は，境内の延長でもあり，遊具でもあり，客席かつ休憩所，また子供の遊び場となる。子供だけでなく風や動物が通り抜ける，開放的な建築を目指した。恒久建築ではあるが，持ってきて置いただけというような，軽やかで遊具的かつランドスケープ的な存在を目指した。全体の色調は，真砂土の色と周辺の色調にあわせて，ベージュ色とした。

Steel plate roof bending due to its own weight like tent

View from west. Pavilion installed in trees at shrine precinct

Place where one can feel almost outdoor as going toward inmost of pavilion

Bezalel Academy of Arts & Design
Jerusalem, Israel
2012–21

SANAA

The site of the new campus for the Bezalel Academy of Arts and Design is located in the Russian Compound, on the top of a hill overlooking the old city of Jerusalem. The Academy includes several departments spatially organized in studios, classrooms, workshops, administration offices and public areas such as exhibition galleries, a store, a café and a cafeteria.

The building is composed of slabs. The slabs are stacked as so to follow the natural gradient of the landscape and are all at different levels. Both at the exterior and in the interior of the building, the slabs are connected through ramps and stairs so that it is possible to walk freely from one to the other, moving horizontally and vertically.

On the exterior, the connected slabs form a terraced roof overlooking the city. On the interior, the slabs are detached from one another to create vertical void spaces throughout the building. The void spaces allow visual connection between the different parts of the program that are hosted on each slab. As a consequence, each part of the building maintains its independence, but at the same time is fully connected with all other parts.

Because of the layout of the slabs, natural light can filter freely through the building both from above and from the sides, penetrating also in those spaces that sit in the middle of the largest footprint areas. The reinforced concrete slabs are supported by reinforced concrete columns.

The scale of the building is determined by its context and by the program. The building volume is composed to fit properly within the city of Jerusalem and, at the same time, it accommodates the necessary spaces for students and faculty of the Academy to work comfortably. The building also fits into the context as it mimics its terraced landscape, and resonates with its color and texture.

1 INDUSTRIAL DESIGN
2 WOOD WORKSHOP
3 METAL WORKSHOP
4 PRINTING WORKSHOP
5 WORKSHOPS
6 FINE ARTS
7 CERAMICS AND GLASS
8 ENTRANCE HALL
9 CENTRAL GALLERY
10 SHOP
11 VISUAL COMMUNICATION
12 FASHION AND JEWELRY
13 PHOTOGRAPHY
14 ARCHITECTURE

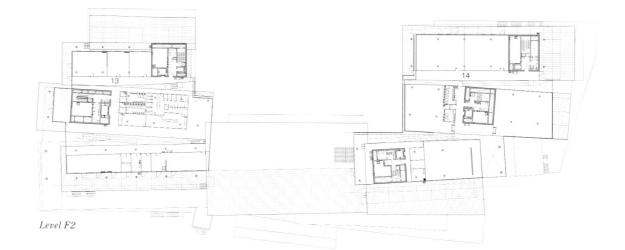

Level F2

Level G2

Level G1 S=1:1200

Overall view

ベツァルエル・アカデミー・オブ・アート・アンド・デザイン
ベツァルエル・アカデミー・オブ・アート・アンド・デザインの新しいキャンパス計画である。敷地はエルサレムの旧市街を見下ろす丘の上，ロシア正教会のある地区に位置する。

　この美術大学には九つの学部があり，それぞれの学部のスタジオ，ワークショップ，クラスルーム，オフィス機能と，全学部で使われるパブリックのワークショップやギャラリー，ショップ，カフェ，レストランなどがあり，周囲に開かれた大学を目指している。

　建物は丘の地形に沿うように，幾つものスラブを積み重ねてつくられている。それぞれのスラブにはプログラムが配置され，建物の周囲や屋上では街を見渡すテラスとなっている。スラブが近づいたり離れたりすることで様々な吹抜けができ，吹抜けにはスロープや階段が設置され，上下左右，室内から室外へと自由に移動することができる。ずれたスラブの合間からは自然光が差し込み，奥行きの深い建物の内部でも明るい空間となっている。吹抜けを介してそれぞれのスラブで行われているアクティビティが連続して見え，各スラブに配置されたプログラムは独立性を保ちながらも，全体としては一つの大学としてのまとまりをもつように，緩やかに繋がったワンルーム空間となっている。

　石張りの建物が広がった歴史的な町並みの中で周辺環境にあった素材を取り入れ，ヴォリュームを抑えながらも，地形に寄り添うように積層することで，ランドスケープのような建物となることを目指している。

In-between space

Lobby

Street view

Library

*Kokusai Soushoku
Headquarters
Tokyo, Japan
2013–*

Office of Ryue Nishizawa

This project was for an one company's own building facing onto a main street of an inner city. The site covers approximately 150 m² and is surrounded by office buildings and apartment blocks, as well as the Metropolitan Expressway running across its facade: a typical space at the heart of a major city. The client's request was to create a building that houses a parking lot and entrance hall on the first floor, office spaces occupying the upper levels, and a private guest house on the highest floor.

Starting from the first floor we installed an entrance hall, then added layers of break rooms, office spaces, conference rooms, and multipurpose spaces before finally placing a guest house on the highest floor which commanded the best view. In total the building was 31 m high, spanning 8 stories. In order to achieve a long, narrow aspect ratio of 4:1, we designed the periphery of the building to have an especially strong surface with a structure containing pillars and braces, and did not install a supportive core. In general we designed each level as one-room structures containing four outward-facing walls. Moreover, through positioning flow spaces such as staircases and ramps on the outside of office spaces, we were able to create expansive rooms which contain nothing to obstruct the gaze.

The entire exterior is cladded in aluminum expanded metal sunshades, providing a 60 cm to 2 m-deep buffer around the building. At the same time, expanded metal screens running along the ramps and terraces that extend from the main building create gaps in the cladding. As a result, even the lower stories which lie in the shade of the capital freeway can take advantage of daylight.

With this project we aimed to create a relaxed office space that lies open to its surrounding environment. In this expansive office, we hope that these work-oriented spaces also feel like homely living rooms for the employees.

国際装飾本社

都心の大通りに面する自社ビルの計画である。敷地は45坪程の大きさで、周囲をオフィスビルやマンションに囲まれ、正面を首都高が横切る大都会の真中のような場所である。クライアントの要望は地上1階に駐車場とエントランスホールを、その上に執務空間を、最上階にはプライベートなゲストハウスが欲しいとのことであった。

1階からエントランスホール、休憩室、執務スペース、会議室、多目的スペース等を順番に積層していき、見晴らしの良い最上階にゲストハウスを配する、高さ31m、8階建ての建物となった。搭状比が4:1の細長い形状を成立させるため、コアはつくらずに外周部に柱とブレースによる構造体の固い面をつくった。原則的に各階一部屋の構成でどの階も四周が外部に面する空間とし、また階段やスロープなどの動線空間も執務空間の外に飛び出すことで、室内に視線を遮る障害物のない見通しの良いワンルーム空間が生まれた。

外装はアルミエキスパンドメタルの日よけで建築全体を覆い、建物のまわりに奥行きが60cm〜2m程のバッファー空間をつくり出した。同時に建築本体から飛び出したスロープやテラスにエキスパンドメタルのスクリーンが沿うことで外装に裂け目ができた。そこから首都高の陰になる下層階に採光をとれるようにした。

落ち着いた執務空間と周辺環境に対しての開放性をあわせ持ち、どこにいても仕事のための空間でありながら同時にみんなのリビングでもあるような開放的なオフィスビルを目指した。

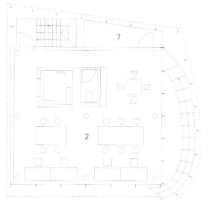
Third floor

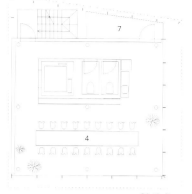
Sixth floor

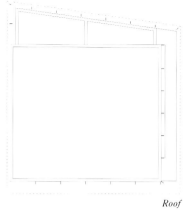
Roof

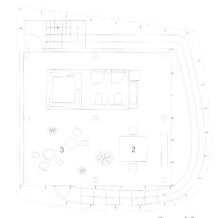
Second floor

Fifth floor

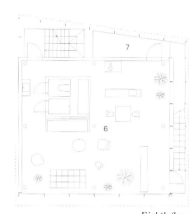
Eighth floor

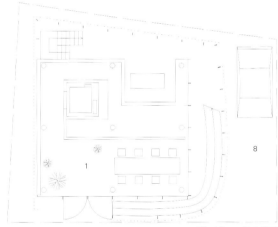
First floor S=1:200

Fourth floor

Seventh floor

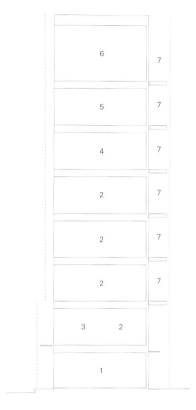

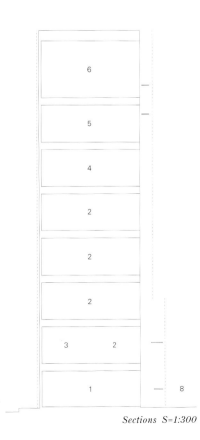

Sections S=1:300

1 ENTRANCE HALL
2 OFFICE
3 BREAK ROOM
4 MEETING ROOM/
   MULTIPURPOSE ROOM
5 EXECUTIVE ROOM
6 GUEST HOUSE
7 TERRACE
8 PARKING

House in Quebradas
Los Vilos, Chile
2012–

Kazuyo Sejima & Associates

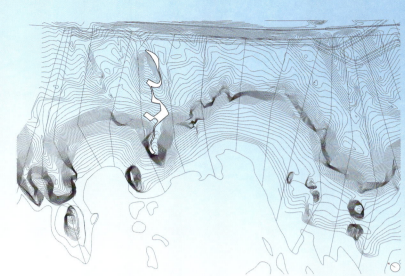

Site plan S=1:4000

Overall view from south

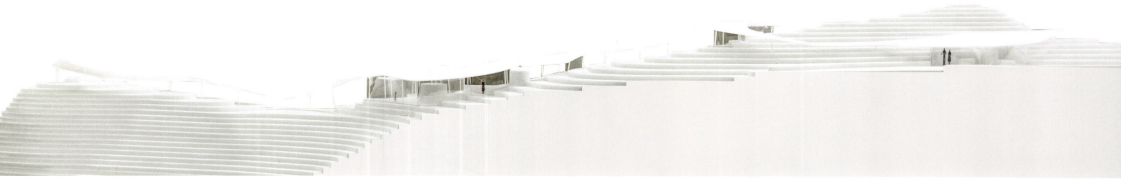

Model: south elevation

South view

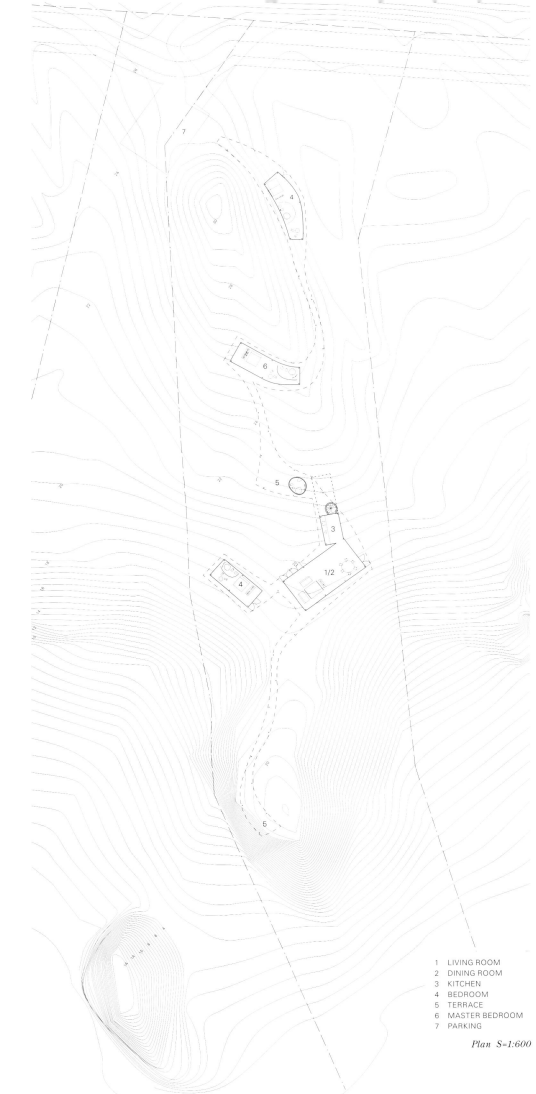

1 LIVING ROOM
2 DINING ROOM
3 KITCHEN
4 BEDROOM
5 TERRACE
6 MASTER BEDROOM
7 PARKING

Plan S=1:600

The project is a weekend house in Los Vilos, Chile.

The site is on a plot of land that faces the Pacific Ocean, a gradually sloping terrain of small bumps and dips with open views in various directions.

We wanted to design a residence that takes advantage of this beautiful piece of land and allows one to fully experience its pleasures.

The site extends toward the sea in east and west directions. We arranged a bedroom on the far side of the hill, another bedroom in the middle of the hill, a terrace to escape from the winter south winds, a bedroom above a cliff, a sunset-view kitchen, and a living-dining room overlooking the ocean.

An expansive roof stretches over the separate rooms, gliding high above into the air and dipping low close to the ground, creating a gradual undulation that not only harmonizes with nature, but also introduces a layer of freshness into the landscape.

The slopes of the roof act as shields to protect from the cold south winds in the winter months, whereas the lower parts of the roof are designed to resist earthquakes.

This construction has allowed us to create a form of environment that harmonizes with nature, with wide, open spaces underneath the roof without braces or load-bearing walls.

Our hope is that the project will evolve from a piece of architecture into a kind of living environment-landscape that resonates with the beautiful wilderness of Los Vilos.

チリの住宅

チリのロス・ビロスに計画している週末住宅である。

敷地は太平洋に面しており，緩やかな傾斜地の中に窪地やこぶのような場所がある．またいろいろな方向に眺望の開かれたところである．

私たちは，このたいへん美しく，魅力的な敷地を最大限体験できるような住宅を考えたいと思った．

東西方向に海へと延びた敷地に，丘の向こう側のベッドルーム，丘の中腹にたつベッドルーム，冬の南風をしのぐテラス，海を間近に感じられる崖の上のベッドルーム，サンセットの見えるキッチン，海が見渡せるリビングダイニングを配置した．

また，敷地に長く広がり，各部屋を緩やかに繋ぐ屋根は，地面から離れ上空を通過したり，地面すれすれを這うような低いところがあったりと，地形に沿ってやわらかく起伏することで，自然と調和し，また同時に新たな風景をつくりだす．

屋根の傾きは冷たい冬の南風をカットし，屋根の低い部分は耐震要素として働く．

このことで屋根下に耐震壁やブレースのない開放的な空間を生み出し，自然と呼応したやわらかな形をつくっている．

ロス・ビロスの美しい荒野に建築というより，なにか風景に近い環境のようなものができればと考えている．

Shogin TACT Tsuruoka
(Tsuruoka Cultural Hall)
Tsuruoka, Yamagata, Japan
2012–17

SANAA
in collaboration with Shinbo Architects Office +
Ishikawa Architects Office

Overall view from northwest

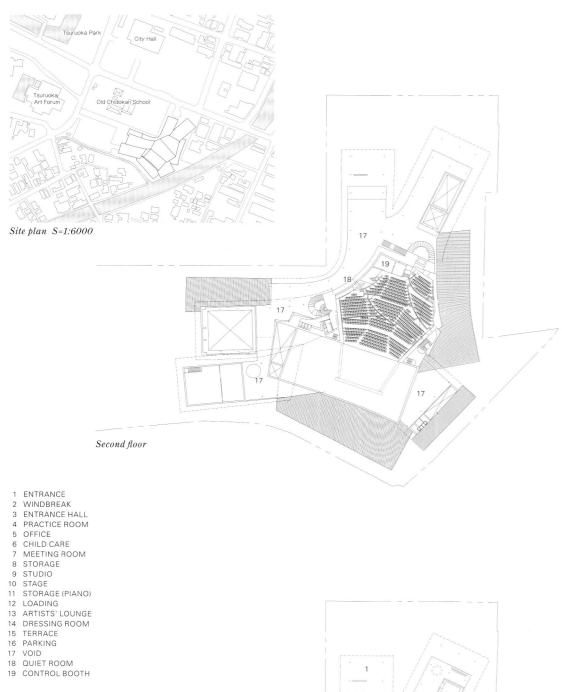

Site plan S=1:6000

Second floor

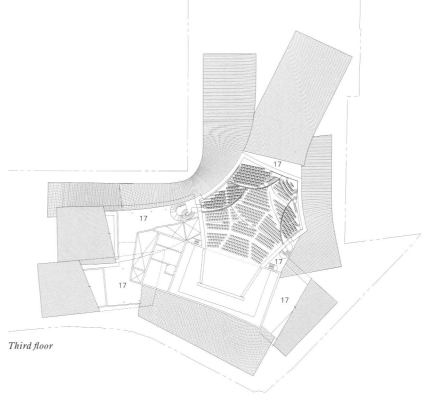

Third floor

1 ENTRANCE
2 WINDBREAK
3 ENTRANCE HALL
4 PRACTICE ROOM
5 OFFICE
6 CHILD CARE
7 MEETING ROOM
8 STORAGE
9 STUDIO
10 STAGE
11 STORAGE (PIANO)
12 LOADING
13 ARTISTS' LOUNGE
14 DRESSING ROOM
15 TERRACE
16 PARKING
17 VOID
18 QUIET ROOM
19 CONTROL BOOTH

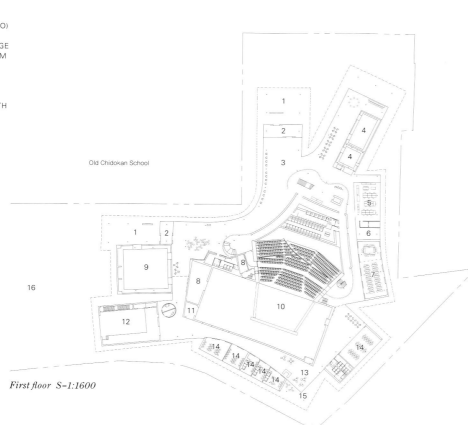

First floor S=1:1600

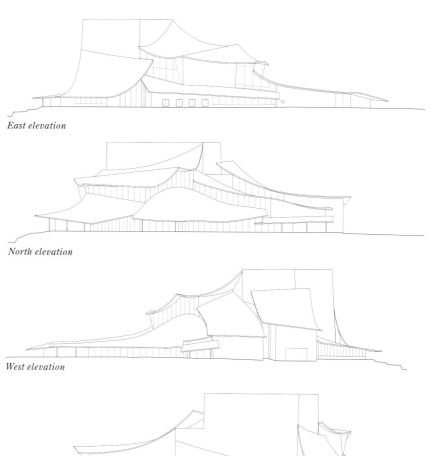

East elevation

North elevation

West elevation

South elevation S=1:1200

View from west

View from north

Entrance hall: view from north

Entrance on north (left); practice rooms on right

This is a reconstruction of a culture hall which acts as the center for cultural and art activities of the region. The site is surrounded by rich nature and is located inside the city's cultural area, and adjoins to the historic building of Chidokan of the Shonai Domain School. The request of the client was to pass on the former culture hall which had long been used by students and local arts groups, while also expanding functionalities that would further enhance such activities.

To create a "hall for the local region" where residents become both spectators and actors, we enveloped the large hall with a surrounding corridor. These corridors will be open to the public with no definite front or back, so that any area can be used freely. For special performances, it can be separated with partitions t the right and left of the stage to temporarily demarcate the front and back.

The large center hall is minimized in depth as much as possible so that it creates an intimate sense of unity between the actors and the spectators. The space is designed in a vineyard style so that live sound reverberates throughout the entire hall, with a composition in which the stage can be accessed directly from any seat.

On the exterior, a group of small roofs cluster to divide the large building into smaller sections. Each of these small roofs slopes down towards the outer perimeter, eventually reaching the height of a single-story building along the street. By controlling the volume in this manner, we aimed for this building to harmonize with Chi-

Entrance hall: practice rooms on right

dokan and the surrounding landscape.

This new hall is full of character and handmade warmth, which are evident in the texture of the sheet metal, concrete finish, and the organic and richly textured wooden louvers. As if to engage and correspond to the natural environment, these features will continue to evolve and change according to the various situations depending on the time and lighting. Like the residents who have fostered and continued to pass on the local culture, the building will also continue to harmonize with its surroundings. We hope that this building will become a lively new center for cultural and artistic activities for the city of Tsuruoka.

Entrance hall: view toward entrance on north

Artists' lounge

荘銀タクト鶴岡（鶴岡市文化会館）

地域の文化芸術活動拠点となる文化会館の建替えである。敷地は，豊かな自然に囲われた市の文化エリアの中にあり，歴史的な建造物である庄内藩校致道館に隣接している。学生や地域の芸術団体の人たちに日常的に親しまれてきた旧文化会館を継承しつつ，その活動の幅をより広げるための機能の拡充などが求められた。

市民の人たちが鑑賞者となり演者にもなる"地域のためのホール"として，大ホールを回廊空間で包む鞘堂形式を採用した。回廊は日常的に市民の方々に開放され，裏表なく色々な場所で活動することができ，特別な公演の際には舞台上下のパーティションによって裏表に区切ることも可能としている。

中央の大ホールは，可能な限り奥行きを抑えることで，客席と演者が一体感のあるホールを目指している。ホール全体に生音が響き渡るワインヤード型とし，どの客席からも直接舞台に降りてくることができる空間構成としている。

建物の外観は，幾つかの小屋根群が集まる形として，建物の大きさを分節している。それらの小屋根は外周に向かって低くなってゆき，道路沿いにおいては1階建てくらいの低さまで高さを抑えている。このようにヴォリュームをコントロールすることで，致道館や周辺の街並みとの調和を目指している。

板金の風合い，コンクリートの左官仕上げ，表情豊かな木ルーバーの自然さなど，人の手がつくり上げた，人の温もりが感じられるこの新しいホールは，自然環境と対話するように，時間や光の加減などの状況によりその表情を変化させていく。地域の方々が末長く文化を紡いでいくように，建物も周辺の風景と調和していき，地域の方々で賑わう鶴岡市の新しい文化芸術活動拠点となればと思っている。

View from artists' lounge: looking north

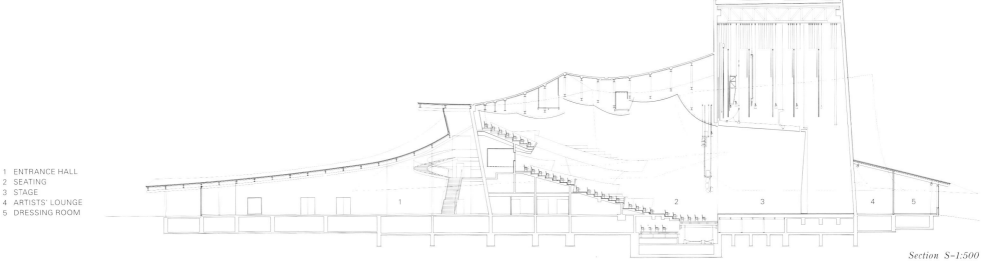

1 ENTRANCE HALL
2 SEATING
3 STAGE
4 ARTISTS' LOUNGE
5 DRESSING ROOM

Section S=1:500

◁ *Entrance hall: view from entrance on west*

Composition of seats

Hall: view toward stage

Hall in wineyard style

House in Los Vilos
Los Vilos, Chile
2012–

Office of Ryue Nishizawa

A residence planned along the beautiful natural coastline facing the Pacific in Chile, South America. This project involves 8 Japanese architects invited to each design a detached house as well as Chilean architects designing 8 houses: a total of 16 houses will constitute an entire community, to which this house will belong.

Located at the tip of a small cape protruding into the ocean, the overall composition of the house consists of an elongated space that corresponds with the cape's long and thin shape, a floor derived from the undulating topography and a roof that tops it all off with its gentle curve in concert with the topography.

It is as if there is just the land and a roof in the midst of an abundant nature. Toward the

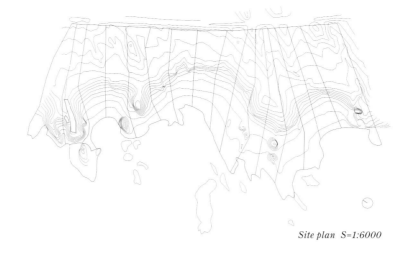

Site plan S=1:6000

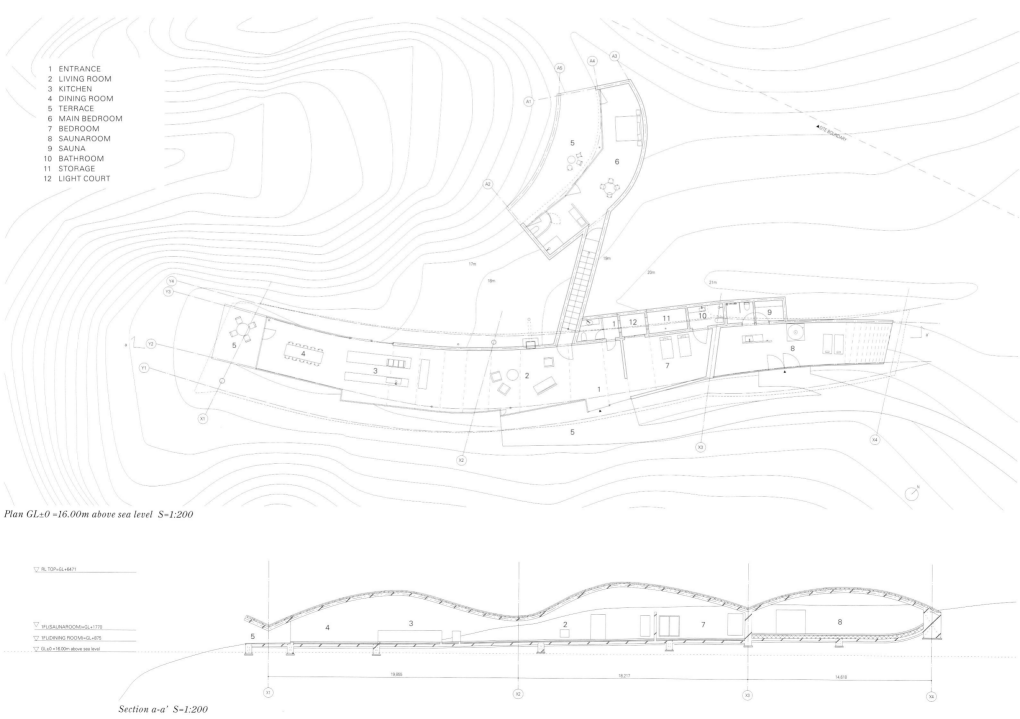

1 ENTRANCE
2 LIVING ROOM
3 KITCHEN
4 DINING ROOM
5 TERRACE
6 MAIN BEDROOM
7 BEDROOM
8 SAUNAROOM
9 SAUNA
10 BATHROOM
11 STORAGE
12 LIGHT COURT

Plan GL±0 =16.00m above sea level S=1:200

Section a-a' S=1:200

tip of the cape facing the magnificent views is the public zone including the dining room, while private spaces such as the bedroom are placed away from the sea in calmness. The concrete roof touches the ground in places, dividing spaces. In terms of structure, arches that connect diagonally-arranged landing points make it possible to create large spans while opening to various directions toward the surrounding landscape.

The space comes with a diversity of openness that can never be achieved with classic arch structures such as the vault roof. It is an effort to establish harmony with the harsh yet beautiful nature through this house's unobtrusive sense of volume that defies the actual 250 m² together with the roof's landscaping continuity.

ロスビロスの住宅

南米チリの太平洋に面した美しい自然の海岸沿いに計画されている住宅である．ここでの計画は，日本人建築家8人が招待されて，各々戸建住宅を設計し，それに加えてチリの建築家が設計する8戸の住宅と合わせて，全16戸の住宅によって一つの住宅地をつくり出すというもので，この住宅はその一部になる．

この住宅のロケーションは，太平洋に突き出した小さな岬の突端である．構成としては，細長い岬の形状に合うように，全体を細長い空間として，起伏する地形の変化を利用して床をつくり，その上に地形に呼応するように緩やかにカーブする屋根をかけている．

豊かな自然の中に土地と屋根だけがあるような建物だ．眺めのよい岬の先端側にダイニングなどのパブリックゾーンを，陸地側の落ち着いた静かな場所に寝室などのプライベート空間を配置する．屋根はコンクリートでつくられ，所々で地面に落ちてきて，空間を分けたりする．構造的には，対角線上に配された着地点を結ぶようにアーチをかけることで，大スパンを飛ばしながら，周囲の風景に対して多方向に開くことを可能としている．

ヴォールト屋根のような古典的なアーチ構造ではなし得ない，多様な開放性をもった空間である．250m²という大きさを感じさせないヴォリューム感と屋根のランドスケープ的連続性によって，荒々しく美しい自然との調和を目指している．

Distant view toward construction site from east

South side of construction site: looking west

Dining room/kitchen. View from west

Shibuya Station Development Plan
Tokyo, Japan
2012–28

SANAA

This is the redevelopment of the Shibuya Station and its surrounding areas. Shibuya is a terminal for the city's buses and multiple train and metro lines including the Tokyu Toyoko Line, Keio Inokashira Line, JR Yamanote Line, Saikyo Line, Tokyo Metro Ginza Line, Hanzomon Line, and Fukutoshin Line, with a large population of commuters and travelers passing through the station every day. This redevelopment project will improve the high- and mid-rise office and commercial buildings, train transfer lines and plaza all under a comprehensive plan. The design is directed by architect Kengo Kuma, Nikken Sekkei Ltd., and SANAA.

We are in charge mainly of designing the western plaza including the Hachiko Plaza, traffic flow connecting each of the stations to the city, and facade of the buildings surrounding them. While efficiently connecting the city to the different train gates dispersed throughout multiple floors, the plan also requires a design that brings about a new kind of appeal to the western plaza, which will become one of the "urban cores" located at key locations of Shibuya.

We thought it would be fitting to design a space that manifests the flow of people coming into the Shibuya Station and then dispersing again. We decided to connect the different spaces—starting from the fourth-floor plaza that lead to both east and west exits, then to the third-floor gates, second-floor passages that connect to the Inokashira Line and other areas of the city, ground-level plaza, and finally to the city itself—with slabs of organic shapes having three-dimensional circulatory traffic flow. A large, flowing roof will cover this, simultaneously unifying the traffic flow and the entire west exit area, creating a symbolic structure visible from anywhere in the city. Furthermore, the mid-level facades are segmented into multiple sections, revealing the inner commotion to the outside while also enclosing the entire west exit and intermingling with various reflections of the city commotion. Various elements will overlap one another, creating a three-dimensional plaza that gently unifies the entire west exit area into a cohesive whole. As one of the most famous terminals of the world, we hope that many people will visit the Shibuya Station and the surrounding area, transforming this place into a stage that instills a whole new generation of culture.

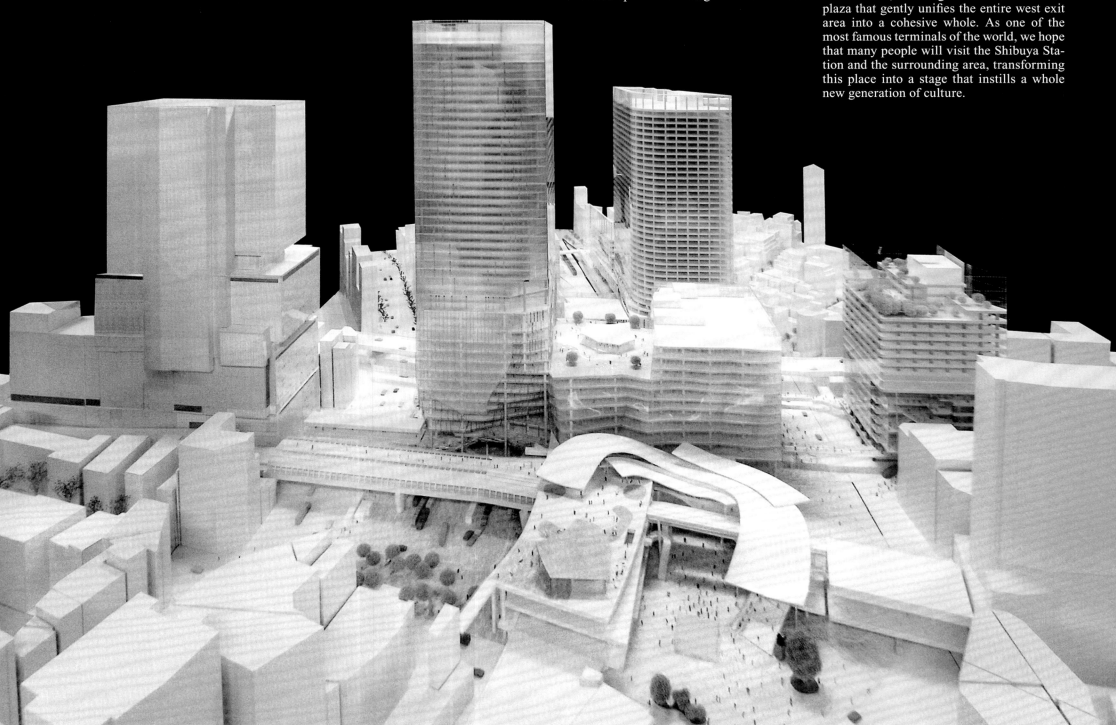

Overall view of Shibuya Station area

Western Plaza area

渋谷駅地区駅街区開発計画

渋谷駅を含む渋谷駅地区駅街区の再開発計画である。渋谷には，東急東横線，京王井の頭線，JR山手線，埼京線，東京メトロ銀座線，半蔵門線，副都心線の各鉄道とバスターミナルの駅があり，毎日多くの人々が利用している。今回の渋谷駅地区駅街区再開発計画は，超高層と中層のオフィスや商業ビル，鉄道乗換動線，広場などを一体的に整備するもので，建築家の隈研吾氏，日建設計，SANAAの3社でデザイン監修を行っている。

私たちは，主にハチ公前広場を含む西口の広場，各駅や街を繋ぐ歩行者動線，そしてそれらを取り囲む中層の建物のファサードを担当している。いろいろなレベルにある各線の改札や街を効率良く結ぶ一方で，渋谷の街の要所に整備されているアーバン・コアの一つとして，西口の広場に新しい魅力を加えることが求められている。

私たちは，渋谷に訪れる多くの人たちが，いろいろなところから駅周辺に集まりまた広がっていく，そのような人の流れをそのまま空間としてつくっていくのが良いのではないかと考えた。東口・西口とも繋がる4階の広場などから，3階の改札，2階の井の頭線や他の街区と繋がる通路，地上レベルの広場，そして街へと，各空間を立体的な回遊性をもった有機的な形のスラブで繋ぐこととした。そして，その上に流れるような大きな屋根を掛け，動線空間と西口全体にまとまりを与えると同時に，街の至るところから見えるシンボルになると考えた。また，幾つかに分節された中層のファサードは，内部の賑わいを街に表出させながら，様々な街の映り込みと混ざり合い，西口を囲っている。様々な要素が重なり合い，西口全体が緩やかに一つにまとまった立体的な広場のようになる。今後も世界有数のターミナルとして，多くの人たちが渋谷駅周辺を訪れ，新しい文化の生まれていく舞台の一つとなることを期待している。

Plan S=1:1200

* *Drawing is as of May 2014 and model photo is as of June 2012.*
図面は2014年5月作成，模型写真は2012年6月撮影。
実際の計画と異なります

Huaxin Financial Plaza
Shanghai, China
2013–19

SANAA

This project concerns a new design for a pair of twin towers on the west coast of Shanghai.

Running along the Huangpu River from the center of the Bund down to the south west, there is an area called Xuhui Binjiang which is undergoing comprehensive development. Plans are in place for cultural and commercial facilities including an amusement park, art gallery, and green parkland to be created on this greenbelt by the riverside. Spreading out from this area are bands of mid- to high-rise buildings. Our site is in the mid-rise area, and commands an unbroken view over the river. Since the region surrounding the site borders the office and commercial district of mid- to high-rise buildings, as well as the riverside park and cultural facilities area, we expect that it will become a thriving hub for various activities.

In this area set to become the gateway to the district currently under development, we set about designing an office building to be occupied by two companies. The client requested an iconic building that would stand out from its surroundings, while also being consistent with local urban planning. A view over the river was also a requirement.

Rather than create two twin towers, we thought it would be more fitting to incorporate the different identities of the two companies while also integrating them into a unified building design. We took seven segmented volumes of different heights and sizes and clustered them together around a central square, arranging them so that their height gradually becomes lower as they approach the river. By positioning these volumes at various angles, we ensured that workers can enjoy a view over the river and parkland from anywhere inside the office space. Furthermore, by placing small volumes at various distances from each other, we created a diverse variety of large floor plans.

The passageway and courtyard running through the buildings gently join the site interior to its surroundings, forming a park-like space with circulating flow. We aimed to create a building that is integrated into the city landscape, and opens itself up towards the river.

Overall view beyond Huangpu River

First floor S=1:2500

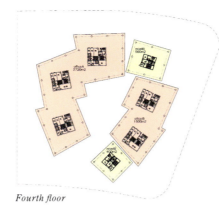
Fourth floor

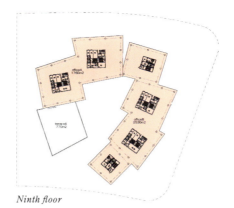
Ninth floor

上海金融センター

本プロジェクトは上海市の西岸に，新しいタイプのツインタワーを計画するものである。

外灘の中心部から南西に下ったところの黄浦江沿いに，徐汇滨江(Xuhui District Binjiang)総合開発地区がある。黄浦江に沿うようにグリーンベルトがあり，自然豊かな公園や美術館，アミューズメントパークなどの文化・商業施設が計画されている。それに並行するように中層エリア，高層エリアが帯状に広がる。敷地はその中層エリアにあり，川を一望することができる。敷地一帯は，中層と高層エリアのオフィス・商業地区と川沿いの公園・文化施設との接点となるため，様々なアクティビティにあふれたエリアとなることが予想される。

そのような開発地区のエントランスとなるような場所に，2社のためのオフィスビルを計画することとなった。街のアイコンとなるような建物，都市計画との調和，そして，川への眺望などが求められた。

私たちは，2本のツインタワーをつくるのではなく，2社のそれぞれのアイデンティティをつくりながらも一つでもある建物がふさわしいと考え，高さや大きさの異なる七つの分節されたヴォリュームを，中央に広場を持ちながら寄り添うように，かつ，川に向かって徐々に低くなるように配置した。それらは，様々な角度にずれながら配置されることで，オフィス空間のどこからでも川や緑地への眺望を楽しむことができる。また，小さな単位のヴォリュームはくっついたりはなれたりすることで多様な大きなかたちの平面をつくり出す。

建物の間に生まれる通り道や中庭は，敷地の中と外を緩やかに繋げ，回遊性のある公園のような空間を生み出す。都市景観と調和しながら川に向かって開くような建物を目指している。

Section S=1:1000

View of courtyard from terrace

Courtyard

Roof terrace

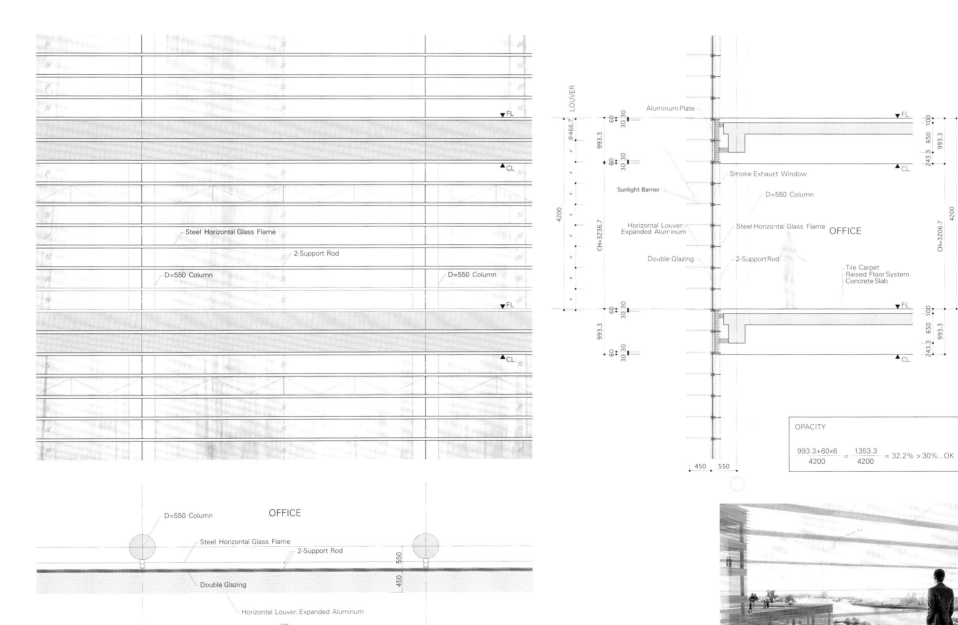

OPACITY

$$\frac{993.3 + 60 \times 6}{4200} = \frac{1353.3}{4200} = 32.2\% > 30\% ... OK$$

Detail: facade S=1:80

Interior

167

Bocconi University New Urban Campus Milan, Italy 2013–19

SANAA

View toward north side of site along street from northeast

Site plan S=1:7500

View toward Reception Center from the public garden

This is the project for a new Urban Campus for Bocconi University in Milan. The university is located at the southern edge of Milan's old city quarter while the site for the new campus stands on a large plot that used to be a milk processing plant adjacent to the south side of the current university. There is a municipal park to the East, where the atmosphere changes from the old city to the suburbs. The new campus includes a number of buildings linked by a park that is open to the public during the day. Each building has its own dedicated functionality, such as faculty space, educational area (masters and executive courses), recreational activities and student dormitories.

Each building has its own courtyard and bold curves so that they are mutually pushed together and pulled apart; at the same time, these courtyards also create a sense of intimacy. We also tried to match this area's spacious atmosphere by arranging the buildings on the park so that they mutually expand as a whole with a sense of tension between one another. The ground floor is arranged to hold public programs, lobbies, bookstores and cafes, with porticos having similar curves to the architecture planned in the park area. One can enjoy the park while being able to traverse its expanse with its horizontal perspectives, as various functions are revealed in a continuous panorama.

The exterior facade of each building have homogenous balconies with expanded aluminum metal screens surrounding them, which act as a filter providing a comfortable environment to every room while creating an integrated facade within the city context.

Ground floor S=1:800

View from northeast

ボッコーニ大学新キャンパス

ミラノのボッコーニ大学の新キャンパス計画である。同大学はミラノの旧市街地の南端に位置し，計画の敷地は現大学の南側に隣接する広大な牛乳工場跡地である。その東には市の都市公園が隣接しており，旧市街地からその郊外へと移り変わっていく空気感がある。新キャンパスは幾つかの棟からできており，日中には開放され公園となる敷地に配置されている。各棟はそれぞれの機能に充てられ，教員スペース，教育用スペース（マスターとエグゼクティブコース），リクリエーションスペース，学生寮となっている。

中庭形式はミラノの一般的な建物形式であるが，この計画ではそれを各棟に継承しつつ，平面を大きく湾曲させ互いにくっつけたり離れたりしながら配置させている。中庭を囲む各棟が各自の親密さを持ちながらも，相互に緊張を持って全体に大きく展開するような平面とすることで，この敷地のおおらかな空気感に合わせようとした。地上部分の多くは，ロビーや書店，カフェといった公共的なプログラムが配され，公園部分には建築と同様に湾曲した平面の回廊が計画されている。公園を楽しみながら，水平的に見通せる広がりの中に，多様な機能が連続して展開していく様を巡っていくことができる。

各建物の外周にはバルコニーがあり，その周りにはアルミエキスパンドメタルのスクリーンが計画されている。それは各室内に心地よい環境をもたらすフィルターとなりながら，都市と呼応する一体的なファサードをつくり出している。

A	MASTER BUILDING	1	ENTRANCE HALL	9	BAR AREA	17	SUNKEN PATIO	25 PARKING
B	RECEPTION CENTER	2	STANDARD CLASSROOM	10	OFFICE	18	VOID	26 FOYER
C	DORMITORY	3	FLAT CLASSROOM	11	POOL	19	LOADING-UNLOADING	27 AUDITORIUM
D	OFFICE BUILDING	4	MEETING ROOMS	12	LOBBY	20	BOOKSTORE	28 CLASSROOM
E	EXECUTIVE BUILDING	5	LOUNGE	13	PORTICO	21	STORAGE	29 KITCHEN
F	EXECUTIVE POD	6	PRIVATE GARDEN	14	PROFESSORS DINING	22	MECHANICAL	
		7	SKYLIGHT	15	MASTER DINING	23	SMALL POOL	
		8	SHOP AREA	16	CAFE	24	SEATINGS	

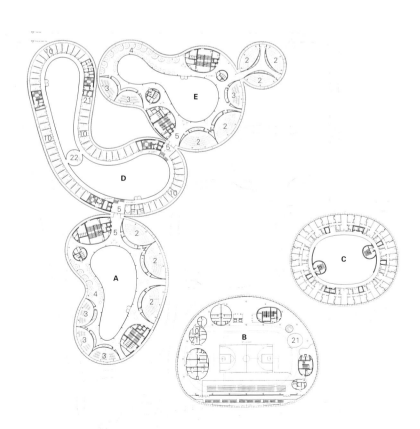

Typical floor S=1:2000

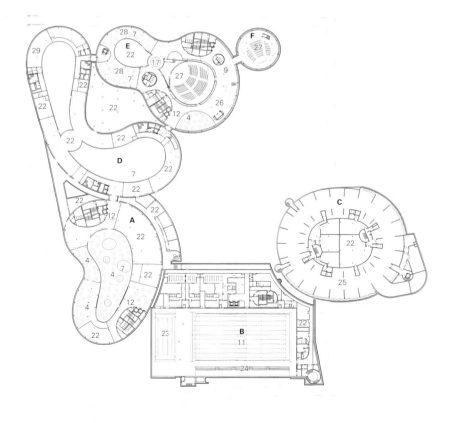

Basement

*Taichung Green
Museumbrary*
*Taichung, Taiwan, R.O.C.
2013–*

SANAA

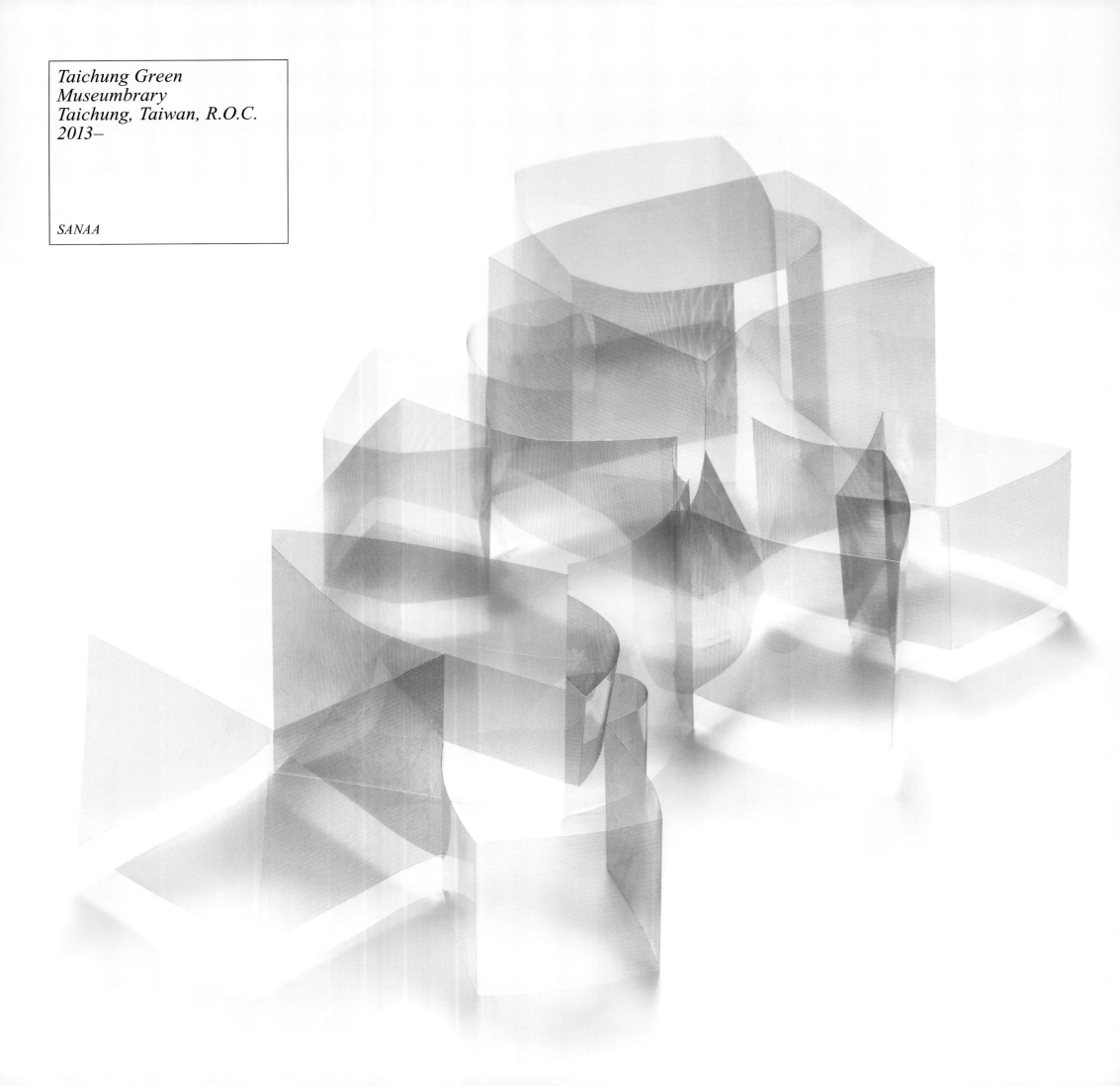

1 MAIN ENTRANCE
2 MUSEUM ACCESS
3 LIBRARY ACCESS
4 MULTI-PURPOSE ACCESS
5 PROJECT ROOM
6 MUSEUM GIFT SHOP
7 MUSEUM PLAZA
8 SHADING PLAZA
9 REFRESHMENT
10 CHILDREN PLAZA
11 CHILDREN READING AREA
12 BOOKS RETURN BOX
13 MUSEUM SERVICE CORE
14 PERMANENT EXHIBITION
15 MUSEUM PLATFORM
16 LOADING
17 MUSEUM TERRACE
18 LIBRARY LOBBY
19 NEW BOOK RELEASES
20 MULTIMEDIA SPACE
21 SENIOR'S READING AREA
22 READING TERRACE
23 LIBRARY ADMINISTRATIVE OFFICE
24 MUSEUM LOBBY
25 SPECIAL EXHIBITION
26 REST AREA
27 SCULPTURE GARDEN (4F)
28 EDUCATION ROOM
29 LITERATURE READING AREA
30 MUSEUM ADMINISTRATIVE OFFICE

Taichung Green Museumbrary is a cultural compound with a public library and fine arts museum at its center, and is planned for construction in Taichung City, Taiwan. It will be located in the north side of Taichung Central Park, which is currently under design by the city authorities, and will contain a convention center in the north-western area, a new urban area in the east, and a bus terminal and train station in the north—making it possible to approach the site from multiple directions.

We divided the requisitioned total floor area of 58,000 m² into 8 volumes per program, floating several of the volumes in order to create a large pilotis space connected to the park. The use of pilotis brings about a comfortable breezy space shielded from Taiwan's strong sunlight; creates a shared entrance at the center to the library and art gallery which can be accessed from multiple directions; and allows the public to move underneath the building to travel directly from the open park into the city.

The floating volumes separate in places and merge together in others, creating diverse interactions on each floor. We hope that the library and art museum also merge together in various ways, providing inspiration for new activities to emerge.

By adopting reinforced concrete structure for underground and rigid steel frame for above, we created an expansive space without anti-seismic walls or braces within the pilotis or indoor areas. Furthermore, by attaching a base-isolation system, potential earthquake damage is reduced, which also made possible the use of an iron frame with an unusually large span for a rigid frame structure.

With this design we hope to create a novel place where the union of public library and fine arts museum brings about cultural innovations. We also aim to realize a dynamic and magnanimous piece of architecture befitting the climate of Taiwan.

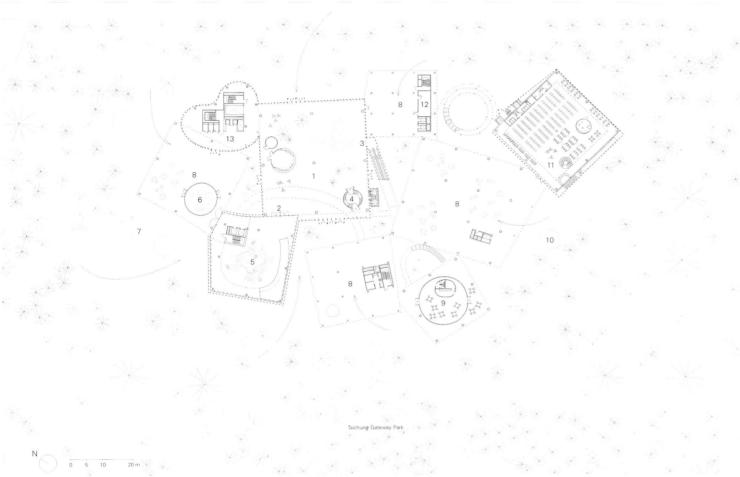

Ground floor S=1:1200

Aerial view

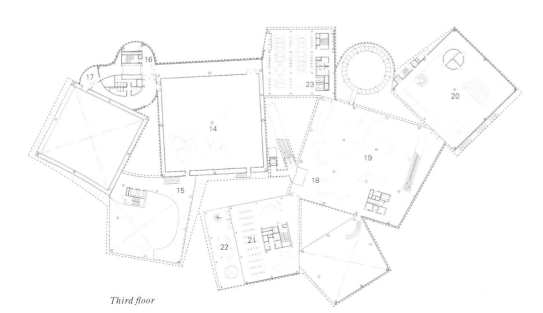

Third floor

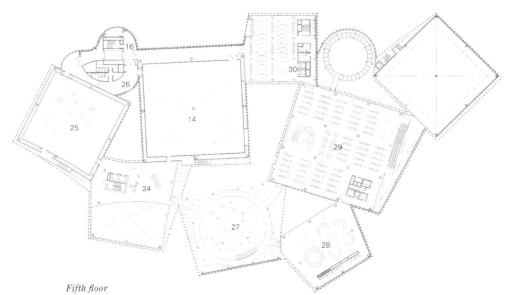

Fifth floor

View from park

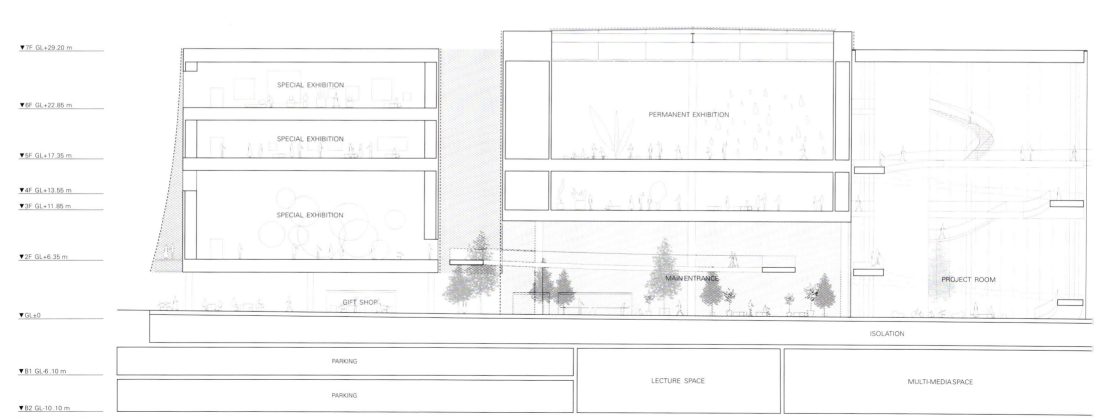
Section S=1:400

Downward view of museum lobby and project room

Taichung Green Museumbrary

Taichung Green Museumbrary は台湾の台中市に計画している図書館と美術館を中心とした複合文化施設である。敷地は台中市が現在計画している台中市中央公園内の北側にあり，敷地の北西にはコンベンションセンター，東には新市街，北には鉄道やバスのターミナルが計画されている．いろいろな方向からアプローチが可能なところである．

　私たちは要求された延床面積の58,000m²をプログラムごとに八つのヴォリュームに分け，幾つかのヴォリュームを浮かし公園と連続する大きなピロティ空間とした．ピロティは日差しの強い台湾では風が通り抜ける快適なシェーディングスペースとなり，中心にはいろいろな方向からアクセスされる図書館と美術館の共有エントランスを配置し，そのまわりにはパブリックにオープンな公園から建物の下を通って街へそのまま通り抜けることもできるようになっている．

　地上に浮かんだヴォリューム同士は離れたりくっついたりし，階によって様々な関係をつくり，図書館と美術館がいろいろなかたちで混ざり合い新たな活動が現れればと考えている．

　また構造は地下をRC造，地上を鉄骨ラーメン造とすることで，ピロティや室内空間に耐震壁やブレースのない開放的な空間をつくり，免震システムにより地震力を低減し，ラーメン造でありながらスパンの大きな鉄骨フレームを可能にしている．

　ここでは図書館と美術館が一体となることで新たな文化が生まれる新しい場所になり，また台湾の気候に合った，おおらかでダイナミックな建築が実現できればと思っている．

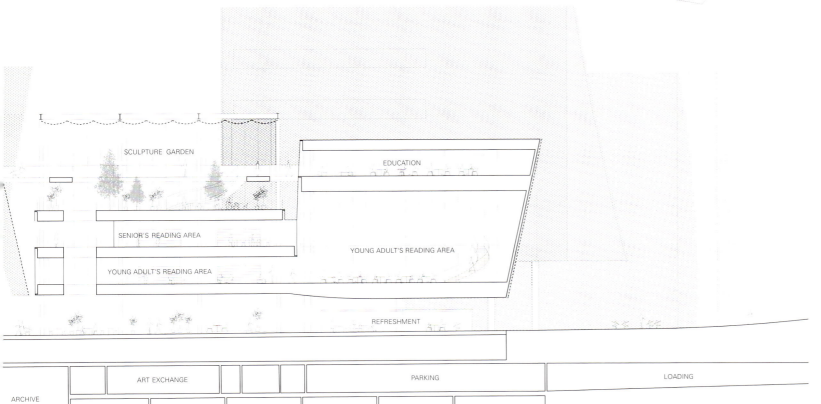

House in Marbella
Marbella, Chile
2013–

Office of Ryue Nishizawa

South elevation S=1:400

Model photo: view from south. Main residence on left and annex on right

This project was for a residence in a resort area in the outskirts of Santiago, Chile. The site is on top of a gentle slope leading up from a golf course, in an area that has mostly been partitioned into rectangular lots. The client requested three bedrooms, space for their three family members to relax together, and a view over the golf course. In response to this, our proposed spatial configuration features several roofs that come together to create the living space. These roofs soar into the sky, dip to the floor, or rise up straight from the ground, creating several interior spaces that feel distinct from each other, yet are connected as part of one large room. Although the exterior of the building looks like a condensed block of several roofs, the interior is linked to the surrounding landscape through multiple gaps in the structure. With this residence, we have aimed to create an open, comfortable space that stands out as an architectural landmark, yet has a smooth relation with the surrounding environment.

マルベーリャの住宅

チリのサンチャゴ郊外のリゾート地に計画されている住宅である。敷地は、ゴルフコースから緩やかに上がっていく斜面の上、ほとんど長方形に分譲区画された土地である。3寝室と、3家族が集まって団らんできるスペース、ゴルフコースへの眺望などが求められた。提案した空間構成としては、何枚もの屋根を集合させて空間をつくるというもので、屋根が上に浮いたり、もしくは着地したり、地面から立ち上がったりするために、ワンルームながら分けられたような、繋がったような、様々な空間ができる。外観としては、複数屋根が凝縮したような集合体に見えるが、あちこちに空隙があるので、室内とランドスケープが繋がる。建築としてのランドマーク性を維持しつつも、建築と環境が連続してゆく、開かれた快適な住空間を目指している。

Model photo: various zigzag roofs covering living spaces

Model photo: interior

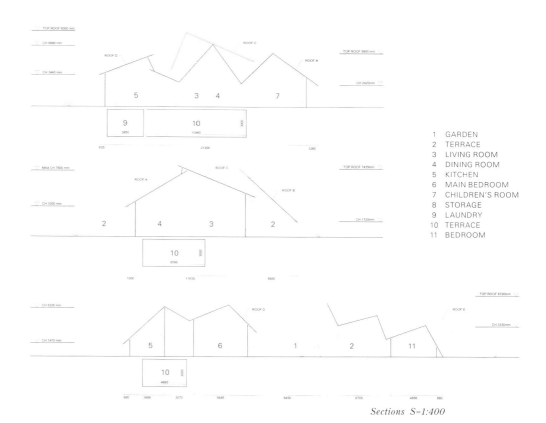

1 GARDEN
2 TERRACE
3 LIVING ROOM
4 DINING ROOM
5 KITCHEN
6 MAIN BEDROOM
7 CHILDREN'S ROOM
8 STORAGE
9 LAUNDRY
10 TERRACE
11 BEDROOM

Sections S=1:400

Plan S=1:400

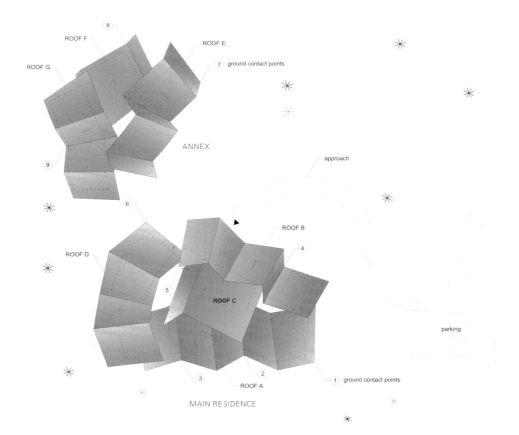
Roof

Hitachi City Hall
Hitachi, Ibaraki, Japan
2013–19

SANAA

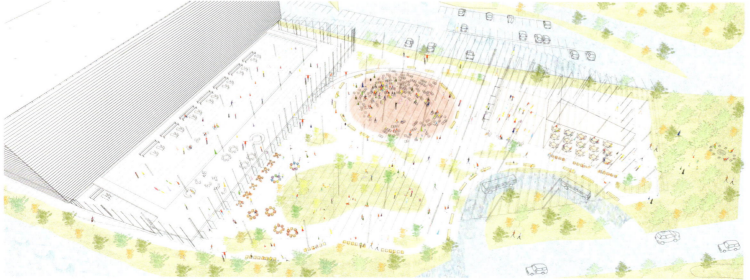

Axonometric

The city of Hitachi extends along a long and narrow north and south line over a gentle inclined slope that spreads between the mountains and the sea. The site is located in the middle section of this area in a place where it opens out, facing Route 6. The existing local government buildings are detached from each other due to repeated expansion over the years; there had been talks of renewal due to aging and service inefficiency, and was finally rebuilt after incurring damages from the 2011 Great East Japan Earthquake.

Our plan called for building a seven-story office on the west side to intersect the existing government offices in phase 1 of the construction, so that these offices can continue to function during the reconstruction. For phase 2 of the construction, we planned a space

Overall view from south

where the local residents could hold activities, centered around a large semi-outdoor roof called the Everyone's Plaza, which would connect Route 6 with the government office.

The government office building would extend lengthwise north to south to face both the ocean and the mountains, with the assembly hall on the highest seventh floor, government functions between the third and sixth floors, and layers of service counters on the first and second floors to facilitate efficient operation. The plans for each floor call for a core at both the north and south ends, with flexible office spaces at its center, and an enclosing outer corridor for circulating around the floor, making it a space where the visiting public and government workers can be continually aware of Hitachi's landscape.

The Everyone's Plaza has a large roof above it with a series of gentle arches that becomes the symbol of the new city, and a bright, open and novel public space underneath the roof for people to gather. It has an indoor multipurpose square comprising waiting areas and galleries for visitors to the service counters, banks, convenience stores, public multipurpose hall, restaurant, outdoor multipurpose square, and other multifunctional spaces. The square gathers various functionalities to create a place of interaction among visitors to the city hall and those who come for leisure and relaxation.

The goal is to create an open government office which not only plays the traditional role of a city hall, but is also identified by the city residents as a place that is designed for their benefit, with the flexibility to respond to changes over time.

Mock-up of large roof

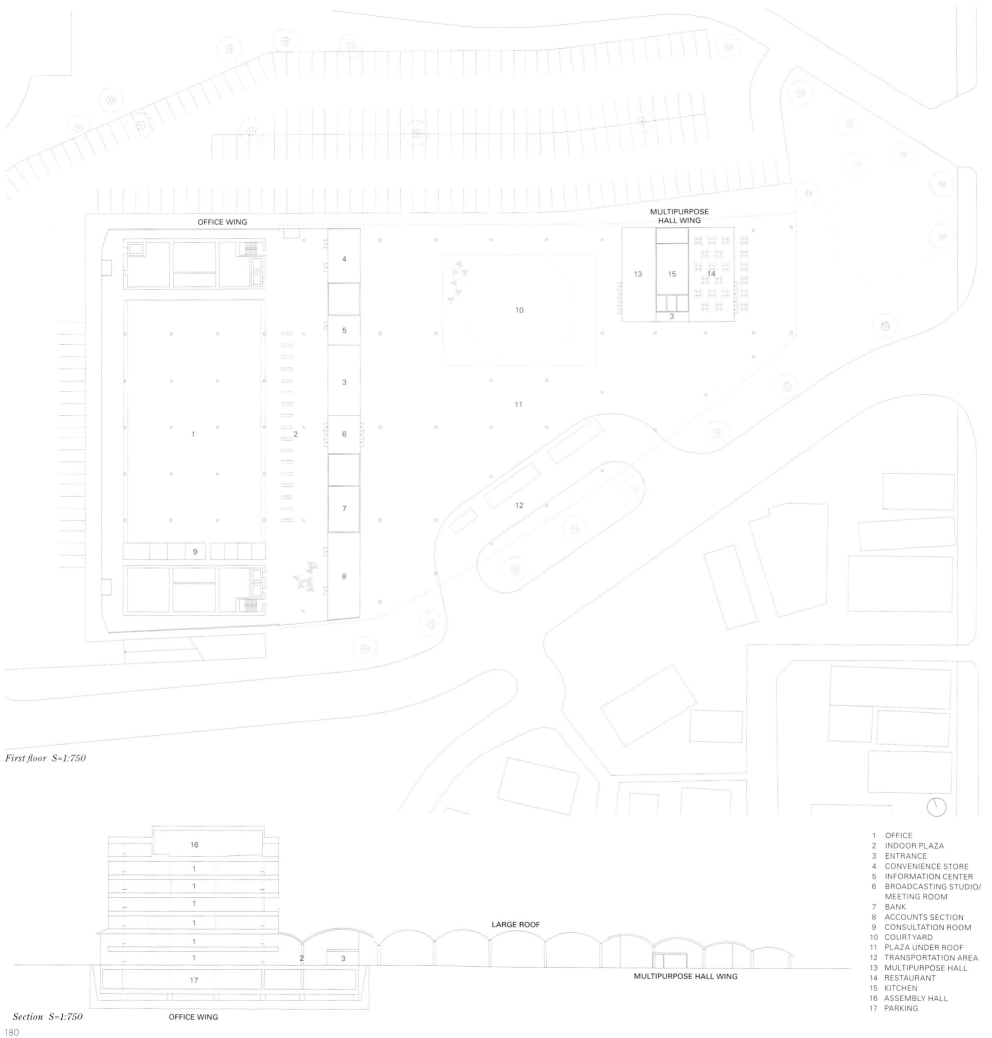

Plaza under large roof: view toward courtyard from transportation area. Multipurpose hall wing on right

Indoor plaza: looking south

日立市新庁舎

海と山に挟まれ南北に細長く伸びる日立の街は，山から海へと続く緩やかな斜面に広がっている。敷地はその中ほどに位置し，国道6号線に面して開けた場所にある。既存庁舎は，増築を繰り返した分棟形式で，業務の効率化と老朽化が指摘され，東日本大震災で被災したことにより建替えることとなった。

庁舎機能を継続しながら建替えを行えるように，第1期工事として，既存庁舎をかわすように西側に7階建ての執務棟を建て，第2期工事として，執務棟と国道6号線を繋ぐように，みんなの広場と呼ばれる半屋外の大屋根を中心とした，市民活動の場を計画することとした。

執務棟は，海と山に面するように南北に長く，最上階の7階に議場，3階から6階に執務機能，1，2階に窓口業務を積層配置し，効率の良いサービスを行うことができる。各階の平面計画は，南北の両端にコア，その中央にフレキシブルな執務スペースを配置し，その周りを回遊することができる外廊下を廻らせることで，訪れる市民や働く職員の人たちが常に日立の風景を意識できるような空間としている。

みんなの広場には，街の新しいシンボルとなるような緩やかなアーチの連続する大屋根がかかり，その下には誰でも集えるような明るく開放的な新しい公共空間が広がる。窓口に来た人たちのための待合スペースやギャラリーからなる屋内広場，銀行，コンビニ，市民の人たちが使うことのできる多目的ホール，レストラン，屋外の多目的広場など，多様な機能が集まっており，市役所に用事のない人でも日常的に多くの市民がみんなの広場に訪れ，憩いの場所となり交流が生まれる。

市役所として，従来の役割だけではなく，今後の長い年月の変化にも対応できるような柔軟性を持ち，市民の人たちから，自分たち，みんなのための場所だと長く愛されるような開かれた庁舎となることを目指している。

Pergola
Okayama, Okayama, Japan
2013–14

SANAA

Okayama University is an international research and educational center that is moving ahead with an environmental improvement plan to achieve a new, beautiful college city that integrates the university with the city and region; the Pergola being part of their improvement plan for the area around the university hall located at the heart of the campus.

The planned site area is one of the central parts of the university where the cafeteria, restaurant, assembly hall, health center, general education buildings and other facilities are clustered, making it a location where many students gather. The northern part of the site has a landscape view of the Handa mountain comprised of the gingko-lined main street running north and south, and a vibrant green belt with the Zasugawa river running east and west. To achieve that beautiful college city, we sought to harmonize the Pergola with the rich natural surrounding environment and create vast spaces that open to the outside.

The main plan was to remove the shorter and middle-height trees as well as the block walls that were placed on the common road running east and west and along the borders of the university, eliminate the border to widen the footpaths, and place concrete benches. We changed the pavement surface from asphalt to brick. The deep significance of the color and materials that are specific to baked bricks would maintain the beautiful landscape in a profound and dignified fashion over time. Our plan was also to incorporate native trees that grow in Okayama around the Pergola in the central square to harmonize with the naturally rich surrounding environment.

The location did not originally cast shadows to the area around the university hall where the Pergola was planned, and was not found to be an outdoor space for relaxing or performing activities. We created a plan, therefore, to locate the Pergola in the middle of the site and create a space to have lunch, rest, dance, read, etc. as a place for relaxing outdoors. The shape is designed so that it spreads out widely across the campus, creating a sense of movement at different heights. To avoid creating a heavy and large structure, steel posts at 60 to 75 mmϕ were merely welded to thin 12 mm steel plates in a simple composition. Roof and posts were butt-welded so that all vertical and horizontal forces are dealt with using only thin posts, without having to install earthquake resistant walls and beams. We also situated the posts randomly with the trees located within and outside the Pergola so that one can experience the entire space and not just the structure itself. With the placement of furniture fixtures, and the growth of trees after a few years, we hope that the space becomes a rich, forest-like shaded area.

Overall view from northwest

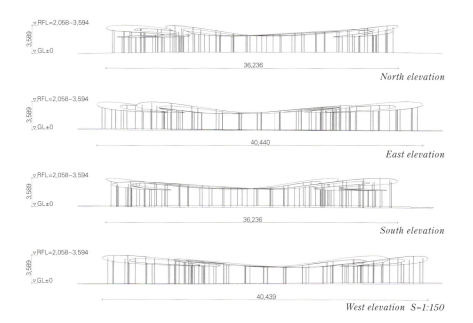

North elevation

East elevation

South elevation

West elevation   S=1:150

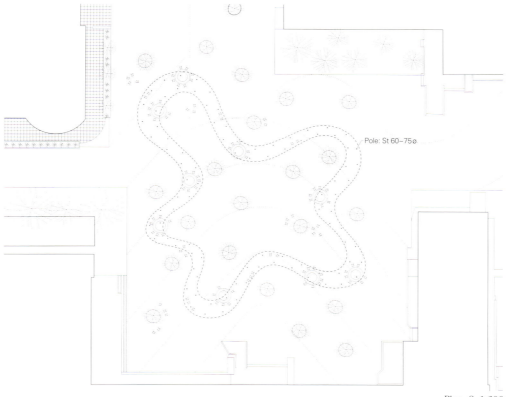
Plan S=1:600

Under the pergola

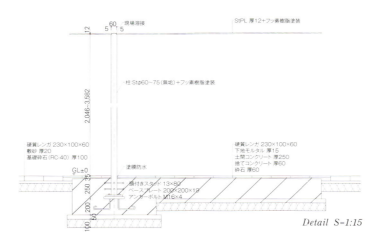
Detail S=1:15

View from north

パーゴラ

岡山大学は国際的な研究・教育拠点として，大学と都市・地域が一体となった新たな「美しい学都」の実現に向けて環境整備計画が進められており，パーゴラはキャンパス中心に位置する大学会館周辺の整備計画の一環として計画された。

計画地周辺はカフェテリアやレストラン，集会場，保健センター，一般教育棟などの施設が集まる大学の中心部の一つで，多くの学生たちが集う場所である。敷地の北部には半田山がキャンパスの借景となっており，銀杏の街路樹が並ぶ南北の主要道路や東西を走る座主川など豊かな緑地帯が形成されている。私たちは「美しい学都」の実現に向けて，この自然豊かな周辺環境に調和し，外部に開かれたおおらかな空間をつくりたいと考えた。

主な計画として，東西を走る一般道路と大学の境界線上にあった低・中木とブロック塀を撤去し，境界をなくして歩道を広くし，コンクリートベンチを配置した。床の舗装はアスファルトからレンガ舗装とした。焼き物特有のレンガの色調と素材としての深い味わいは，時が経っても重厚で品格のある美しい景観を維持できるのではないかと考えている。そして中央広場にはパーゴラと，岡山に生育する樹木をまわりに取り込み，自然豊かな周辺環境に調和させた計画としている。

パーゴラが計画された大学会館周辺にはもともと日陰になるような場所があまりなく，外でゆっくり休憩をしたり活動できるスペースが見当たらなかった。そこで敷地の中央にパーゴラを配置し，お昼を食べたり，休んだり，ダンスをしたり，本を読んだりと，もっと外でくつろげるような空間を計画した。形状はキャンパス全体に大きく広がっていくような，高低差のある動きのあるかたちとし，重みのある大きな建物とならないように12mmの薄い鉄板に60～75mmφほどの鉄骨柱を溶接するだけのシンプルな構成としている。屋根と柱を突き合せ溶接とすることで，耐震壁や梁などは設けずに細い柱のみで全ての鉛直力と水平力を処理している。また建物だけではなく空間全体を感じられるように，パーゴラ内外に配置された樹木と相まったランダムな柱配置とした。今後，家具が配置され，数年後には樹木がもっと成長し，森の木陰のような豊かな空間になることを望んでいる。

The Roof & Mushrooms project is a temporary construction planned in conjunction with the joint exhibit of nendo and the Office of Ryue Nishizawa, held by the Kyoto University of Art and Design. Although the plan at the beginning was only for an indoor exhibit, potential for an exhibit using outdoors space was proposed during discussions held between Kyoto University of Art and Design's executive director Yutaka Tokuyama, the planning office director for curating Kayo Tokuda, and nendo, which led to reconsidering the place of installation. The Office of Ryue Nishizawa took charge of the architecture, while nendo handled the furniture, interior, smaller items, handrails and other elements of the surrounding space. Its major function was as a temporary pavilion within nature, with a learning facility and rest area for students to enjoy the natural setting.

The site sits on a steep slope nestled on the side of a mountain behind the university campus. We envisioned this structure as rising up along the slope, with only the roof floating atop, based on this specific location which stands on a natural incline. The roof has a tertiary curve in order to follow the slope of the mountain, and floats in such as way as to cover the surface contours (flat land, slope, existing concrete steps, retaining wall and overgrowth, for example) with its existing inclines. The roof and ground surface make a gradual incline, mutually approaching and separating from each other, as we attempted to create a variety of places between both of them.

We built it as a wooden structure in order to make it easy to build on an incline. It is a wooden architectural structure combining modern building methods, yet held together by traditional column and beam framing. More specifically, a myriad of columns were arranged using an anchoring method in line with the various surface shapes; a delicate cross beaming was built to create a framework forming gentle wooden curves; and thin wood boards are fitted on top in double layers, folding naturally into each other so that they intersect in two directions to maintain rigidity.

Each board is carefully processed and stacked in a way so that they fit into the tertiary curved shape and adhere to the top of the roof with a steep, cliff-like incline, resulting in a roof that feels both strong and generous. Parts of the existing rotating ball joints were also reworked for the column and beam joints through mockups and combined experience of the contractors and carpenters, which enabled us to create a detail that uses a relatively simple mechanism for the complex tertiary curved roof.

After talking with the contractors and carpenters who specialize in building tea ceremony houses, superior solid wood, as opposed to the ordinary run-of-the-mill plywood, was employed for the materials. Based on their wish, we agreed that the project should be made entirely of solid Japanese cypress wood. The structure was finished fully with untreated Japanese cypress wood so as to fit the surrounding nature with the passage of time. Our goal was to create a structure that harmonizes with the surrounding environment while being different from nature; is artificially created by our hands but possessing natural qualities; a space that enables human beings to develop something new within nature. Since the project in its entirety was technically difficult to complete as it follows along the slope of the mountain, this time we were completed about one-third of the overall plan.

森の屋根ときのこ

京都造形芸術大学で開催された，nendo＋西沢事務所の共同展覧会にあわせて計画された，仮設建築のプロジェクトである。当初は屋内展示のみの企画であったが，同大学の徳山豊専務理事とキュレーションをされた企画室長の徳田佳世さん，nendoとの話し合いの中から，屋外の土地を使った展示の可能性が提案され，設置場所から考えることになった。建築部分を西沢事務所が担当し，家具，インテリア，小物，手すりなどの身の回りの空間をnendoが担当している。主な機能としては，学生たちが自然を楽しめる学習施設であり，かつ休憩所でもあるような，自然の中の仮設パヴィリオンである。

敷地は，大学キャンパス裏手の山の中腹で，激しい勾配をもった傾斜地だ。自然の中の斜面に建つという特別な立地から，屋根だけが浮かんで斜面に沿って上がって行くような建築を考えた。屋根は山の傾斜に沿うために3次曲面となり，それが既存の斜面が持つ様々な地面形状（たとえば平地や

Roof and Mashroom Pavilion
Kyoto, Japan
2013

Office of Ryue Nishizawa

Plan S=1:250 Section S=1:300

斜面，既存コンクリート階段や擁壁，雑草地など）を覆うように浮かぶ。屋根も地面も傾斜しつつお互いに近づいたり離れたりして，屋根と地面の間に様々な場所をつくり出そうとしている。

構造は斜面上でのつくりやすさという観点から木造とした。構成としては，伝統的な柱・梁という軸組を持ちあわせつつも，現代的な工法を組み合わせた木造建築である。具体的には，様々な地面形状に合わせた固定方法で無数の柱を配置し，繊細な断面の梁を架けていくことで，木のしなやかなカーブがつくり出すやわらかな架構をつくり，その上に2方向に交差するように薄い板材を二重に張り込むことで，屋根の剛性をつくるというものだ。

カーブした屋根形状のため，3次曲面に馴染むように大工さんたちの熟練した技術によって，崖のような斜面にかかる急傾斜した屋根の上で，張り付くような姿勢の中，1枚1枚が丁寧に加工され張り込まれていくことで，とてもおおらかでありながら何か力強さも感じる曲面屋根をつくることができた。また，柱と梁の接合部は，ボールジョイントという回転する既製品の工具の部品に少し手を加え，施工の方や大工さんとモックアップや実験を重ねることで，複雑な3次曲面の屋根に対して単純な仕組みで納まるディテールとすることができた。

材料は，数寄屋建築を得意とする施工者や大工さんとの話で，今回一緒につくるのであれば，合板のようなものでなく，得意とする木のムク材を使ってつくりたいということもあり，全てヒノキのムク材としている。仕上げは，時間の経過とともに周囲の自然と馴染んでいくように，ヒノキをそのまま使った総素木造りとした。周囲の環境と調和しながらも，自然が持つものとは異なる，人間がつくり出せる人工的でありながらも自然的でもあるようなもの，自然の中に，人間が新たに何かを開拓していくような空間を目指した。山の斜面に張り付くような建築で，プロジェクト全体としては大きく難しいものなので，今回は，全体の約3分の1が部分的に実現したものだ。

View from west. Roof rising upward along incline with straddling existed stairs

Roof covering steep-sloped surface

Roof winds following terrain. Mushroom-formed furniture designed by nendo

View from west

Maru
Kanazawa, Ishikawa,
Japan
2014–16

SANAA

Downward view from west

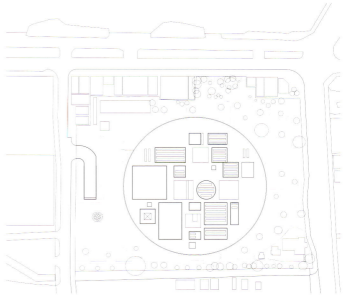
Plan S=1:3000

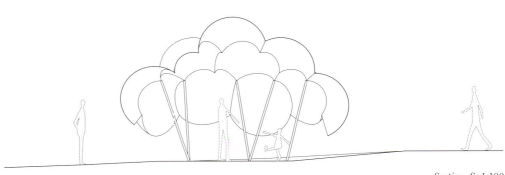
Section S=1:100

View from inside toward museum

To commemorate the 21st Century Museum of Contemporary Art, Kanazawa's 10th anniversary, the making of Maru was planned to create a rest space within the museum campus.

The cloud-like roof of the building was created by combining sixteen hemispheres made of stainless steel into one shape. To be specific, stainless steel plates of 6 mm and 8 mm thickness were processed into three dimensional curved shapes, and welded together so the hemispheres themselves became the structural body upheld by ten stainless steel columns.

Its outer mirrored surface reflects the museum and the landscape of the city, while the inner surface creates a slightly dull reflection that captures the scenery while softly reflecting the spheres back at each other.

It is my hope that this building will become a new landmark within the city, and that the many visitors of the museum, from young children to the elderly, will think fondly of this structure.

まる

「まる」は，金沢21世紀美術館の開館10周年に際し，美術館に新たなイメージを付加する休憩スペースとして美術館の敷地内に計画された。

この雲のような形の屋根は，ステンレスの半球が16個集まり全体として一つのかたちをつくっている。具体的には，厚さ6mmと8mmのステンレスの板材を3次元曲面に加工し，溶接することで半球自体が構造となり，それを10本のステンレスの柱が支えている。

鏡面仕上げの外観は美術館や街のランドスケープを映し出し，内部では少し鈍い鏡面が，外の風景を取り込みながら球同士をやわらかく反射する。

この建物が美術館を訪れる子どもからお年寄りまで沢山の人に親しまれ，街の新たなランドマークになればと思っている。

Jining Museum
Jining, China
2014–

Office of Ryue Nishizawa

Overall view from northwest

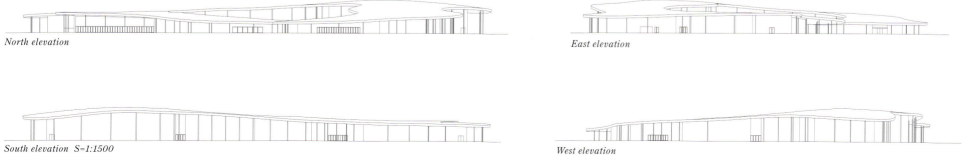

North elevation

East elevation

South elevation S=1:1500

West elevation

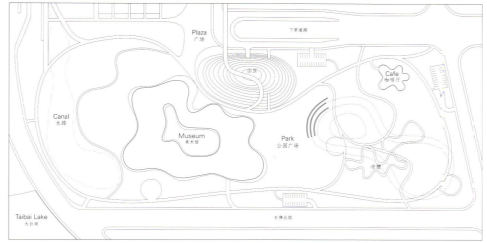

Site plan   =1:5000

Under-construction

View from northeast

This is an art museum currently planned for the city of Jining, Shandong province, China. The project is planned on a site around a large lake, located about twenty minutes from the city center. The master plan calls for four cultural facilities consisting of a library and three different types of museums, as well as commercial facilities and a public park. The art museum was to be built within the public park on the southern side and located separately from the other buildings.

The art museum is a single-story building with a massive roof designed to be in harmony with the environment of the park. Beneath the large roof, various large and small exhibition spaces and other rooms are placed independently from each other. Glass corridors run between and around these rooms, expanding as it connects to the semi-outdoors space underneath the eaves, courtyard, and outdoor plaza. The roof shape is designed to further include a large courtyard, and margins around the perimeter of the building for spaces that can be used as gardens. The building captures natural light and outside scenery, illuminating the inner rooms through the corridor spaces that can be seen from one end of the building to the other. At the same time, eaves of the large roof also create shady areas. These spaces under the eaves become rest areas for people visiting the park as well; walking through the building, there are various spaces where one can sense and enjoy light and shadow. The goal was to create a building that is in continuous harmony with the surrounding landscape, has a large and generous roof, and is open for everyone to enter and enjoy freely.

済寧市美術館

中国の山東省済寧市に計画中の美術館である。敷地は市街地から車で20分程の大きな湖のまわりに計画されている。今回のマスタープランでは図書館, 芸術館, 博物館, 美術館の四つの文化施設と商業施設と公園が計画されている。美術館は他の建物とは別に南側の公園の中に計画されることになった。

美術館は, 公園の環境と調和するようにおおらかな大屋根を持つ平屋建てとした。大きな屋根の下には, 大小様々な展示室や各諸室が独立して配置され, その間をガラスの回廊空間が包み, 軒下の半屋外空間や中庭, 屋外広場といった周辺環境と連続しながらひろがっていく。また, 大きな中庭を持ち, 建物周辺にも庭をつくり出すことができるような屋根形状とした。建物の端から端まで見通すことができる回廊空間によって, 内部へ自然光や外の景色を取り込むことで, 建物は明るく開放的でありながら, 同時に大きな屋根の軒によって日陰の空間もつくり出している。軒下空間は公園を訪れる人々にとっても憩いの場となり, 建物の中を歩きながら, 光と影が感じられる様々な場所をつくり出している。おおらかな大屋根を持ち, 周辺のランドスケープと調和しながら連続する, 誰でも気軽に立ち寄ることができる開かれた建物を目指した。

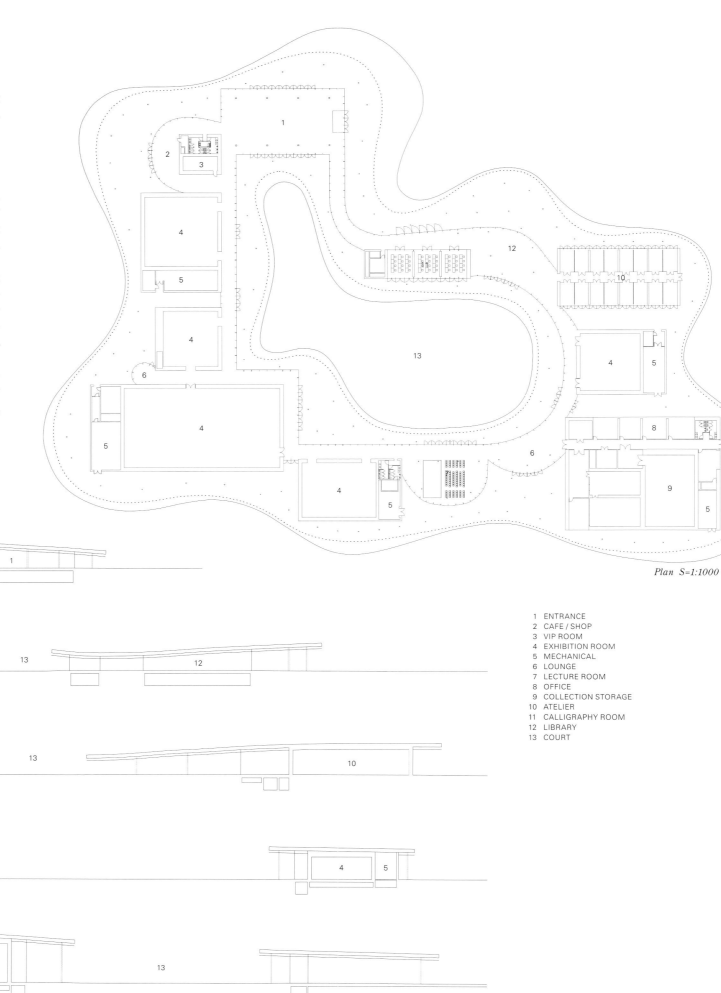

Plan S=1:1000

1 ENTRANCE
2 CAFE / SHOP
3 VIP ROOM
4 EXHIBITION ROOM
5 MECHANICAL
6 LOUNGE
7 LECTURE ROOM
8 OFFICE
9 COLLECTION STORAGE
10 ATELIER
11 CALLIGRAPHY ROOM
12 LIBRARY
13 COURT

Sections S=1:1000

Entrance

Court

O House
Tokyo, Japan
2014–18

Office of Ryue Nishizawa

This project is a house designed for a young couple. The site is located in Tokyo's residential area, a bright and pleasant hilltop neighborhood with a nearby park. The client wanted a large living area for entertaining guests, a rooftop garden with views from about 10 m above ground, and spaces that include the bedrooms and a garden with spaces to install their collection of furniture and artworks.

The space consists of two levels: one underground, and one above ground. The basement floor includes bedrooms and other private spaces, and the ground floor was made into an expansive space with 10 m-high ceiling. By reserving a large air volume, the space above ground becomes open and expansive, providing ample room to showcase large-scale artworks. Further, the high ceiling pushes the rooftop garden to a height of about 10 m, allowing the residents to capture a view above the neighboring roofs. Because the space can be accessed directly from the street, it is suitable for inviting guests and hosting parties. The large void can also be converted into a children's room in the future. We are currently in the process of adding windows into this concept, and our goal is to introduce sunlight from multiple directions so that the house becomes bright and garden-like. Conversely, the private spaces of the basement are quiet and peaceful, tucked away and separated from the street side. I hope that, by blending two contrasting characteristics of quietness and expansive openness, the house becomes a rich and fulfilling environment.

Site plan S=1:1000

View from southeast

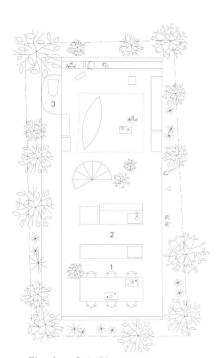

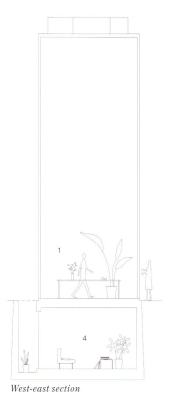
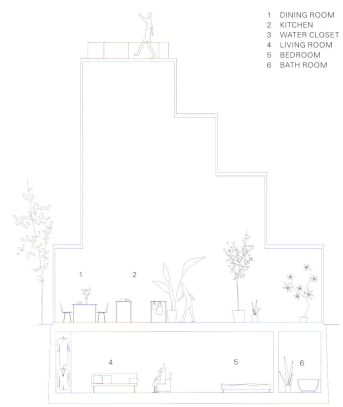

1 DINING ROOM
2 KITCHEN
3 WATER CLOSET
4 LIVING ROOM
5 BEDROOM
6 BATH ROOM

First floor S=1:150

Basement

West-east section

South-north section S=1:150

Aerial view from east

Overall view from southwest

View from northwest

Under construction

193

O邸

若い夫婦のための住宅である。都内の丘の上の住宅地にあり、近くには大きな緑園もある、気持ちよく明るいところである。要望としては、ホームパーティを開くこともできるような大きなリビング空間と、眺めのよい屋上庭園を地上10mくらいの高いところに欲しいということと、現在所有の家具や美術作品などを設置できる空間、寝室、庭などであった。

空間構成としては、地下1階地上1階の2層構成で、地下を寝室その他のプライベートな空間とし、地上1階部分を天井高10mくらいの非常に大きな空間とした。地上に大きな気積の空間をつくることで、空間的な広がりと開放感を得ることができ、大きな作品を設置することもできる。また屋上庭園レベルが地上10mくらいの高さとなって、屋上に立てば隣家を飛び越して眺望を得ることができる。道路から段差なくダイレクトに出入りすることができる場所なので、友人が集まってパーティをしたり、にぎやかに使うこともできる。吹抜け部分は、将来の子供室の増築スペースとして考えている。窓をどう開けてゆくかは現在検討中だが、あちこちから立体的に光が入ってくるような、庭のような明るい空間をイメージしている。地下のプライベート空間は、その逆に穏やかで安定した空間となって、通りから一歩離れた静かな場所となる。静かな空間と大きく開放的な空間という、個性の異なる二つの場所をもつことで、全体として豊かな住まいになれば、と考えている。

Sectional view

Looking north on first floor *Dining/kitchen on first floor, living below* *Dining/kitchen on first floor*

Morimoto House
Aichi, Japan
2014–

Office of Ryue Nishizawa

Aerial view from northeast

This is a project for a house which was planned to be built in collaboration with Misawa Home's A Project department. The site is located in a regional city, nestled among a rural landscape with sprawling rice fields and rich greenery with mountains farther behind. The house was created for a family of four, whose requests included a bright and spacious living room, plenty of play room for the children, and a layout that allows individuals to pursue their solo projects while having a sense of togetherness with the rest of the family.

We thought it would be interesting to intertwine the existing model with handmade design, and combined Misawa Home's wooden panel method with conventional construction. The entire composition consists of a two-story, box-like volume built with the wooden panel method, and a light, wooden wrap-around porch spanning around all four sides of the perimeter.

The outside of the first floor is a porch-like area that is slightly raised from the ground, with a bright living and dining room area to the south, and an open work space to the north. The box-like space connected to this porch area includes the slightly closed functionalities such as the kitchen and bathroom, with the most private bedroom situated on the second floor.

Moreover, the eaves of the roofs covering the outer perimeter all face the yard, allowing residents to enter the house from all sides. While small, we aimed to create a house in which the spaces offer a consistent change of quality, from the closed areas to the semi-closed porch, extending to the greenery of the yard in a rich, continuous flow.

By wrapping the porch around the box-like model, we were able to adjust the shape of the house according to the site conditions and functional necessities, while simultaneously creating comfortable surroundings like the yard. We hope that this home becomes a prototype for the ever-diversifying future, with a construction that is based on mass production yet still retains the freedom and flexibility to adapt to the local site conditions.

View from east

View toward living room

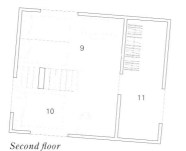

Second floor

1 ENTRANCE
2 VERANDA
3 LIVING ROOM
4 DINING ROOM
5 KITCHEN
6 BATHROOM
7 DRAWING ROOM
8 WORK TERRACE (STUDY)
9 BEDROOM 1
10 BEDROOM 2
11 CLOSET
12 GARDEN

森本邸

ミサワホームAプロジェクト室と協働でつくる住宅である。敷地は地方都市の，後ろには山，目の前には田園の広がる緑豊かな場所にある。住まい手はご家族4人で，明るくて広いリビングを持つこと，子どもたちと遊ぶ場所があること，家族がそれぞれ別のことをしていても一つの場所に集まっているような空間があることなどが望まれた。

私たちは，型式のものと手づくりのものが組み合わさることでおもしろい住宅ができるのではないかと思い，ミサワホームの木質パネル工法と在来工法を組み合わせた構成を考えた。全体としては，真ん中に木質パネル工法でつくられた2階建てのハコがあり，そこから外側にのびるように軽やかな木造の回廊がぐるりと四周に架かっているという構成である。

1階の外周部分は，地面から床が少し上がった縁側のような空間で，明るい南側はリビング・ダイニング，開けた北側はワークスペースとなる。そこに連続するハコの空間は少し閉じた性格をもったキッチンやお風呂や客間となり，もっともプライベートな空間として2階に寝室をもつ。

また，外周部分の屋根の軒先はすべて庭に面していて，どこからでも出たり入ったりすることができる。小さい住宅でありながらも，閉じられた落ち着いた部屋から少し開けた縁側，そして緑の庭へと異なる質の場所が連続的に展開する豊かな空間をつくりたいと考えている。

型式のハコのまわりに回廊をつくるという構成は，敷地や機能に合わせて形をつくることができ，同時に庭などの周りの環境も魅力的につくることができる。大量生産住宅をベースにしながらも，自由なかたちと敷地に合ったやわらかさを持った，多様化するこれからの時代に向けた住まいになれば，と思っている。

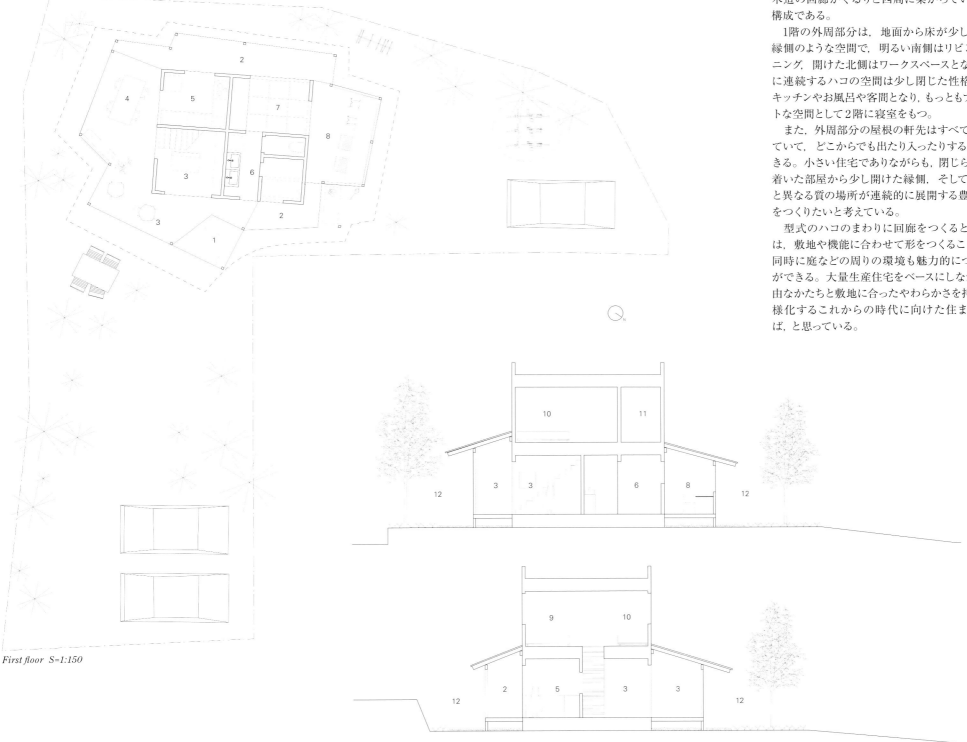

First floor S=1:150

Sections S=1:150

Cawaii Bread & Coffee
Tokyo, Japan
2014

Office of Ryue Nishizawa

In a block of apartments and offices near the Tokyo Station, we renovated the first floor of a small building into a coffee shop and bakery. This building had previously been used as a small printing factory, and then as a garage. Running next to the building is a canal whose surface reflects the surrounding scenery, giving a sense of charm to this inner city location.

Our client's request was for a shop that would connect both with the street and canal, with a friendly atmosphere that invites passers-by to drop in. Since half of the small shop would be taken up by the bakery, our study focused on how to smoothly demarcate the bakery and shop, while linking them together in a bright, pleasant space that formed a bridge between the street and canal.

To this end, we installed a large entrance on the street side and opted for a bright, open spatial construction to maximize the visibility of the canal behind the shop. We designed an arabesque-print wallpaper to adorn the wall that is visible from the street: this was intended to act as a sort of signboard informing passers-by that a shop is present here. The walls are decorated with various artworks for customers to enjoy alongside their coffee and the view of the canal. The bakery is sectioned off with movable doors and glass panes which allow the inside to be seen from the street. Here the bakers can make bread in a bright, comfortable space looking out over the canal. Through smoothly connecting the shop to its surrounding environment, we aimed to create a space where people would get a sense of brightness and comfort from both outside and within.

Site plan S=1:4000

View from west (above), shop interior (below)

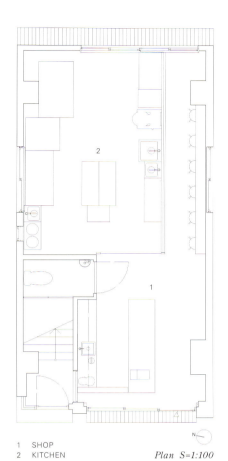

1　SHOP
2　KITCHEN

Plan　S=1:100

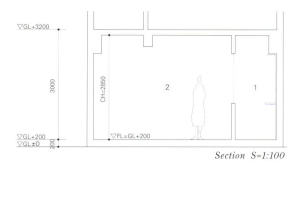

Section　S=1:100

カワイイブレッド＆コーヒー

東京駅からほど近い，マンション，オフィスビルが立ち並ぶ街区に立つ小さなビルの1階を，パン屋とコーヒー店舗へ改修した。既存のビルは，小さな印刷場で，その後はガレージとして使われていた。ビルのすぐそばには運河が流れていて，水面には風景が写り込み，都心でありながらとても魅力的なロケーションである。

クライアントからは，街と運河とも繋がり，誰でもふらっと立ち寄ることができるお店を要望された。小さな店舗の半分を工房スペースが占めるため，私たちは，工房と店舗を上手く分けながらも明るく快適に繋がることができ，街と運河とも繋がることができる空間を目指してスタディをした。

その結果，通り側には大きく開口を設け，奥に流れる運河まで見渡すことができる，明るく全体が繋がった空間構成となった。通りから見える壁一面にはアラベスク模様の壁紙をデザインし，通りを歩く人々にも，どこか店の雰囲気が感じられる看板のかわりになるような壁を考えた。壁にはアートが飾られ，アートや運河を眺めながらゆっくりとコーヒーを飲むことができる。工房は可動式の扉とガラスで仕切り，通りからも中が見える。職人は，運河が見えるとても明るく快適な工房でパンを焼くことができる。周辺の環境と上手く関係を築くことで，内からも外からも明るく快適な雰囲気が感じられる場所を目指した。

Arabesque-printed wallpaper on wall of shop

Night view over canal from east

Pink-hued east facade along canal

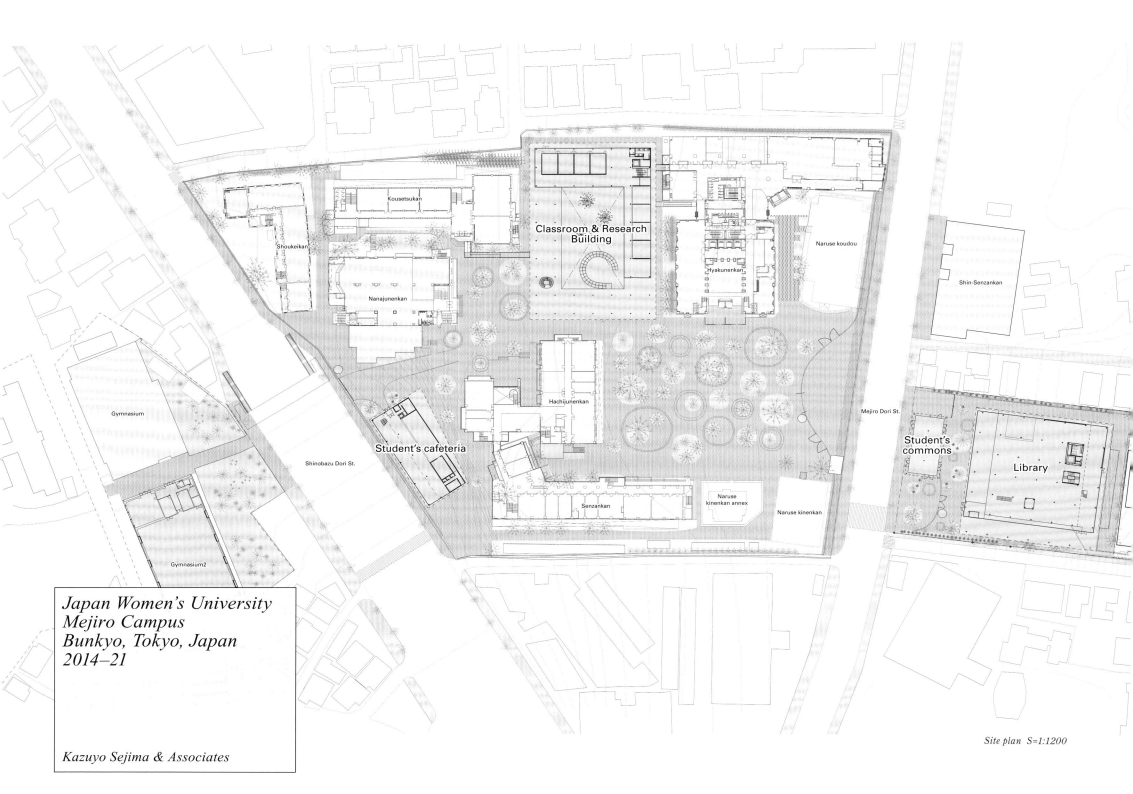

*Japan Women's University
Mejiro Campus
Bunkyo, Tokyo, Japan
2014–21*

Kazuyo Sejima & Associates

Site plan S=1:1200

It will be 120 years since the founding of Japan Women's University. The project involves consolidating the university's Mejiro campus and Nishi-Ikuta campus, with plans for building additional spaces for the students.

The Mejiro campus is surrounded in lush greenery despite being in the center of the city. The two avenues of Mejiro Dori and Shinobazu Dori cuts through the campus, and it is divided into three different districts of kindergarten, Senzan, and gymnasium. Numerous buildings of various heights cover the area as a result of repeated extensions and reconstructions.

For this project, we planned new buildings for the library, research and classrooms, gymnasium facility, and new students. Also, as part of renovating the plaza and existing buildings, we decided to create a flexible common area for the students called the "learning commons" dispersed throughout the indoors and outdoors. This enables us to gently connect the various buildings, as well as the three different districts into one, loosely unified campus.

The idea was to create a place where the common areas for the students such as the new plaza, cafeteria, club activity areas, spaces between the classroom hallways, pilotis, and library expand organically throughout the campus, allowing the students to have an open, active school life.

日本女子大学目白キャンパス
創立120周年を迎える日本女子大学の目白キャンパスに、西生田キャンパスを統合し、新しい学生の場所を計画するプロジェクトである。

目白キャンパスは、都心の中において緑に恵まれた環境にある。その中を目白通りと不忍通りが通り、キャンパスは、幼稚園地区、泉山地区、体育館地区の三つに分かれている。キャンパス内には、建替えや増築を繰り返した建物が高層や低層の分棟となって並んでいる。

今回、新しく図書館棟、教室研究室棟、体育施設棟、新学生棟を計画するとともに、広場の整備や既存建物も含めて、「ラーニング・コモンズ」というフレキシブルな使い方ができる学生滞在スペースを建物内外に散りばめることとした。そうすることで、独立して建っているそれぞれの建物を、さらには三つの地区を緩やかに繋げていく。

新しくつくられる広場や、食堂、クラブスペース、教室の廊下の間、ピロティ、図書館内などの学生の滞在の場所がキャンパス内に有機的に広がり、オープンで活発な学生生活が送れるように考えた。

Classroom & Research Building

There are a number of relatively large buildings standing inside the Senzan area of the Mejiro campus. The site for the classroom and research building is nestled within these buildings, and the project required that we design one that houses the research labs, classrooms of various sizes, and communal spaces for four different departments. On a plan that expands to the edge of the site, we designed a building with four floors: three above ground, and one underground. It has a courtyard with a large atrium to allow as much light and air, and is designed to harmonize with the volumes of the surrounding buildings with the least amount of influence on the campus's line of flow and the neighboring residences.

Communal spaces and small classrooms are located on the first floor, many parts of which are designed as pilotis to connect with other "learning commons" dispersed throughout the campus. Descending the large staircase, one enters the courtyard and sunken garden, and the underground classrooms and communal spaces surrounding this are unified with the floors above ground. The second and third-floor labs are sandwiched between the surrounding terraces and the courtyard, having a bright, well-ventilated space.

While serving to fulfill the classroom and research activities, this building is designed as a space that connects to the entire campus as a place that can be shared among many students for a diverse range of activities.

教室・研究室棟

目白キャンパス・泉山地区には比較的大きい建物が並んでおり，教室・研究室棟の敷地はそれらの建物に囲まれた場所に位置している。そこに四つの学科の研究室，大中小の教室，学生滞在スペースなどが求められた。私たちは，周囲の建物のヴォリュームに調和しつつ，キャンパス内の動線や住宅地への圧迫感を抑え，また建物内の採光や風通しを良くするように，敷地いっぱいの大きさの平面に対してなるべく大きな吹抜けの中庭をもつ，地上3層，地下1層の建物を考えた。

1階には学生滞在スペースと小教室があり，多くの部分がピロティとなっていることで，キャンパス全体に広がっているラーニング・コモンズと連続した空間になっている。また，大階段を降りると中庭とサンクンガーデンが広がっており，それを取り囲む地下1階の教室・学生滞在スペースと地上階は一体的な関係をもつ。2, 3階の研究室は外周のテラスと中庭に挟まれた，明るく風通しの良い空間になっている。

授業や研究活動のために求められる機能を満たしつつ，より多くの学生が多様な活動のために共有できるような，一つの完結した建物ではなく，キャンパス全体に連続した空間として計画している。

1. COURTYARD
2. STAY SPACE FOR STUDENTS
3. MECHANICAL
4. CLASSROOM FOR 200 PEOPLE
5. SMALL CLASSROOM
6. CLASSROOM
7. TRAINING ROOM
8. MEASUREMENT ROOM
9. REFERENCE ROOM
10. VISUAL ROOM
11. PILOTIS
12. LABORATORY
13. CENTRAL LABORATORY
14. SEMINAR ROOM
15. DEPARTMENT OF PSYCHOLOGY PLAYROOM
16. COMMON LABORATORY
17. BROWSING ROOM

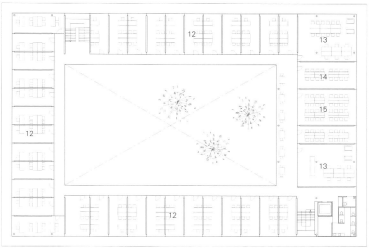
Second floor / third floor

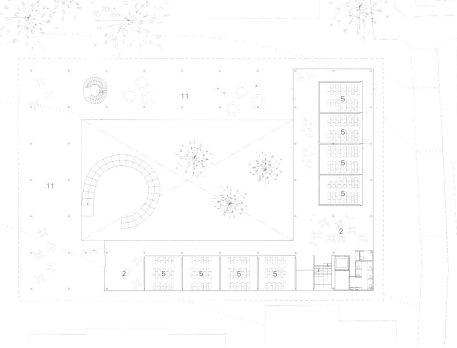
First floor S=1:600

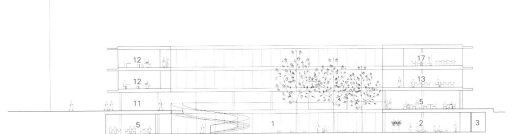
Section S=1:600

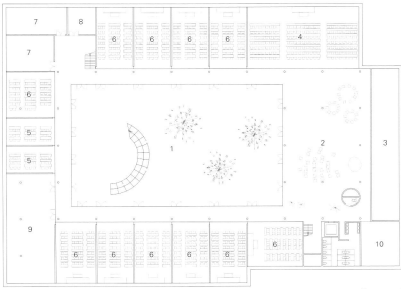
Basement

Student's cafeteria

The new student's cafeteria is located near the entrance facing the Shinobazu Dori, and is one of the main buildings of the Mejiro campus. The request was to design a building that can be flexibly transformed from a cafeteria into a large lecture hall and other special events.

The site is a gentle incline that amounts to a total of about 3 m in height difference at both ends, and starts near the Shinobazu Dori toward the campus center. Here, we created a two-story building with a terrace that can be entered from two different directions on the two floors, so that students can access the facility effortlessly. A symbolic, lightweight vault roof gently envelops the various activities within the building.

Within the various "learning commons" on campus, this particular building facilitates social activities among a large number of people. We hope that it will become a place that encourages various types of interactivity, serving the students as both a cafeteria and a large communal space.

新学生棟

新学生棟は不忍通りに面した入口の場所にあり，目白キャンパスのもう一つの顔となる建物である。普段は食堂として使われ，時には大人数のためのレクチャーなどのイベントにも使えたりするような，フレキシブルな建物を求められた。

敷地は不忍通り側からキャンパスの内部に向かって上り坂になっており，3mほどのレベル差がある。そこでテラスのある地上2層の建物とし，レベルが違う2方向からのアプローチを可能にし，学生たちが自然と建物を使えるような構成にした。その上にシンボルとなるようなヴォールトの軽い屋根によって，様々な活動をやわらかく包み込む。

キャンパス内の様々なラーニング・コモンズの中で，この建物は大人数のための交流の場となるため，食堂でもあり一つの大きな学生滞在スペースでもあるような，いろいろな人々の交流のきっかけになるような場所になればと考えている。

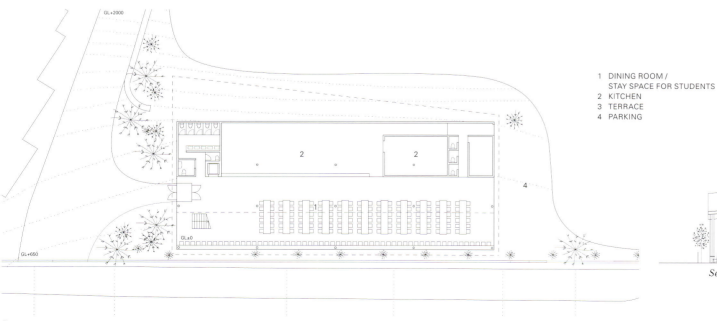

First floor S=1:400

Basement

1 DINING ROOM / STAY SPACE FOR STUDENTS
2 KITCHEN
3 TERRACE
4 PARKING

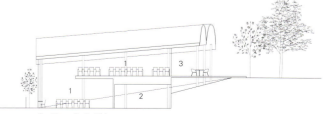

Section S=1:400

202

Aerial view

Library

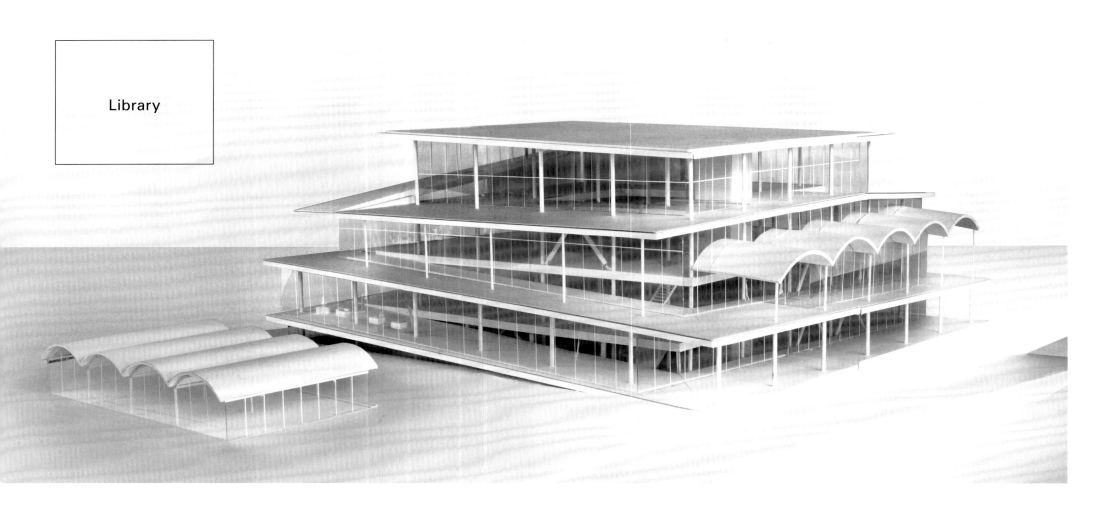

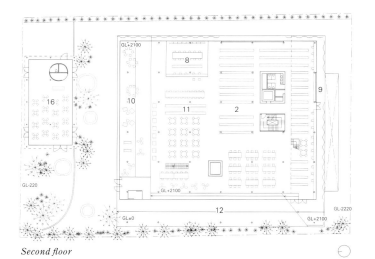

Second floor

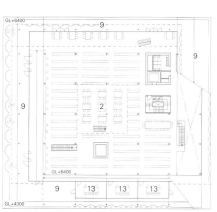

Third floor

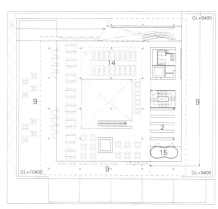

Fourth floor

Basement

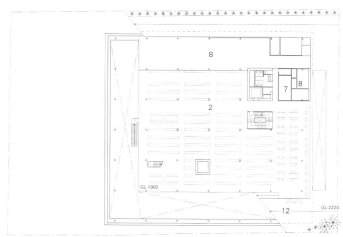

First floor S=1:800

1 COMPACT SHELVING / READING SPACE
2 FIXED SHELVING / READING SPACE
3 JAPANESE BOOKS ROOM
4 STORAGE ROOM FOR MICROFILM
5 MECHANICAL
6 DRY AREA
7 RARE BOOK ROOM
8 OFFICE
9 TERRACE
10 STUDENT'S COMMONS
11 EXHIBITION / LOUNGE SPACE
12 PILOTIS
13 GROUP STUDY ROOM
14 LECTURE / READING ROOM
15 AUDIO-VISUAL ROOM
16 STUDENT'S COMMONS WING

Since the library building faces the Mejiro Dori, it was important for this building to not only provide new spaces for the students to interact and learn, but to also become a new symbol of the university.

Rather than a conventional layered design, we thought it would be better to use slopes and open ceilings to vertically connect the different floors, which would foster an integrated experience as the students search for books and socialize in the building.

The slope begins from the campus plaza and circles around each floor. As terraces and private rooms are placed along the slope's path, and by changing its width here and there, its utility and character are designed to change depending on each location.

Spaces connect seamlessly like a single large room, starting above ground and leading down to the underground compact shelving areas, fixed shelving on the mid-level floors, and lecture and browsing spaces on the top floor. Students are able to enjoy various experiences in this building, from attending lectures to relaxing on the terrace. We hope that, as the library continues to serve the school over many years, it proves to be a kind of facility that can adapt to the evolving community and changing times.

図書館棟

図書館棟は，目白通りに面しており，大学の新しいシンボルとなるとともに学生の新しい学習や交流の場所となることが求められた。

私たちは，従来のような積層の図書館ではなく，スロープや吹抜けによって上下階を繋ぐ構成として，一体的な体験の中で本を探したり交流が生まれたりするような図書館がよいのではないかと考えた。

スロープは，キャンパスの広場から連続しフロアの周りを回遊していくように設けられ，その動線の途中にテラスや個室を設けたり幅を変えたりしていくことで，場所ごとで性格が変わっていくようなものとした。ワンルーム空間のように地上から地下の集密書架スペース，中間層の固定書架スペース，最上階のレクチャー，閲覧スペースが連続的に繋がっていき，レクチャーを聞きにいったりテラスに休憩しにいったりと，いろいろな体験を図書館の中に織りまぜるようにした。

長く使われていく中で，周辺地域や時代によって使われ方が変わっていくことを許容できるような，新しい大学図書館のあり方を期待している。

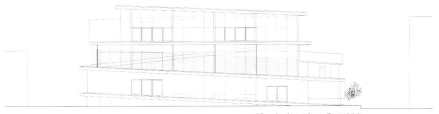

North elevation S=1:600

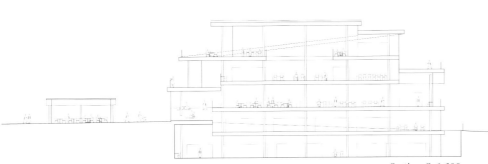

Section S=1:600

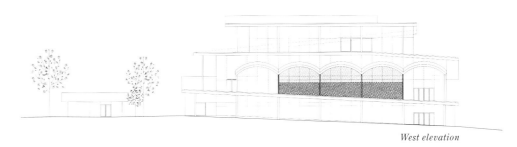

West elevation

*Auckland Castle Walled
Garden Project
Auckland, U.K.
2014–*

SANAA

This project is for a garden, greenhouse and restaurant in a 17th c. walled garden. It is on the grounds of Auckland Castle in the north of England, home to the Prince Bishops of Durham for 900 years. The site is composed of three parts: a flower garden on the top terrace, a vegetable area to the south and an orchard to the west.

The building is a cluster of glass bubbles that sits close to the historic Castle Lodge, inciting curiosity without disrupting views from the Castle to the landscape through the Wyatt screen. Visitors are first immersed in coloured flowers set against the green of the surrounding parkland.

The bubbles sit independently at the top of the site, the organic geometry reflecting vegetation, historic brick walls and sky. The building billows across a steep slope, establishing a sequence of spaces that slide between interior, greenhouse, terrace and garden. The structure is made up of 13 intersecting spheres, each with a diameter of 6 m. This geometry creates a split-level buffer zone for both people and plants.

From the entrance on the mezzanine visitors can enjoy the scented tree-tops and view of the river; below they are immersed in a citrus forest. Reminiscent of the greenhouse structures that have characterised the site throughout its history, the bubbles blur the line between building and landscape creating a series of dining spaces that adapt to seasonal shifts.

Carved out of the ground the design uses natural materials and earthy colours to create a Mediterranean garden bursting with colour throughout the year. Very thin 6 mm glass creates the skin of the building: almost invisible from inside, softly reflective from outside it floats above the ground like a transparent cloud.

Terrace on ground floor

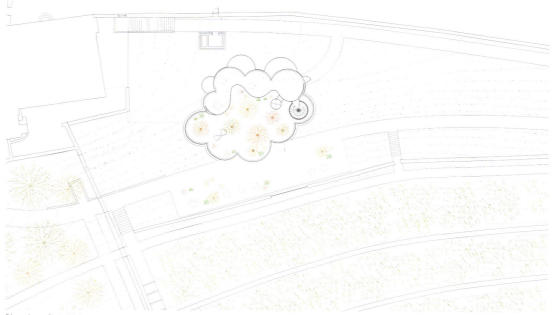

Site plan S=1:600

オークランド・キャッスル・ウォールド・ガーデン

このプロジェクトは，17世紀のウォールド・ガーデンに温室と一体となったレストランとランドスケープをつくる計画である。敷地はイングランドの北部，オークランド・キャッスルにあり，庭はトップテラスの花畑，南側の野菜畑，西側の果樹園の三つのエリアから構成されている。私たちは傾斜した庭の全体が見渡せるところに，ガラスの球体をランダムに積み重ね，ランドスケープに馴染みつつ，同時に独立した雲のような形の温室を考えた。

温室は直径6mの球体13個からできており，それぞれの球体は厚さ6mmの薄いガラスとガラスのフレームを兼ねたメッシュ状の小梁で構成され，それら球体同士は柱梁に支えられ，ワンルームの温室を繊細なストラクチャーで覆っている。そのことで，温室内の植物と建築とランドスケープとが連続した環境として捉えられるような空間になればと考えている。

メザニンレベルのエントランスラウンジへは花畑を通ってアプローチし，そこから温室内の植物越しに遠くまで広がった庭が望める。そして，柑橘類の木々が生い茂る温室に降りるとレストランとテラスがあり，テラスに出てパーティーをしたり，レストランで植物を楽しみながら食事をしたり，植物の中で訪れた人はゆったりとした時間を過ごす。

人々は1年を通して鮮やかな地中海の植物を楽しむことができ，歴史的な庭や周囲の建物群とランドスケープの中に，植物と人のための明るく透明な空間が現れることを目指した。

Mezzanine

View toward restaurant from terrace

Restaurant on ground floor

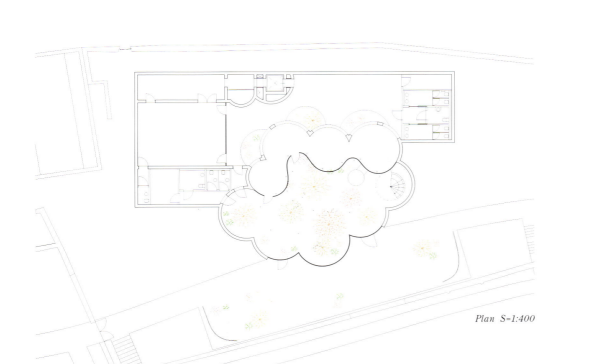
Plan S=1:400

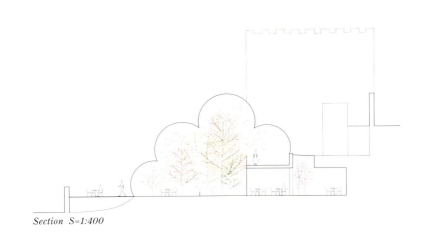
Section S=1:400

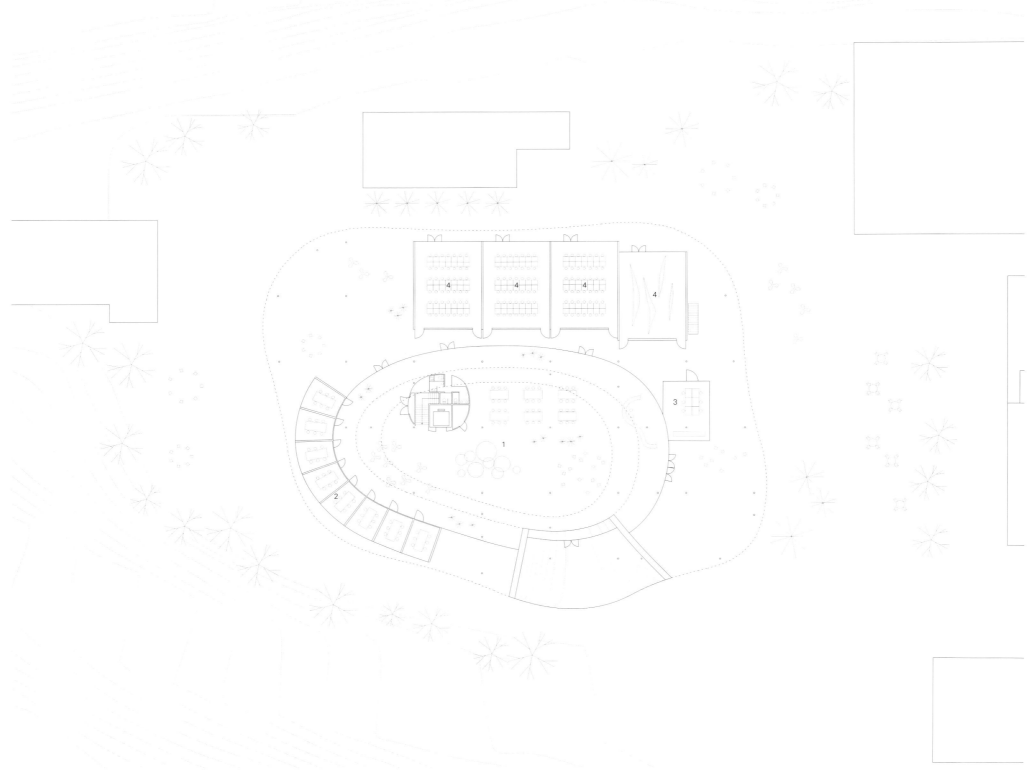

First floor S=1:500

*Osaka University of Arts,
Art Science
Osaka, Japan
2015–*

Kazuyo Sejima & Associates

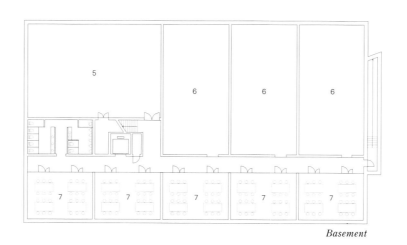

Basement

1 LABORATORY
2 PROFESSOR'S ROOM
3 OFFICE
4 CLASS ROOM
5 MECHANICAL
6 GALLERY
7 STUDIO

Site

View from approach

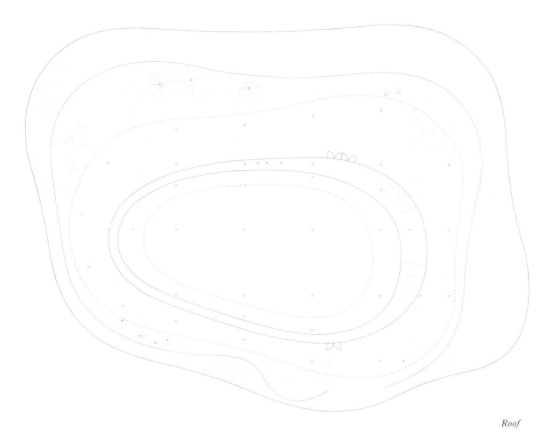
Roof

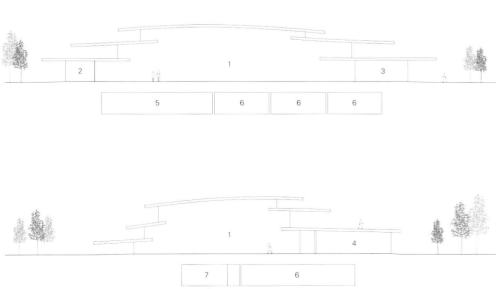
Sections S=1:600

This is the department building for the Art Science Department which recently opened inside the Osaka University of Arts campus, located in the mountains approximately one hour by train from the Osaka Station.

The site is found at the very top of a hill as one approaches the campus, having lush greenery and a vista of the city. The request was to create a building that houses a gallery for video artworks, lecture halls, and an atelier-like communal space that can be shared with the students of other departments as well.

The mountain has been cut through to create a flat site; we designed a building that corresponds to the topography, with a large roof that captures the light and wind, and expands continuously with the surrounding environment as if it is part of the landscape. The roof is stacked in three layers and has gentle undulation; it curves slightly along the site topography and, as it connects with a large open void, creates a large single space that intermingles with the surrounding environment. Furthermore, interior and exterior are gently linked together as the roof comes down and lands on the ground, allowing one to freely walk over the rooftop; underneath this space is also a large semi-outdoors space that opens to the rest of the campus.

The structure is made with a 3D curved surface concrete slab for the roof, under which pillars are positioned on a 9-m grid. This created a tense, transparent space that connects both with the landscape as well as the existing grid of the campus, enabling the building to become part of the environment while also retaining a sense of independence.

With architecture that harmonizes with the local landscape like a mountain, our goal was for this building to become a new landmark and a creative environment that fosters interaction between students of all departments.

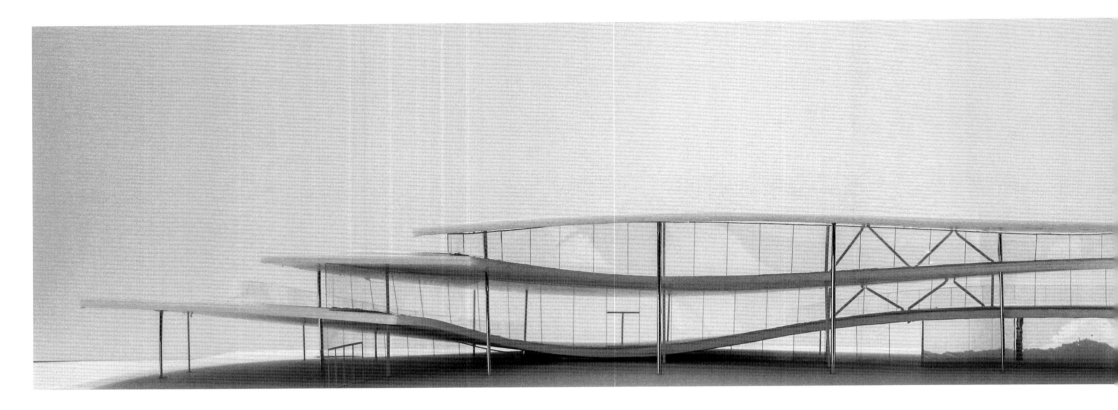

Section model

大阪芸術大学アートサイエンス学科棟

大阪駅から電車で1時間程の山の上にある大阪芸術大学のキャンパスに新たに開設された、アートサイエンス学科のための学科棟の計画である。

敷地は、キャンパスへのアプローチである坂道を登りきった、多くの緑に囲まれ、まちを一望することができる。そこに、映像作品などのためのギャラリー、講義室、また他学科の人も利用できる大きな工房のような共有スペースなどが求められた。

私たちは、山を切り崩した平坦な敷地に、地形と連続しながらも、光や風を取り込めるような大きな屋根をかけ、周囲の環境と連続するランドスケープのような建築を考えた。屋根は3枚に積層され、緩やかな起伏をもち、敷地に沿ってやわらかくカーブし、大きな吹抜けで繋ぐことで、周囲の環境と混ざりあった大きなワンルーム空間をつくる。また、屋根が地面に着地したところから屋根の上を回遊することができ、その下にはキャンパスに開放された大きな半屋外空間が生まれ、内部と外部を緩やかに繋げる。

構造は屋根を緩やかな3次曲面のコンクリートスラブとし、柱を9mグリッドに配置することで、緊張感のある透明な空間をつくり、グリッドで計画された既存のキャンパスと地形の両方と連続することで、独立しながら周囲に溶け込む。

このランドスケープと連続した山のような建築が、新たなランドマークとなり、他学科の学生との交流が生まれる創造的な環境となることを目指している。

Interior

View from street

Tokuda House
Kyoto, Japan
2015–16

Office of Ryue Nishizawa

This is a renovation project for a machiya (townhouse) in Kyoto. The existing building is a Kyomachiya (traditional townhouse in Kyoto) in the style of two row houses, which share the same wall and is around 100 years old. Parts of the building were renovated over time, and even though the building is old and deformed, it still preserves the original appearance and special characteristics like degoushi and mushiko-mado (different types of lattice windows) and a tori-niwa—a narrow path of earth that continuously connects the street to the garden that is at the back of the site. It was the request of the owner to renovate this old machiya to create a living space and a spacious place where friends and neighbors can gather.

We proposed to remove the flooring of the second floor in the south building, transforming it into a big space as a two-storey void, to restore the tori-niwa in the north building and to connect the south and north by opening the shared wall. The south building becomes a large spacious place, which is suitable to be used as a small assembly hall where people can gather, and the north building is designed as a residential unit with a tori-niwa. However, depending on the situation, the hole in the boundary wall could be utilized to join the two machiyas into one big residence, or the second floor could be used as a private space while guests could use the first floor. We wanted to incorporate the freedom to accommodate different lifestyles while using the existing body of the architecture.

The large space in the south building and the tori-niwa in the north building both directly face the street and garden, and since the two-storey void has a rooftop window, it brings in the natural elements of light and wind, and also the presence of the street deep into the building. By referring to and restoring the traditional space structure of machiyas in Kyoto, we hope that this will be a residence that notably matches with the lifestyle in Kyoto.

1 PASSAGE (TORI-NIWA)
2 MEETING ROOM
3 LIVING ROOM
4 VERANDA
5 COURT
6 BEDROOM
7 MEZZANINE
8 VOID

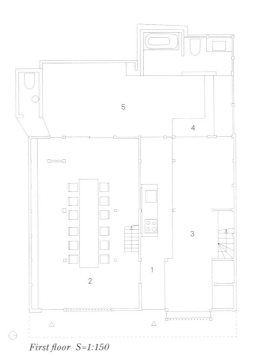

First floor S=1:150

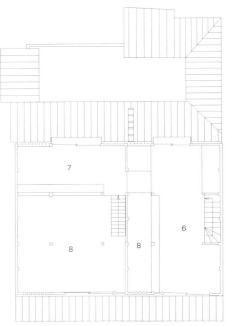

Second floor

Mezzanine

Meeting room with double height removing slab of second floor

徳田邸

京都の町家改修の計画である。既存の建物は二つの住居が壁1枚を共有している二軒長屋形式の京町家で，築100年くらいのものであった。長い時間の中で改造されてしまった部分もあり，建物も古く歪んでいたが，京都の町家が伝統的にもっている出格子窓や虫籠窓といった特徴的な外観や，通りから敷地の奥の庭まで連続した細長いタタキの土間空間である通り庭といったものが一部残っているという状態であった。お施主さんからの要望としては，そのような古い町家を改修し，住むところと地域の仲間が集まる広い場所をつくりたい，というものであった。

私たちが提案したのは，南棟では2階の床をとりはずして2層吹抜け大空間として，北棟の方は土間部分を吹抜けさせて通り庭形式を復活させる，ということと，南北棟を分ける界壁に穴を開けて南北を繋ぐ，というものだ。南棟は大きな空間となるので，人が集まる集会所として使うのに適していて，北棟の方は通り庭付き住宅と考えられる。しかし場合によっては，界壁に開けた穴を利用することで二軒町屋全体を一つの大きな住宅にしたり，または2階をプライベート空間，1階をゲスト用空間にしたりと，既存の躯体を利用しながら様々な住まい方ができる自由度を持ちたいと考えた。

南棟の大きな空間も北棟の通り庭も，通りと庭に直接面しており，また吹抜けと天窓を持っているので，光や風といった自然環境や，街の気配を建物の奥深くまで取り入れることができる。京都の町屋の伝統的空間構成を参照し，それを復活させることで，京都の暮らしによく合った住まいになれば，と考えた。

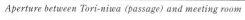
Aperture between Tori-niwa (passage) and meeting room

Tori-niwa with kitchen: view toward court

Tori-niwa (passage in earth floor): looking toward street

Bathroom

Corridor on bathroom. Sunlight comes through gaps of wood panels

Court

1　PASSAGE (TORI-NIWA)
2　MEETING ROOM
3　LIVING ROOM
4　VERANDA
5　COURT
6　BEDROOM
7　MEZZANINE
8　VOID

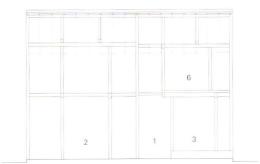
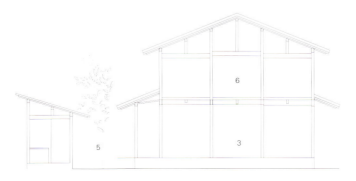
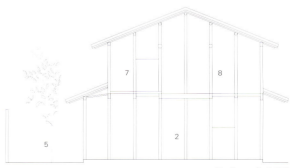

Sections S=1:150

House in Kyoto
Kyoto, Japan
2015-

Office of Ryue Nishizawa

This is a house under way in Kyoto for a young couple and their children. The site is a shape typically described as unagi no nedoko (eel's nest), with a frontage of 5.5 m and a depth of 24.5 m. The 6- to 8-m-tall houses standing on either side, as well as the office building over 20 m tall that towers behind, fully occupy their own sites. The clients requested a spacious living room for gathering friends, along with a dining room, kitchen, bedroom, children's room, bathroom, guest room, parking lot and storage. At the same time, the house was to be an architecture that can be considered a contemporary Kyoto machiya.

Our proposal is a house with a tori-niwa (passage garden), which fully occupies the site and enjoys an 8.5-m-tall atrium. The house, being a little taller than the surrounding buildings, can take in elements of the natural environment like light and wind. As a result, the south-facing atrium space becomes a tori-niwa that acts as an environmental device. With the wind blowing in summer and the sun warming up the space in winter, it creates a well-lighted, exterior-like environment that is pleasant throughout the year. As all the rooms face the passage garden, liveliness from the street and the turn of the seasons can be perceived from anywhere in the building. When the fittings that divide the rooms are cleared, the space can also be used as a single, extended living room. By embracing Kyoto's traditional housing typology, we wish that this project will become a house in which the joy and richness of life in Kyoto can be experienced.

West edge

East edge

South elevation

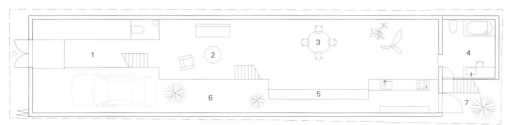

First floor S=1:200

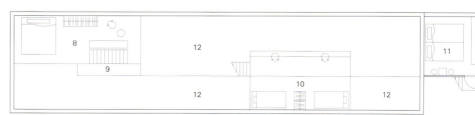

Second floor

Sectional view

京都の住宅

京都に計画中の，若い夫婦と子供たちのための住宅である。敷地は間口5.5m，奥行き24.5mほどの細長いうなぎの寝床のようなかたちをしており，左右には高さ6～8mほどの住宅が，奥には高さ20mを越すオフィスビルがそれぞれ敷地いっぱいに建ち並んでいる。お施主さんからは，知人が集まれるような広いリビング，ダイニング，キッチン，寝室，子供部屋，浴室，ゲストルーム，駐車場，倉庫などが求められると同時に，現代の京都の町家とも呼べるものをつくって欲しいとの要望があった。

私たちが提案したのは，敷地いっぱいに建つ，高さ8.5mの吹抜けを持った通り庭形式の住宅である。周辺の建物より少し背を高くし，そこから光や風といった自然環境を取り入れることで，南に面した吹抜け空間である通り庭全体が環境装置となり，夏は風が流れ，冬は陽だまりのできる，1年を通して快適に過ごせる，明るい屋外のような環境をつくっている。全ての部屋が通り庭に面しているので，建物のどこにいても，通りからのにぎわいや季節の移ろいを感じることができる。室内との間の建具を開け放てば，全体を一つの大きなリビングとして使うこともできる。京都の伝統的な住居形式によって，京都で生活する楽しさや豊かさを感じられる住まいになれば，と考えた。

Downward view from master bedroom

Tori-niwa (passage)

Living room on first floor

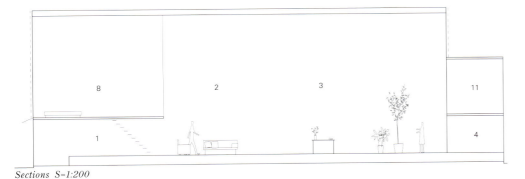
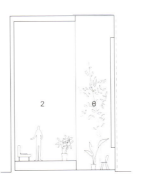

Sections S=1:200

1 ENTRANCE
2 LIVING ROOM
3 DINING ROOM
4 BATHROOM
5 VERANDA
6 PASSAGE (TORI-NIWA)
7 COURT
8 MASTER BEDROOM
9 TERRACE
10 BEDROOM
11 GUEST ROOM
12 VOID

New National Gallery,
Liget Budapest
Budapest, Hungary
2015–

SANAA

Southwest elevation

Northeast elevation S=1:1200

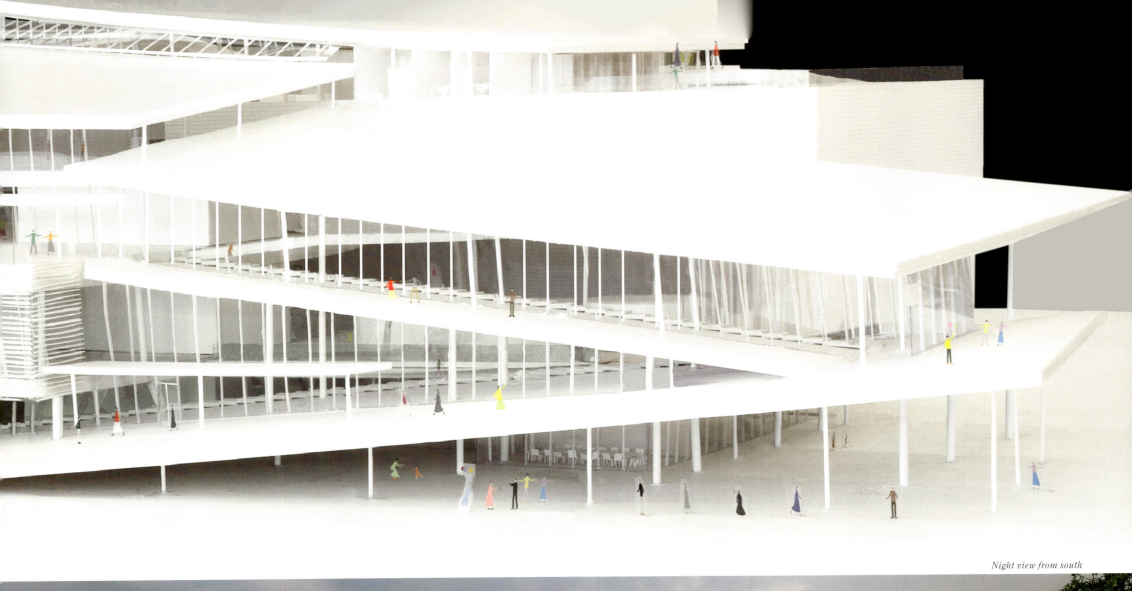

Night view from south

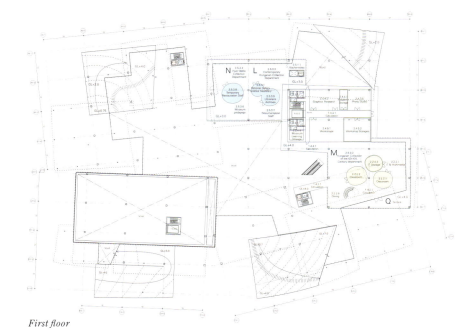
First floor

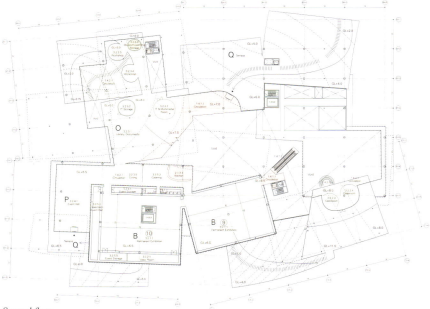
Second floor

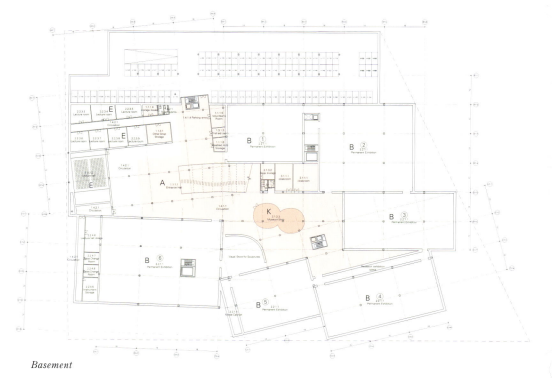
Basement

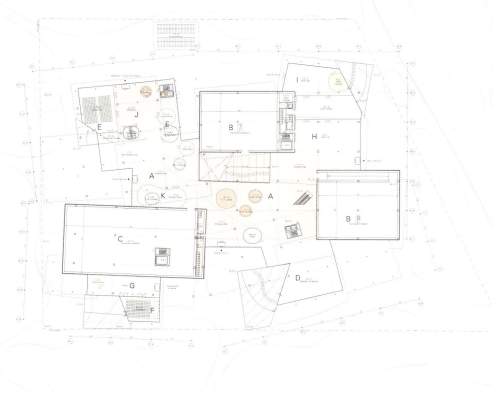
Ground floor S=1:1500

Aerial view

This project is for a museum located inside the Városliget public park at the center of the city of Budapest, Hungary. With a rich forest expanding throughout, this historic park is the world's first public park, and has long been enjoyed by residents of the city and tourists.

The site for this museum is located close to the center of the park, and can be reached from various directions through the park's forests and grassy open areas. Our idea was to create a museum that would enable visitors to enjoy art with the same sense of ease and relaxation of visiting the park. By staggering box-shaped exhibition spaces, slabs and slopes in a three-dimensional fashion, various spaces are created above and between the boxes which also connect to the park as well. This enables one to enjoy the scenery and light of the park from any place in the building.

Inside the exhibition space, artworks are displayed in sequence from the 1800's to today, enabling visitors to view the collection as a sort of "time gallery" arranged from the past to the present. On the other hand, each exhibition space can also be accessed directly from the continuous slope which leads from the park through the

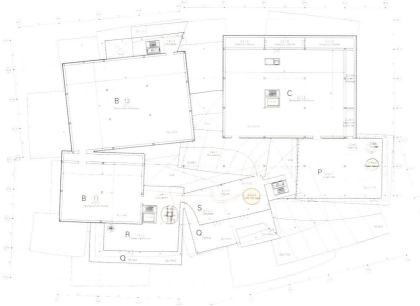
Fourth floor

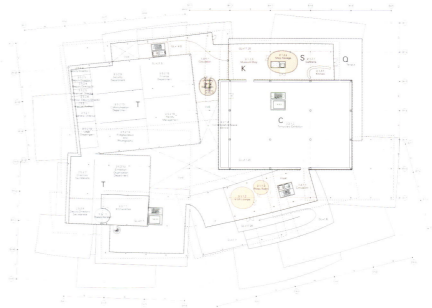
Fifth floor

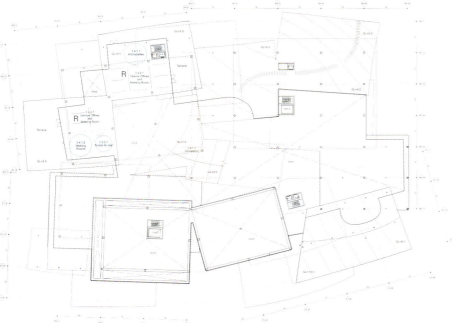
Third floor

Entrance hall

Entrance hall: slope to first floor

entrance, creating a sense of continuity as if the visit is an extension of a leisurely walk. Furthermore, the cafe, restaurant, and workshop spaces located above the boxes and the slab can be widely used by visitors to both the museum and the park.

Our hope is that the project will seamlessly integrate to become one with the park, creating new relationships between people and art inside a comfortable, park-like setting.

A ENTRANCE HALL
B PERMANENT EXHIBITION
C TEMPORARY EXHIBITION
D EXHIBITION OF STATUES
E LECTURE SPACE
F CINEMATEQUE
G FOYER
H GAIA LAB
I GAIA HALL
J BRASSERIE
K SHOP
L CONTEMPORARY HUNGARIAN COLLECTION
M HUNGARIAN COLLECTION OF XIX-XXI. CENTURY
N POST 1800S COLLECTION
O LIBRARY, DOCUMENT
P EVENT HALL
Q TERRACE
R CELLULAR OFFICE AND MEETING ROOM
S CAFETERIA
T OFFICE

View from foyer

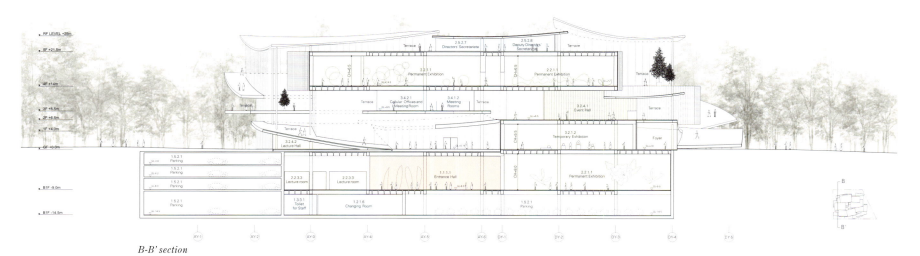

B-B' section

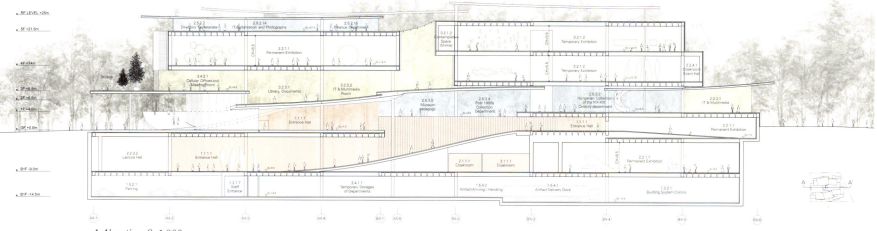

A-A' section S=1:800

新国立美術館 リゲット・ブダペスト

ハンガリー・ブダペストの中心市街地にあるVárosliget（市民公園）に建つ美術館の計画である。豊かな森が全体に広がるこの公園は，世界で初めて計画された歴史の古い市民公園であり，街の人々や観光客に長く愛されている。

美術館の敷地はこの公園のほぼ中央に位置し，公園の森の中や芝生広場を通って様々な方向から人々が訪れることができる。そこで，公園に訪れている雰囲気のままアートを鑑賞することができるような美術館がふさわしいのではないかと考えた。箱状の展示室，スラブ，スロープを適度にずらしながら立体的に並べることで，箱の上やそれぞれの間などに公園と連続した多様な空間が生まれる。そのことにより，建物のどこにいても公園の風景や光を感じることができる。

展示室は1800年頃から現代までのアートを時代順に体験するように連ねられており，来館者たちは，タイムギャラリーとして過去から現代まで通して鑑賞することができる。一方で，公園からエントランスを通って続くスロープなどの動線から，散歩の延長のように各展示室に直接アプローチすることもできるような構成となっている。また，箱の上やスラブの上にあるカフェやレストラン，ワークショップスペースなどの各機能は，美術館の施設でもあり公園の施設としても広く利用されることとなる。

美術館が公園の中に溶け込んでいき，公園にいるような居心地の良さの中で人々とアートの新しい関係を築くことができればと思う。

Sectional detail S=1:120

Sloped terrace connecting various museum spaces

*Shiga Museum of Modern Art
Shiga, Japan
2015–*

SANAA

The Museum of Modern Art, Shiga is located inside the Biwako Culture Park that lays between the Biwa Lake and its southern-side mountains. The museum is to be reinvigorated through the restoration and the construction of new extension with comparable size of the existing building.

The original museum is surrounded by nature, and is composed of separated buildings that include a Japanese garden and corridor for outdoor exhibitions. Our idea is to follow the existing composition of a circuit-style garden museum which becomes landscape with nature while adding new elements.

The new building is designed with a pitched roof that blends into the existing facilities and the surrounding scenery. By constructing separated buildings, the entire complex can be configured to match the local topography, and seamlessly connect to the sequence of the park. The project is designed so that people can experience nature while navigating through various exhibitions.

Exhibition spaces were expanded to include rooms with open views to the pond and outdoors scenery, as well as those that allow natural light, where collections including Beauty of God and Budda, Art Brut, and Modern and Contemporary art will be displayed. The placement of some corridors enables to install flexible exhibitions, and makes visitors feel of unity with various attractive exhibitions.

Areas adjacent to the library are renovated into an auditorium and workshops, and a restaurant, information center and other social functions are built on the opposite side of the pond. As a result, the museum can be approached from various points of the park, and the whole park will be a place where provides new experiences.

Within this open circuit surrounded by Shiga's mountains and waterside nature, the museum will be re-established as a place to stimulate new communication, and experience Shiga's beauty from the past to the future.

Aerial view from northeast: existing wings with hipped roofs, white volumes are new wings by SANAA ▷

View from southwest

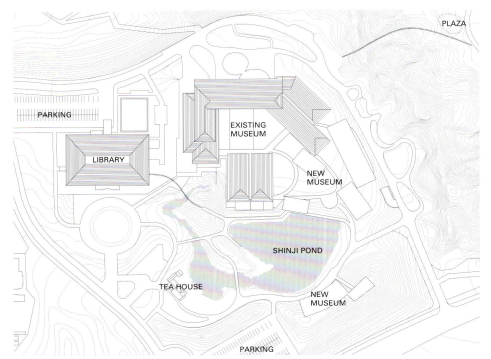

Site plan S=1:3000

Exhibition room

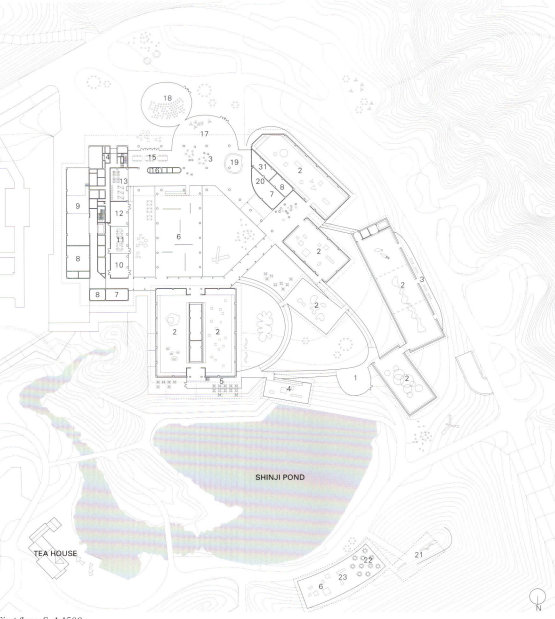

First floor S=1:1500

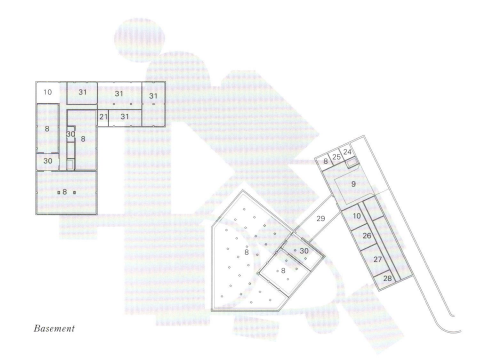

Basement

1 ENTRANCE/SHOP	12 CHILDREN'S ROOM	23 INFORMATION DESK
2 EXHIBITION SPACE	13 REFERENCE ROOM	24 GARBAGE ROOM
3 LOBBY	14 SECURITY OFFICE	25 WAITING ROOM
4 COMMISSIONED WORK	15 WORKSHOP	26 RESTORATION ROOM
5 CAFE	16 BOOKSHELVES	27 REFERENCE ARCHIVE
6 GALLERY	17 ENTRANCE HALL	28 INFORMATION MANAGEMENT
7 WC	18 AUDITORIUM	29 CARGO HANDLING
8 STORAGE	19 TICKET COUNTER	30 ACCLIMATION ROOM
9 LOADING DOCK	20 LOCKER ROOM	
10 CULTURAL OFFICE	21 OBSERVATION PLATFORM	
11 SHARED OFFICE	22 RESTAURANT	

Cafe: towrad annex over pond

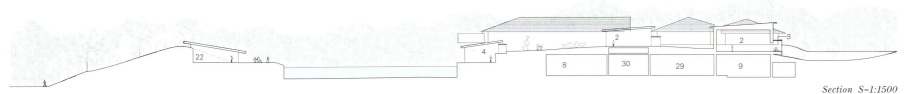

Section S=1:1500

滋賀県立近代美術館・新生美術館

滋賀県立近代美術館は，琵琶湖とその南側の山々の間に広がるびわこ文化公園の中に位置し，既存と同規模程度の増築と既存の改修を行い，それらが一体となって新生美術館として生まれかわることとなった。

既存の美術館は，周囲を自然に囲まれ，幾つかの分棟と日本庭園や屋外展示を巡る回廊による構成となっている。私たちは新しい要素を加えつつ，その構成を継承し，自然とともに風景をつくり上げるような回遊式庭園美術館がよいのではないかと考えた。

既存の建物や周囲の風景に調和するような勾配屋根とし，分棟形式とすることで周囲の地形に寄り添い，公園全体の回遊性と連続する。いろいろな展示を巡りながら，周囲の自然を感じることのできる計画とした。

展示室としては，既存の展示室の他に，池や風景に開いた展示室，自然光を取り入れることのできる展示室などを加え，そこに「神と仏の美」「アール・ブリュット」「近代・現代芸術」などを展示する。幾つかの回廊によってフレキシブルな展示計画が可能となり，異なる魅力をもつ展示を一体的に感じることができる。

図書館に隣接する既存部分を改修してワークショップや講堂を設け，池の向こう側にはレストランと情報交流室などの交流機能を設けたりすることで，公園のいろいろなところから美術館へとアプローチしやすくするとともに，公園全体が新しい経験をつくり出す場となる。

山々や水辺などの滋賀の魅力に開かれた回遊の中で，過去から未来までの滋賀の美を体感し，新しい交流が生まれる拠点となる。

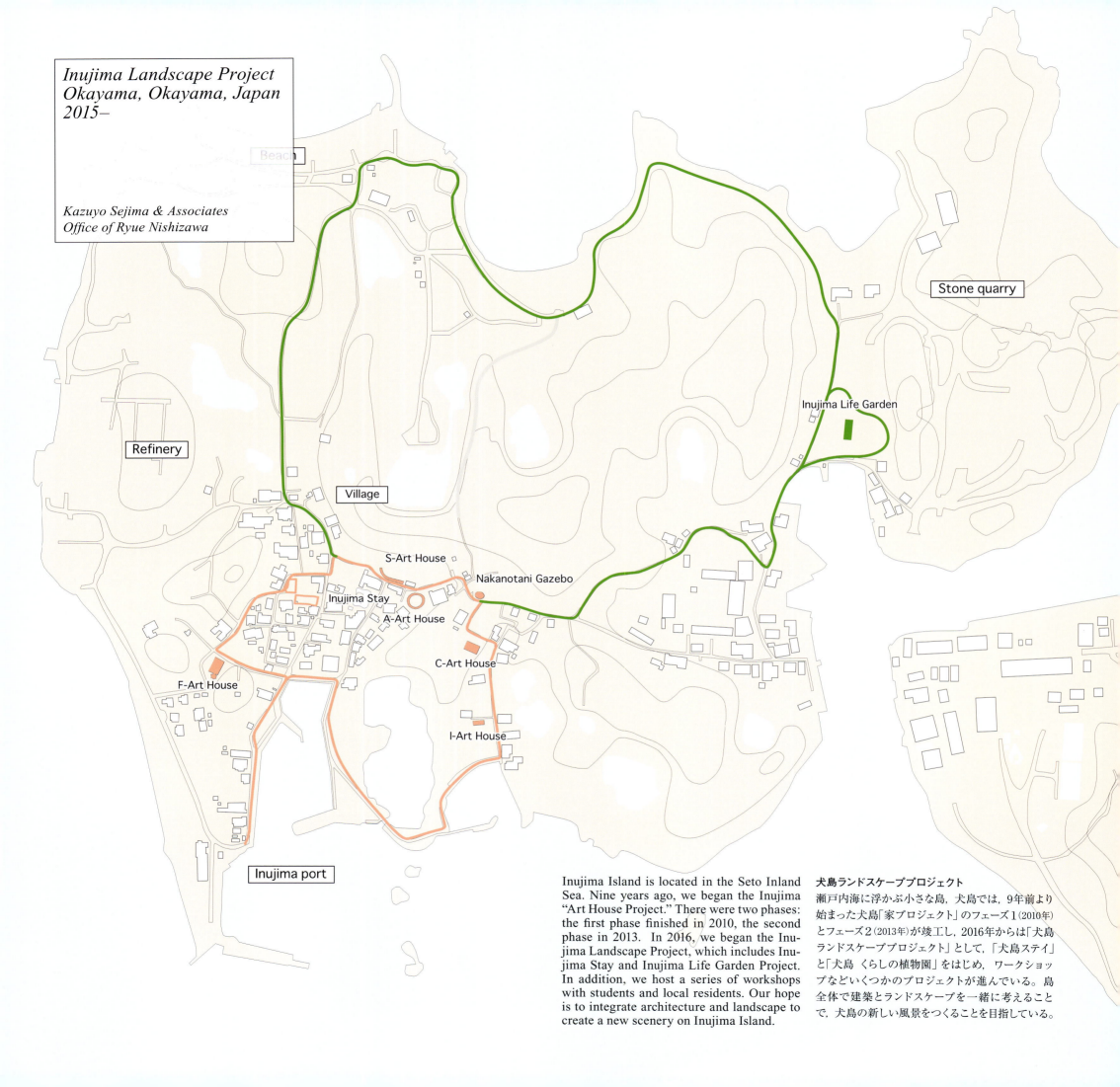

Inujima Life Garden

Kazuyo Sejima

View from garden

1. GREEN HOUSE
2. TERRACE
3. KITCHEN
4. OUTDOOR KITCHEN
5. BIOTOPE
6. BIOSWALE
7. ORCHARD
8. VEGETABLE GARDEN
9. HEARB GARDEN

Plan S=1:800

Inujima Life Garden is located slightly outside of the village on the western part of the island, about twenty minutes by foot from the harbor. This project is a collaboration with the client Fukutake Foundation, and gardener "Akarui heya."

Since the site had been left untouched for a long time, we first began by removing the stones that were intermixed with the earth, and fixing the glass-made greenhouse that had been abandoned for a while. The project is still a work in progress; in 2016, it opened in tandem with the Setouchi Triennale, with tables and chairs underneath a shady pergola next to the greenhouse, fruit orchard, herb and vegetable garden to the western side, and bio-geo filter and biotope for filtering drainage on the eastern side. In 2017, a small drink stand opened in the spring and a pizza oven in the summer; the house also began to raise chicken in the yard. Plants that were sparse during the opening have grown, and the plan is to create an animal house that will be used for composting as well.

The goal here is to create a landscape that intimately relates to a life among plants and animals. We hope that this environment system will naturally spread to the rest of the island in the future.

犬島 くらしの植物園

犬島 くらしの植物園は，港から歩いて20分ほどの島の西側，集落から少し離れたところにある。プロジェクトはクライアントである公益財団法人 福武財団とガーデナーの明るい部屋と一緒に進めている。

私たちはまず，敷地は誰も手をつけていない状態だったため，土に混ざった石を取り除き，また長年手つかずであった既存のガラス温室を綺麗にするところから始めた。プロジェクトは現在進行形で，ガラス温室の横に日陰をつくるパーゴラ，その下に休憩用のテーブルと椅子，温室の西側にハーブや果樹の庭と菜園，東側に排水を浄化するバイオジオフィルターとビオトープをつくり，2016年の瀬戸内国際芸術祭秋会期にあわせオープンした。そして，2017年春には飲み物を販売する屋台小屋，夏にはピザ窯をつくり，庭で鶏を飼い始めた。オープン当初，まばらだった植物は生い茂り，今後は堆肥小屋を兼ねた動物小屋ができる予定である。

ここでは，植物と動物が共生する生活とより親密に関係したランドスケープを目指している。そして，ここでの環境システムが将来的に自然と島全体に広がっていけばと考えている。

Inujima Workshop

Inujima Stay
Kazuyo Sejima

This project is for a shared communal space where visitors to the Inujima Island can stay and gather during their mid- to long-term stay. For the first stages of the project, we are planning two buildings for the visitors to stay inside the village, as well as a shared communal space for both visitors and the local residents.

The communal space houses the dining and kitchen, spacious bathroom, and relaxation and eating space which are all arranged around a courtyard. The roof opens and closes towards the street, fruit orchard and other residences, corresponding to the surrounding environment and creating a sense of various distances. The building flexibly responds to the surrounding situations: for example, if the building next-door becomes a library in the future, some of the spaces under the roof can be transformed into a reading space.

The communal space is slightly larger in scale than the neighboring buildings. We hope that it will become a space where visitors and locals actively interact, creating scenes and landscape as a new landmark for the Inujima Island.

犬島ステイ

犬島を訪れる人たちが中長期の滞在もできるように，泊まるところや集まれる共有スペースをつくるプロジェクトである。その始まりとして，集落の中に，泊まるところ2棟と，それらのとなりに来島者と島民の共有スペースを計画している。

共有スペースについては，ダイニングキッチンと，ゆったりとしたトイレ，食べたり休んだりできる屋根下空間が中庭を囲うように配置されている。屋根は道や果樹園や民家に対して開いたり閉じたりすることで，様々な距離をつくり，まわりの環境と連続する。例えば将来，隣の建物が図書館に変われば，それに合わせ屋根下空間が閲覧室になったりと，周囲と柔らかく呼応する。

周りの建物よりも少し大きな共有スペースは，犬島の新たなランドマークとなり，来島者と島民が積極的に交流する，犬島の新しい風景をつくる場所になればと考えている。

Scenes from Inujima Workshop

"Stay 01", "Stay 02" / Inujima Stay

Ryue Nishizawa

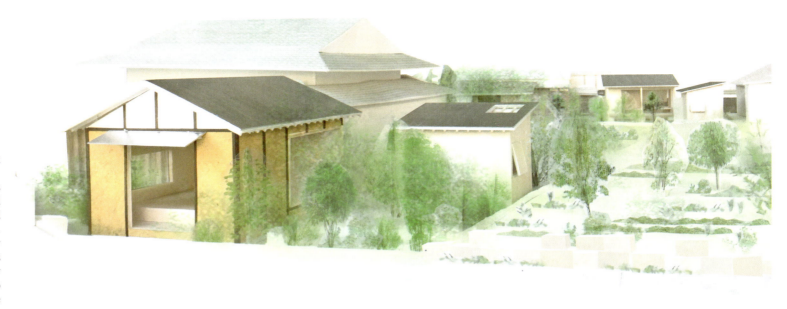

This is a project on Inujima, a small island in the Seto Inland Sea.

Inujima Island is a place where numerous different artworks can be found dotted throughout the tiny settlement, integrated into the lifestyles of the people living there. The resident population is only around fifty people, but on weekends around 200 visitors descend upon the island, causing its scenery to undergo a dramatic change. Due to increasing visitor numbers to Inujima, there are currently plans to create places for visitors to stay overnight and interact with the locals. Much like the artworks, there are several different projects scattered about the tiny settlement, among which are two cabin-cum-lodging-spaces designed by our office.

The two cabins we propose to build are both small wooden structures surrounded by picturesque greenery, and come with their own accompanying gardens. One will be a refurbishment of an old, gable-roofed house that has been unoccupied in recent years; the other will be a new construction with a raised floor and slanting roof, in the garden of an existing traditional Japanese house. Both of these cabins will be small, one-story lodges that can hold one or two lodgers. Their gardens will be accessible via large apertures, allowing guests to feel connected to the scenery of the village from inside. At the same time the lattice doors, storm shutters, rattan blinds and lush, enclosed garden create a private space which nonetheless remains gently tied to its surroundings via the seasons, time of day and weather. We hope that these transparent, open spaces with malleable boundaries become an integrated part of the landscape of Inujima, and help guests fully experience the lifestyle and scenery of this island.

ステイ 01, ステイ 02／犬島ステイ

瀬戸内海に浮かぶ小さな島である，犬島でのプロジェクトである。

犬島は小さな集落の中にアートが点在している，アートと人々の生活が一体となったような島だ。人口は50人ほどであるが，週末になると200人ほどのビジターがやって来て，島の風景を一緒につくっている。ビジターの増加にともない，犬島では現在，訪れた人々が滞在したり，住民の人々とシェアしながら交流できる場所をつくる計画が進んでいる。アートと同様に小さな集落の中にいくつか点在する計画で，西沢事務所ではそのうち宿泊機能をもった小屋二つの設計を担当している。

私たちが提案している二つはどちらも，美しい緑に囲まれた，庭付きの小さな木造の建物だ。一つは空家となった切妻屋根の古い建物を改修したもので，もう一つは新築，上げ床式の片流れの建物を民家の庭に新たに建てるというものである。どちらも共通して，一人か二人ほどが滞在できるような小さな平屋の建物で，大きな開口部を通して庭と繋がり，建物の中にいながら集落の風景を感じることができる。同時に格子戸や雨戸，簾，また美しい緑に囲まれた庭により，季節や時間，天気に応じて，周辺と緩やかに繋がりながらもプライベートな空間をつくることもできる。やわらかな境界を持った透明で開放感のある空間をつくることで，訪れた人々が犬島の生活や風景を体験できるような，そして全体として犬島の風景の一部となれるような建築を目指している。

Site plan S=1:400

Interior

Site section

> Sydney Modern Project
> Sydney, New South Wales,
> Australia
> 2015–21
>
> SANAA

The Art Gallery of New South Wales sits at the top of the gentle hill of Sydney's Domain, adjacent to the Royal Botanic Gardens, overlooking Woolloomooloo bay. This Gallery gradually grew over the past century, making multiple extensions to accommodate their diversifying collection. The Sydney Modern is a new extension for the Art Gallery of New South Wales which is planned to the North of their existing building at the junction of many vital pathways— pedestrians crossing the site to go to work in the morning and cars running through the highway crossing below.

The new extension is composed of various sized roofs which sit lightly on the site, mixed in with gallery volumes. These low and calm roofs step and shift gently along the natural topography to preserve existing trees and sight lines to form a connection between the Woolloomooloo Bay and the Domain along with a large plaza between the existing and new buildings.

This plaza is a shaded outdoor space which serves as not only the main entrance for the new building but also a shared space connecting surrounding neighbors—Royal Botanical Gardens, CBD, the Domain, Woolloomooloo, and Potts Point. It is a large open space which many activities can simultaneously spill into. We envision a space where residents and school groups can gather casually to relax, meet new people and prepare for their visit to the Gallery. The shifts and slopes of the roofs create spaces of various scales and views. From the entrance foyer, visitors see into an atrium that connects the entire gallery. Some roofs are accessible. While the visitors meander through the new extension they can step out to the open terraces or enclosed glass galleries and enjoy the view to the harbor. By integrating art, the existing site, and the surrounding landscape of Sydney, we hope to make a new art viewing experience for the visitors of the Art Gallery of New South Wales.

Aerial view (Sydney Opera House by Jørn Utzon on right)

Site plan S=1:6000

View from southwest: plaza (left) and gallery (center) on upper level (entrance level)

Entrance plaza: view from Art Gallery Road on west

Welcome gallery
Initial design concept of the Sydney Modern Project as produced by Kazuyo Sejima + Ryue Nishizawa / SANAA, 2016

```
1  PLAZA        6  ARTIST COMMISSION
2  TICKET       7  CAFE
3  CLOAK        8  KITCHEN
4  GALLERY      9  FOYER
5  TERRACE     10  MULTIPURPOSE
```

Lower floor S=1:1500

シドニー・モダン・プロジェクト

ニューサウスウェールズ州立美術館はシドニーのロイヤルボタニックガーデン，ドメイン公園に隣接し，ウルムル湾を見下ろせる緩やかな丘の上にある。100年来この美術館はコレクションが増えるとともに建物も増改築を繰り返し行ってきた。そして今回，さらなる増築を既存建物の隣に計画することになった。

新しい美術館は幾つかの大きさの異なった屋根とボックスでできている。この低く緩やかな建物は，高低差のある敷地に沿って木々を残しながら，連なり広がる。それらの屋根はウルムル湾を望むテラスになったり，広場をつくったりし，ドメイン公園とウルムル湾を繋いでいる。

公園からアプローチするとエントランスプラザが来館者をむかえる。エントランスプラザは日差しを柔らかく遮る屋根に覆われた屋外広場で，新しい美術館，既存美術館，周辺環境を繋ぐ公共空間である。美術館の一部でありながら，都市的なスケールで地域の中心となる活気ある場所をめざしている。何枚かの傾いた屋根は，連続した空間と風景をつくり出している。エントランスから大きな明るいアトリウムが見え，さらに奥に進むと一つ下にあるランドスケープが見えてくる。各階から屋根にアクセスすることができ，外に出られるテラスになったりもする。訪れる人々が展示室に入ったり，屋外に出たりという体験を繰り返しながら，展示とシドニーの自然を楽しむことができるよう，ランドスケープと建築が混じり合った建物を目指している。

Overall view from east

Middle floor   *Upper floor (entrance level)*

View from west in morning glow (above), northeast view from ship approaching port (below)

Naoshima Port Terminal
Naoshima, Kagawa, Japan
2015–16

SANAA

This terminal is for small passenger ships, located in the Honmura section of Naoshima. A new terminal with a waiting area, parking and toilet facilities were required as the existing terminal was suffering from its age.

A significant number of the island residents of Naoshima have settled in Honmura, and it is also becoming an attraction for many tourists, given the many Art House Projects scattered throughout the area. We thought of the terminal as becoming the local landmark so that the island residents and tourists who first visit the island would immediately identify the pier within the port itself.

We randomly piled 4 m diameter fiber reinforced plastic (FRP) spheres on top of a wooden beam frame assembled in a lattice structure to create a 3D form that resembles a bank of clouds, standing at a height of 8 m. This allows the port to be located from a great distance away by those headed to the pier or by those approaching the island by boat. We also thought about realizing an airy, bright and comfortable space where exterior light cascades throughout the interior voids by creating the spheres using translucent FRP that are 5 mm in thickness.

It is our hope that this place becomes the new symbol of the area where residents and tourists who come to the island gather together as a result of this terminal.

直島港ターミナル

直島の本村にある，小さな旅客船のためのターミナルである。既存のターミナルが老朽化したため，待合所，駐輪場，トイレの機能を持つ新しいターミナルが求められた。

本村は直島の多くの島民が住む集落でもあり，家プロジェクトが点在していて多くの観光客が訪れる場所でもある。島に住んでいる人にも，島を初めて訪れる観光客にも，港の中で船乗り場がすぐにわかるように，まちのランドマークとなるように考えた。

格子状に組んだ木の柱梁のフレームの上に，直径4mの球体のFRPをランダムに積み上げて，高さ8mの入道雲のような立体的な形をつくった。そうすることで，船乗り場に向かう人々や，船で島に近づく人たちが，遠くからでも港をすぐに見つけることができる。また球体を厚み5mmの半透明のFRPでつくることで，外からの光が内部空間全体に広がり，ふんわりと明るく快適な空間となるように考えた。

このターミナルのもとに，島に住んでいる人たちや島を訪れた観光客が一緒に集まり，この場所がまちの新しいシンボルとなることを望んでいる。

Morning view from sovth before sunrise

View from southwest

Detail of structure

Plan S=1:400

Elevation S=1:400

Section S=1:400

Aerial view from east. Site for Museum of the 20th Century located between New National Gallery designed by Mies van der Rohe (left) and Berlin Philharmonie designed by Hans Sharoun (right)

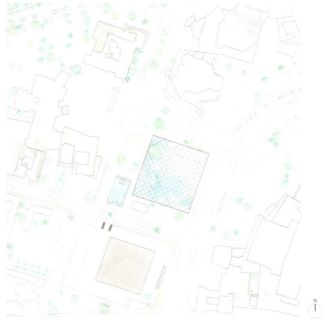

Site plan S=1:5000

South view

The site is located in the center of Berlin's central cultural district, sandwiched between the city's two important landmarks of the Tiergarten and the Landwehr Canal. There are symbolic architecture in this area with important cultural meaning such as the New National Gallery by Mies van der Rohe, Berlin Science Center by James Stirling, and Berliner Philharmonie by Hans Scharoun. Nestled among such symbolic buildings, we proposed an open museum park in which the museum itself becomes a central park that links together the nearby buildings and their public spaces.

On the ground floor of the open museum park, we planned a large winter garden enclosed in glass. Winter garden is an urban park-like space that houses Berlin's native trees and plants. It also creates a unique landscape that can be used throughout all seasons, even during the harsh natural conditions of the summer and winter. Inside we designed cafes and multipurpose halls which can be utilized by everyone whether they are visiting the museum or not, creating an open museum park that can be easily enjoyed by the public.

The exhibition spaces can be accessed via the platform located in the center of the winter garden. The space is designed as an open entrance where a view of the surrounding scenery beyond the winter garden can be enjoyed from the top of the platform. The special exhibition space on the mezzanine is directly connected to the winter garden, and can be expanded into the winter garden itself depending on the occasion. Furthermore, natural light filtered through the dry area, illuminating the underground exhibition space and foyer to create a relaxing atmosphere for the visitors.

Our goal was for this open museum park to become part of the local environment while also inspiring a new landscape, creating a place that opens up to the city where various people can come together and interact with one another.

Museum of the 20th Century 設計競技案

敷地は，ベルリンのティーアガルテンとラントヴェアー運河，二つのベルリンの重要なランドマークの間にある，ベルリンの主要文化地区の中心に位置している。敷地周辺にはミース・ファン・デル・ローエのニューナショナル・ギャラリーやジェームズ・スターリングの科学センター，ハンス・シャロウンのベルリン・フィルハーモニーなどといった，歴史的に重要な意味を持つシンボリックな建物が集まっている。私たちは，このように様々なシンボリックな建物が周囲に建ち並ぶ中で，美術館そのものがセントラルパークとなり，それぞれの個性豊かな建物とそのパブリックスペースを繋ぐ，オープン・ミュージアムパークを提案した。

オープン・ミュージアムパークの1階には，ガラスで囲われた大きなウィンターガーデンを計画した。ウィンターガーデンは，ベルリンに自生する既存の樹木や植物を残し，都市の中にある公園のような場所であり，また夏や冬の過酷な自然環境の中でも1年間通して使える，ユニークなランドスケープをつくっている。中にはカフェや多目的ホールのような，美術館を訪れない人々にも開かれた場所を設けて，誰でも気軽にオープン・ミュージアムパークを訪れることができるように考えた。

展示室へはウィンターガーデンの中央にあるプラットフォームの上からアクセスできる。プラットフォームの上からは，ウィンターガーデン越しに周辺の風景を一望できる，開放的なエントランス空間となるように計画した。中2階にある企画展示室はウィンターガーデンと直接繋がっていて，展示内容によってウィンターガーデンまで展示室を拡張することができる。またドライエリアから自然光を取り入れ，地下の展示室やホワイエも明るく，美術館を訪れた人々にとって居心地のいい場所となるように考えた。

私たちはオープン・ミュージアムパークが，周囲の環境になじみながらも新たな風景をつくり，また様々な人が集まって交流が生まれる，まちに開かれた場所になることを目指した。

Ground floor S=1:1000

Southeast elevation S=1:2000

NEW NATIONAL MUSEUM　　MUSEUM OF THE 20TH CENTURY　　BERLIN PHILHARMONIE

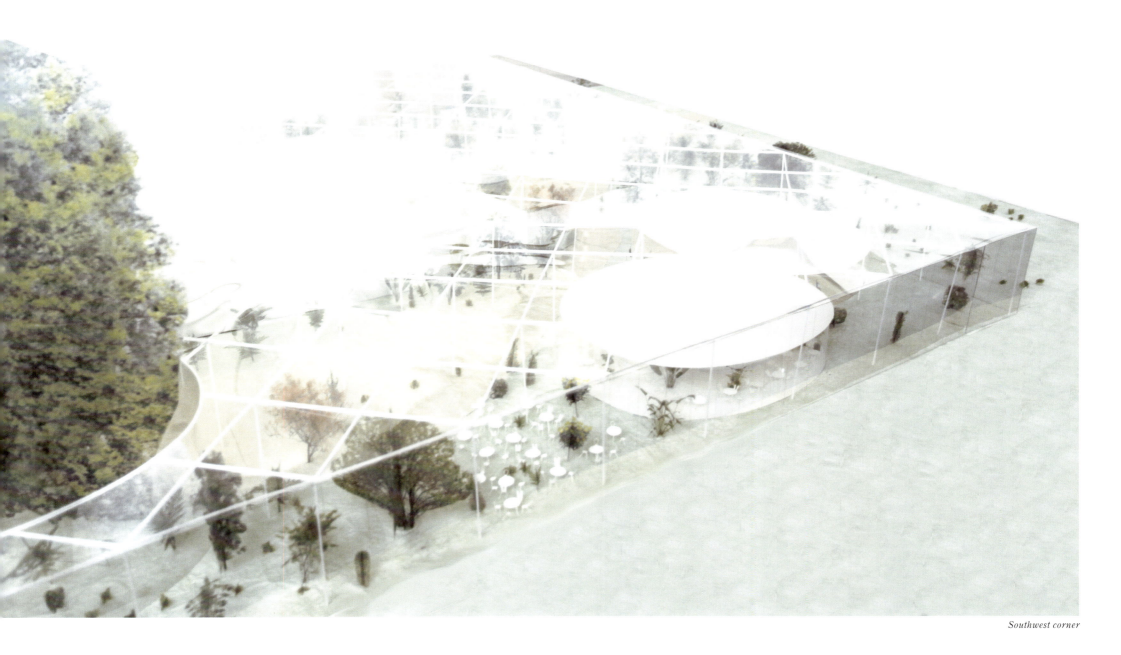

Southwest corner

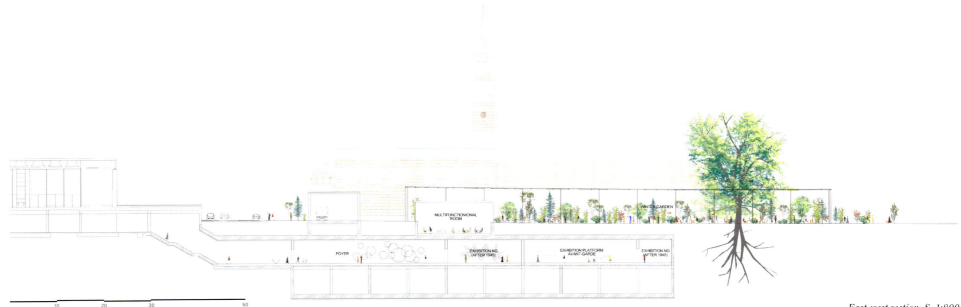

East-west section S=1:800

I House
Nagano, Japan
2016–

Office of Ryue Nishizawa

This is a new residence currently planned in a quiet housing estate. The neighborhood streets are lined with residences surrounded by spacious plots.

The clients are a married couple whose requests included a study for their vast private library, a bright and open living room, a classroom for running English classes, a bedroom for the wife on the upper floor, and a sense of connectedness throughout the home. The clients are sensitive to sounds and vibrations, so above all, it was important to create a serene living environment.

This was originally a single-story plan, but we eventually realized that meeting size requirements would result in a building comparatively much larger than neighboring houses. The building would also cover the entire plot, which would give it a claustrophobic feeling.

In response, we felt that by arranging the desired room-functions into distinctly sized living spaces and stacking them like building blocks, the layering would create a compact building with a spacious garden in a scale consistent with neighboring residences. By considering the surrounding structures, gardens and their relationships, we are aiming to create a structure that, while at a glance seems free-standing, is also in harmony with the surrounding environment.

Each spatial volume faces multiple directions so that there is no front or back. Various apertures and the spaces between rooms allow air and light to filter through from the surrounding garden. By stacking volumes of different sizes, we also created a split-level design with floors of various heights layered both internally and externally. As each room faces the open-ceiling living area at the core of the building, the home is an open space that feels connected three-dimensionally.

As for the structural design, reinforced concrete construction creates an interior environment protected from external noise and vibrations, with light, steel-frame box stacked above. This difference in construction is also visible externally. The plan is designed so that proximate rooms will support each other like they are holding hands to sustain a well-balanced composition.

We hope that by freely combining multiple spaces, from the open-plan areas to the rooms protected from external commotion, this residence will become a cozy, nest-like home that inspires new spaces to be born with the changing seasons and environment.

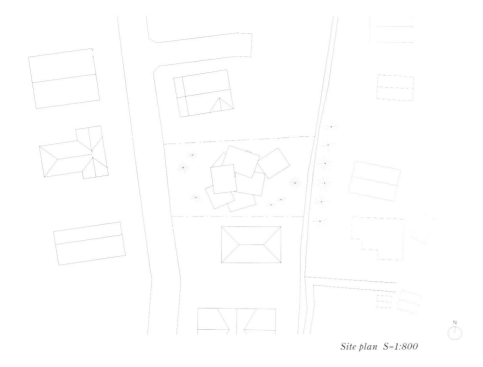

Site plan S=1:800

I邸

閑静な分譲住宅地に計画中の住宅である。周辺にはゆったりとした土地の中にぽつんと置かれたような住宅が建ち並んでいる。

住まい手はご夫婦2人で、要望としては、たくさんの蔵書を納められる書斎、開放的で明るいリビングルーム、英会話教室を開くためのクラスルーム、上階に奥さんの寝室を設けること、全体として繋がりが感じられる住宅であること、などが望まれ、何より音や振動に敏感な住まい手のために安定した居住環境が必要であった。

当初は平屋の案も検討していたが、必要な大きさを平屋の建物で計画すると周囲に比べてとても大きく、敷地いっぱいに建物が広がることでどこか息苦しさを感じた。

そこで私たちが考えたのは、求められた各機能をヴォリュームに分け、積み木のように積んでいくというもので、積層させることで周辺の住宅同様に広い庭を持つコンパクトな建物とした。周囲の建物や庭との関係を考えながらヴォリュームを配置することで、一見フリースタンディングな建物でありながら環境と調和した住宅をつくろうとしている。

各ヴォリュームはいろいろな方向を向いているので、表裏がなく、開口部や部屋と部屋の隙間を通して周囲の庭から光や風を取り込むことができる。また、大きさの違うヴォリュームを積んでいったので、内外にいろいろな高さの床があるスキップフロアの建物となった。それぞれの部屋は中央の吹抜けのリビングルームに面しているため、全体として立体的に繋がりのある空間となっている。

構造計画としては、RC造で外部の音や振動から守られた環境をつくり、その上に鉄骨造の軽い箱を載せる構成としている。また、構造の違いがそのまま外観に現れるようにしている。平面的には隣り合う各部屋が手を繋ぐように支え合うことでより安定した構造となるよう計画している。

開放的な空間から外部の喧騒から守られた空間までいろいろなものが自由に組み合わさり、季節の変化や周辺環境とともに様々な居場所が生まれることで、快適な巣のような住宅になれば、と思っている。

First floor S=1:150

Second floor

1 LIVING
2 LIBRARY
3 CLASS-ROOM
4 TATAMI-ROOM
5 TEA-ROOM
6 ANNEX
7 SHOWER-ROOM & TOILET
8 BATHROOM
9 DRESSING ROOM
10 TOILET
11 KITCHEN
12 ENTRANCE
13 BED ROOM
14 STORAGE
15 DEN
16 TERRACE
17 STUDY-ROOM

Section S=1:150

Spring
Daigo, Ibaraki, Japan
2016

Kazuyo Sejima & Associates

Plan S=1:500

Section S=1:500

Daigo town's Old Asakawa Onsen is located on a gentle slope leading down from the mountains to the Kuji River, in the midst of the idyllic landscape in the north of Ibaraki Prefecture. Here one can find a large old wisteria tunnel alongside the hot springs, and there is an atmosphere here that the locals have used this as a gathering place since long ago.

Climbing up the steep road at the entrance to the site, a vista of tranquil scenery and a natural footbath greets your eyes. The footbath is shaped like a mirrored aluminum dish, with a diameter of 10 m. The surrounding landscape and sky are mirrored in both the whitish surface of the reflective aluminum, and the gently swaying water surface of the hot spring, causing these features to overlap in curious manner. Visitors are able to enjoy the footbath while surrounded by reflections of different intermingled sights. We hope this will create new relationships between the people, hot spring, and scenery, leading to become a place where people gather naturally.

Spring（KENPOKU ART 茨城県北芸術祭）
大子町の旧浅川温泉は，山から久慈川へと続く緩やかな斜面の中程に位置し，県北の美しくのどかな風景の中にある。そこには温泉とともに古く大きな藤棚もあり，地域の人たちが長くこの地に集ってきた雰囲気を敷地からどことなく感じることができる。

敷地の入口の急な坂道を登り切ると，目の前にその穏やかな風景とともに足湯が広がる。足湯は，直径10mの鏡面のアルミのお皿のような形をしている。白っぽく反射するアルミの面と緩やかに揺れるお湯の面にそれぞれ風景や空が映り込み，不思議な風景の重なりが生まれる。訪れた人たちはその風景の重なりの中に入り，足湯を楽しむ。人とお湯と風景の新しい関係が生まれ，自然に人が集まることのきっかけとなってくれればと思う。

Both water surface and mirror finishing bottom of footbath reflect natural light

Footbath made by aluminum plate of 5 mm in thickness

Entrance completed in 2013

Entrance: view from east

Shodoshima-Fukutake
House
Shodoshima, Kagawa,
Japan
2016

Office of Ryue Nishizawa

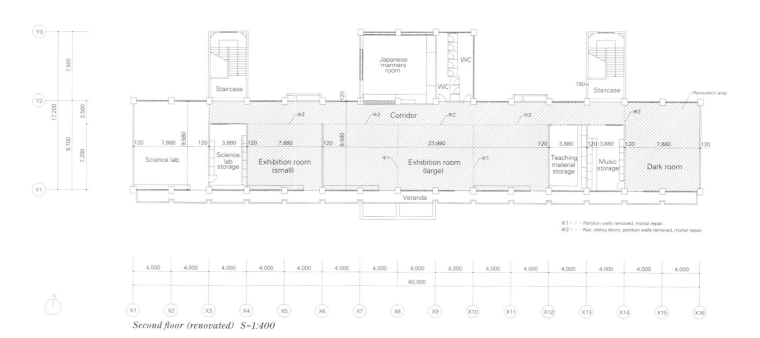

Second floor (renovated)   S=1:400

246

Exhibition room (large) on second floor

Exhibition room (small) on second floor

Dark room on second floor

This is a renovation of the second floor of the former Fukuda elementary school building in Shodoshima.

Since 2013, the site has been used annually for the display of artistic works of Asia. On the occasion of the 2016 Setouchi triennale, the client requested that a part of the building be renovated to make an exhibition space to eliminate the school image and make it more suitable as a proper art exhibition site. The client also requested that the second floor of the building be converted into a single exhibition space in which artists could work and stay in the future, and where local citizens could freely enjoy themselves.

The classrooms, hallway, dividing walls, ceiling and fixtures were removed as much as possible to create a large open space that exceeded the scale and feel of the former elementary school building.

Bright, natural sunlight pours in from the southern windows lining the former classroom walls as well as the northern windows lining the former hallway, providing a large spacious area in which artists can create and exhibit their works. Visitors can freely move about the space among the artworks on display as soon as they enter the second floor.

We hope that this place will become a place where visitors can feel free to enjoy art during exhibitions, as well as a place of interaction among artists and local residents during other seasons as well.

小豆島福武ハウス一部改修

小豆島にある旧福田小学校の校舎2階の改修である。

敷地は2013年から毎年校舎にてアジア美術作品の展示が行われてきた場所であり，クライアントからは，2016年の瀬戸内国際芸術祭をきっかけに学校のイメージを払拭して美術展時にふさわしい建物にしたいということで，展示会場となる部分の改修を求められた。また将来的にはアーティストが制作，滞在できるスペースとしたいということ，地元の方々にも気軽に遊びにきてもらえるようなスペースとしたいということ，校舎の2階全体を一つの展示スペースとしたいという希望があった。

2階の教室や廊下の仕切り壁や天井，建具をできるだけ取り払い，小学校の校舎のスケール感を超えた大空間をつくった。

小学校の教室の南側の壁一面に配置された窓と廊下側であった北側の壁一面に配置された窓から明るい自然光が差し込む中，アーティストたちは大きな空間を使い制作や展示活動を行うことができる。展示を見に会場を訪れる人々は，校舎の2階へ上るとすぐに，アート展示が広がる中を自由に移動することができる。

展示会場を訪れた人々が気楽にアートを楽しめるような，また芸術祭会期以外でもアーティストや地域の方々の交流の場としても使われる場所となることを期待している。

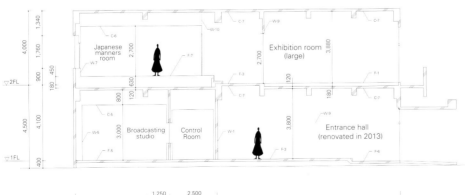

Section (renovated) S=1:200

Atelier
Tokyo, Japan
2016–17

Office of Ryue Nishizawa

Office

Office: looking north

This is a renovation project to convert the top two floors of a building into an office space.

The building is situated just one block behind the main street, and luckily had good ventilation and natural lighting from three sides of the property, as well as a large terrace attached on the south side of each floor.

The office will be shared mainly among three companies for various uses, serving as the main office for some, and as a secondary place of work and activity for others.

Some of the requests from the client included: a large, one-room working space that allows people to feel each other's presence with freedom to move around for a change of mood; a separated meeting area; FAB Room; and a terrace space where everyone can gather. We removed all partition and transformed the space into a large studio while retaining as much of the existing structural frames as possible. This allowed natural light to filter through the large, terrace-facing opening, and the staircase that connects the upper and lower floors, creating a bright and expansive one-room space.

Rooms that needed to be enclosed were gathered at the north side of the property, and open, display-type working spaces were also assembled nearby. Furniture of different styles were arranged around the terrace. This spacious open area can be used for various activities, whether to work individually or to hold meetings with other members. The large, existing terrace on the fifth floor was already comfortable and open, so we installed a movable canopy rooftop and furniture to create a multifunctional space that can also be used to hold outdoor meetings.

By extending flexible, multifunctional spaces on both indoors and outdoors, our intention was to create a place that inspires activities that feel even more free and diverse.

Terrace on fifth floor

FAB Room. Terrace on left

FAB Room

1 OFFICE
2 TERRACE
3 KITCHEN
4 WC
5 STORAGE
6 FAB ROOM
7 MEETING ROOM

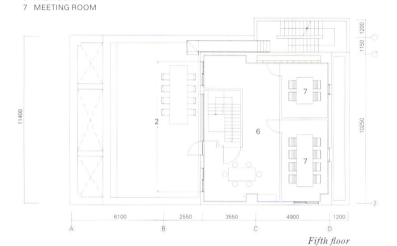
Fifth floor

Meeting room

Terrace on fourth floor

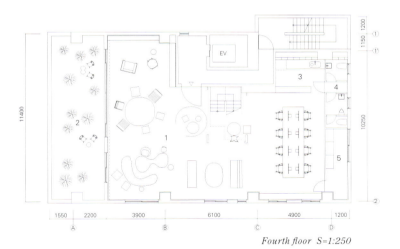
Fourth floor S=1:250

Office: south side

Office: view from entrance

アトリエ

ビルの最上階である4,5階のメゾネット住居をオフィスに改修する計画である。

建物は，大通りから1本入ったところに建ち，3面で通風や採光がとれ，それぞれの階の南面には大きなテラスがあり，とても環境に恵まれていた。

オフィスは，主に3社で利用し，それぞれ，拠点であったり，必要な時に利用する場であったり，いろいろな用途で活用する場所となる。

要望は，みんなの気配が感じられ，いろいろな場所で気分転換しながら仕事ができるワンルーム空間，仕切られたミーティングスペース，FAB ROOM，みんなが集えるテラス空間などであった。私たちは，間仕切り壁を全て取り除き，できる限り既存の躯体をそのまま残したワンルーム空間とした。テラスに面する大きな開口や，上下階を繋ぐ階段室からは自然光が入るようになり，とても明るく，広がりのあるワンルーム空間となった。

北側には閉じる要望が求められた部屋をまとめ，その近くにディスプレイで作業するスペースをまとめて設け，テラス側にはいろいろなスタイルの家具を並べた。一人で作業したり，みんなで打合せができたりと，多様に活動ができるオープンスペースが広がる。5階のテラスは，とても広く，開放的で気持ちの良い場所であった。そこに，可動式のテント屋根を設け，家具を並べ，外部でも打合せができる多目的な空間となった。

内部，外部にわたり多様なスペースが広がることによって，より自由でより多様な活動が生まれる空間になれば，と考えた。

Shizuoka City History Museum
Shizuoka, Shizuoka, Japan
2017–

SANAA

This project was for the Museum of Shizuoka History and Culture.

The site lies next to Sunpu Castle Park, which stands at a little distance from the Shizuoka Station. A sense of history permeates the area thanks to the stone castle walls, moat, Tatsumi Turret and Higashigomon East Gate. One approaches the site along a path running between the trapezoid stone walls, guided by the dense greenery lining the moat.

Here we were asked to create a proposal for a building that would duly respect its Edo-period historical surroundings, and also provide a link between the city center and the historical and cultural zone.

Our proposal was for a building consisting of two volumes: one for general exhibitions and community exchange, and one for historical exhibitions, as well as an open, low corridor. The size of the two volumes perfectly bridges the small scale of the park and castle turrets, and the grand scale of the city. The wall surfaces are segmented so that they do not excessively oppress the surroundings. Furthermore, through an echelon formation that allows room for a plaza in one corner of the site, we have ensured a direct line of sight from the city to Sunpu Castle Park and Tatsumi Turret. This open street space invites the city people to come and visit the park.

The corridor leading from the plaza continues the city's continuous direction of flow, looking out onto the community exchange area and cafe as a welcoming space which opens up towards the city. Beyond the corridor lies the large atrium of the historical exhibitions area. From here, visitors climb a slope while appreciating the various displays, and gain access to the temporary and permanent exhibition areas. After browsing the exhibits and emerging onto the observation lobby on the highest floor, visitors can enjoy a panoramic view over modern-day Sunpu Castle Park and Shizuoka City.

We designed this museum so that visitors could experience a series of exhibitions spanning the past to present day, and gain a sense of familiarity with the history of Shizuoka and Sunpu City. With this building we aimed to create a space that remains connected to the city, while offering a simultaneous experience of the present and future.

Aerial view

Street view

静岡市歴史博物館

静岡市の歴史文化施設の計画である。

敷地は静岡駅から少しはなれた駿府城公園に隣接している。周辺には石垣やお堀，巽櫓，東御門などが歴史的景観をつくっており，雁行する石垣の間の道やお堀沿いの豊かな緑に導かれて敷地にアプローチする。

このような江戸時代から続く歴史的景観に配慮するとともに，ここでは街の中心地と歴史文化ゾーンとを繋ぐ拠点となる提案が求められた。

私たちは展示・交流棟と歴史体感展示棟の二つのヴォリュームと開放的で低い回廊からなる建物を提案した。二つのヴォリュームは，公園や櫓の小さなスケールからまちの大きなスケールを繋ぐような大きさで，そして壁面を分節化することでまわりへの圧迫感を抑える。また，敷地の角に広場を持つように雁行配置とすることで，駿府城公園や巽櫓への視線の抜けをつくり，まちから駿府城公園まで人々を引き込むような街路空間となる。

広場と連続する回廊空間は雁行するまちの動線をそのまま連続させたような空間で，市民交流スペースやカフェなどが面し，まちに開かれた空間となっている。回廊空間の先には大きな吹抜けのある歴史体感展示室があり，展示を見ながらスロープを上がっていき，企画展示室と常設展示室にアクセスする。そして，展示を見終えて，最上階の展望ロビーへと出ると現在の駿府城公園や静岡市のまちが広がっている風景を見ることができる。

過去から現在に至るまでの一連の展示を体験することによって，駿府や静岡の歴史がより身近に感じられるよう計画した。まちと連続した空間をつくり，現在と未来を同時に体験できるような建物を目指した。

Looking over moat of castle

Sanya MOCA Project
Sanya, Hainan, China
2017–

SANAA

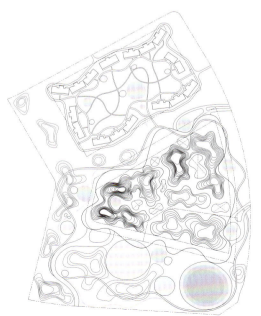

Site plan S=1:9000

Fifth floor

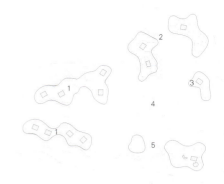
Sixth floor

Third floor

Fourth floor

The city of Sanya on China's Hainan Island is a popular resort known for its warm, tropical climate that can be enjoyed throughout the year.

This project involves a masterplan for one of the city districts in the Haitang district, as well as for a museum inside this area. Here, an apartment complex, boutique hotel, Ascot Hotel, artist's residence, and a museum will be built under the theme of "Art and Living," with the entire project spanning over a total of 140,000 m².

Since the weather is warm and gentle, there was an idea to create large terraces for enjoying the outdoors, which eventually led the way to our masterplan concept. We designed a configuration in which bright and open terraces link together, with a slab that gradually sets back as it extends upward. Furthermore, the positioning and shape of each building were determined by making sure that each unit had both privacy and good views. This resulted in a mountain range-like configuration and volume. It is our hope that this organic configuration and design that takes advantage of the uniquely warm climate will inspire new experiences, encouraging the people to engage with art in unprecedented ways.

三亜MOCAプロジェクト

中国の海南島にある三亜市は熱帯モンスーン気候で1年を通して暖かく，リゾート地としても有名な都市である。

海棠区の一つの街区のマスタープラン計画と，その中の美術館の設計である。この街区に「アートと暮らし」をテーマとして，集合住宅，ブティックホテル，アスコットホテル，アーティストレジデンス，そして美術館の合計約14万m²の建物を計画する。

温暖な気候であるため，テラスを大きくとって外部空間を楽しめる計画がいいという建築のアイディアからマスタープランを考えていった。明るく開放的なテラスが連続していき，スラブが上に行くにつれてセットバックしていくような形にした。また，ビューとプライバシーの関係から各々の棟の形，場所を決定していった。その結果，山なみのようなヴォリュームの配置計画となった。有機的な形態の配置計画とこの温暖な気候だからできる外部空間の使い方が，暮らしの中で新しいアート体験をつくり出し，これまでにない人とアートの関わりが生まれてくることを期待している。

First floor S=1:6000

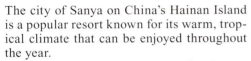
Second floor

1 RESIDENTIAL APARTMENT
2 COMMERCIAL HOTEL
3 BOUTIQUE HOTEL
4 ARTIST STUDIO AND RESIDENCE
5 MUSEUM OF CONTEMPORARY ART

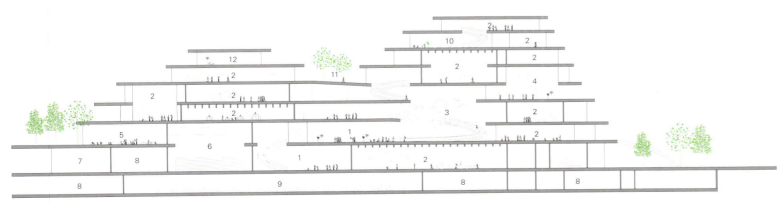
Section S=1:1200

1 LOBBY
2 GALLERY
3 ATRIUM
4 SCULPTURE GARDEN
5 LIBRARY
6 THEATER
7 ADMIN
8 BACK OF HOUSE
9 PARKING
10 RESTAURANT
11 ROOFTOP GARDEN
12 VIP SPACE

Louna Music Hall Project
Guizhou, China
2017–

Office of Ryue Nishizawa

The project is a music hall built inside a village in the idyllic countryside of Louna, Guizhou Province. It is located just outside of a tunnel which serves as the entrance to the village. When visiting the site, one is left with an impression of an expansive field of yellow rape blossoms and the beautiful mountains surrounding the village. We designed a new music hall where the architecture in this natural environment fuses with nature.

We proposed a building which has a gentle, unified space that is also divided, under one large roof that connects with the ground in one area and breaks open in another. Various large and small spaces are built under a single sheet of freely curved concrete. There is a large hall and a small hall beneath the swollen roof, and an open space for a foyer and a catering area underneath the extended roof. A break in the roof serves as the main entrance, and an outdoor performance area is located on top of the roof where it forms into a conical shape. People can walk over the roof, enter the building from a gap where the roof rolls back, roam about and exit to the outside from the cut, continuously experiencing the landscape and architecture as they crisscross one another in two or three layers both externally and internally. Also, by simultaneously creating the closed space of the music hall and the open space of the landscape, we believed we could create a concert experience embedded within beautiful nature. Our aim was to create a music hall architecture which, by corresponding to the village's unique landscape of the gentle valley surrounded by tall mountains, would become a new space that leaves a lasting impression.

Overall view

South elevation S=1:800

West elevation

Site section S=1:1200

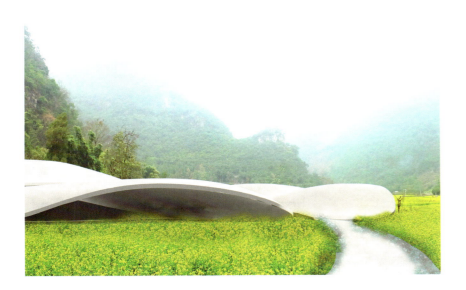

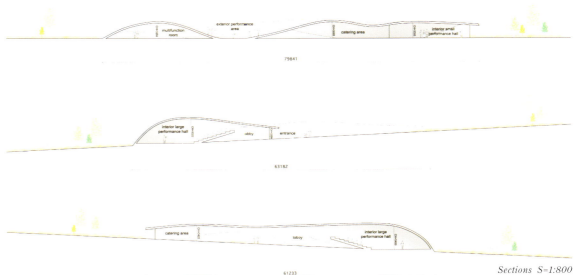

Sections S=1:800

1 ENTRANCE HALL
2 LARGE PERFORMANCE HALL
3 SMALL PERFORMANCE HALL
4 EXTERIOR PERFORMANCE HALL
5 MULTIFUNCTION ROOM
6 REHEARSAL ROOM
7 CATERING AREA
8 ROOF TERRACE
9 ARTISTS TERRACE
10 CAFE TERRACE

Plan S=1:1000

楼納音楽ホールプロジェクト

貴州省の楼納にある牧歌的な田園風景の農村に建つ音楽ホールである。敷地は村の入口となるトンネルを抜けた先に位置している。敷地を訪れると，村を囲む美しい山々と一面に広がる黄色の菜の花畑が印象的であり，この自然環境の中に建築と自然の融合した新しい音楽ホールの空間を考えた。

私たちが提案するのは，大きな1枚の屋根が着地したり切れ目が入ったりすることでできる，分かれつつも緩やかな一体の空間をもつ建築である。1枚のコンクリートを自由にカーブさせて，その下に大小様々な空間をつくる。大きめにふくらんだ屋根の下には大ホールと小ホールが入り，そこに連続する屋根の下にホワイエやケータリングエリアなどのオープンスペースが入る。屋根の切れ目はメインのエントランスとなり，すり鉢状に囲まれた屋根の上は屋外パフォーマンスエリアとなる。人々は屋根の上を歩いて，ひらりとめくれた隙間から建築の中に入り，めぐり歩くと切れ目からまた外に出たりと，外と中を立体的に行き交い2層か3層に重なった建築とランドスケープを連続して体験する。また，音楽ホールの閉じた空間とランドスケープに開かれた空間を同時につくることで，美しい自然の中のコンサートの体験をつくることができるのではないかと考えた。この地域特有の高い山に囲まれた緩やかな谷と呼応する音楽ホールの建築が，この村を印象づける新しい空間となることを目指している。

Interior

Aerial evening view over Tianshi Lake from west

**Suzhou Shishan Square Art Theater and Museum
Suzhou, China
2017–**

SANAA

This is a project for an art theater located in Suzhou City, China.

The site was formerly an amusement park, which was redeveloped as a public park and a cultural center of the city. The park is surrounded by abundant nature such as the Lion Mountain and the Tianshi Lake. The Art Theater is located in the center of this urban municipal park, and the building needed to become a new symbol within this setting.

We thought the building should link with the park and the surrounding nature as both a symbol and as a functional facility within the park.

We proposed a structure with a roof shaped like flower petals or an iceberg that softly enclose the fly tower, seating volume in the hall, and a portion of the park. It is visible as a symbol from a distance; from nearby, it creates a variety of expressions reflective of the abundant surrounding nature and human activity.

A 1,200-seat opera house, 400-seat theater and small 200-seat playhouse were placed under the large roof, and the corridor spaces connected to the park resulted in a unified space. Interior, semi-outdoor spaces and courtyards spread out underneath the roof, allowing visitors to pass through the building. This structure functions as a sunshade during the daylight hours, transmitting indoor activities and outdoor scenery; at night, the interior lighting softly brightens the park and the streets like a lantern.

Our goal was to create a building that connects to the park and city, reflecting the surrounding landscape and human activity through its changing expressions.

1 ENTRANCE LOBBY
2 FOYER
3 INFORMATION
4 AUDITORIUM
5 FLY TOWER
6 STAGE
7 STORAGE
8 REHEARSAL ROOM
9 SHOP
10 CONTROL
11 CAFE
12 KITCHEN
13 RESTAURANT

蘇州獅山広場芸術劇場

中国蘇州市の芸術劇場の計画である。

かつてのテーマパークを街の文化の中心としての公園に再開発する。公園は獅子山と天獅湖などの豊かな自然に囲まれた環境である。芸術劇場はその都市公園の中心に位置している。そのような環境の中で，新しいシンボルとなるような建物が求められた。

私たちはシンボルとなりながらも，公園の一つの施設として公園や周囲の自然に連続していくような建物がよいのではないかと考えた。

花びら，あるいは氷山のような形の屋根がホールのフライタワーや客席のヴォリューム，そして公園の一部を柔らかく包み込むような建物を提案した。遠くから見ると都市のシンボルとなり，近くからみると周辺の豊かな自然や人々の活動を映し込み様々な表情をつくっている。

大きな屋根の下には1,200席のオペラ劇場，400席の大劇場，200席の小劇場があり，公園と連続する回廊空間によって一体的な空間となっている。屋根の下には内部，半屋外空間，中庭など多様な空間が広がっているため公園を訪れた人が建物を通り抜けていくことができる。昼は日よけとして機能しつつも内部での活動や周辺の風景を透過し，夜は内部の照明によってランタンのように公園やまちをやさしく照らす。

都市公園やまちと連続し，周辺の風景や人々の活動によって表情が変わっていくような建物を目指した。

Ground floor S=1:1000

Cafe

Volumes are connected by undulating roof

New Express Train
2018

Kazuyo Sejima & Associates

Interior image

Entrance image

Image of aluminum body

In this project we directed the design for the new express train cars for Seibu Railway.

The goal was to innovate a new express train that would itself become a destination and purpose of the trip, as opposed to another means of travel. The landscapes along the Seibu railway is characterized by its uniquely diverse scenery, as it changes from nature to suburbs, and suburbs to city. We wanted to design an express train that would paint a new scenery while gently harmonizing with such natural and urban landscapes. The interior of the train car was designed so that passengers can relax as if sitting in their own living rooms; it features a bright space lined with large windows and seats colored in a yellow-based palette.

We hope that the express train will become a familiar presence in the community, traveling every day as it becomes part of the ever-changing natural and urban landscapes.

新型特急車両
西武鉄道の新型特急車両のデザイン監修。

新しい価値を創造し、ただの移動手段ではなく、目的地となる特急が求められた。西武沿線は、自然から郊外、郊外から都会へと変化に富んだ風景がとても印象的である。そのような自然や都市の風景の中にやわらかく溶け込み、新しい風景となるような特急になればと考えた。室内はみんながくつろげるリビングのようなインテリアを目指した。大きな窓のある明るい室内に、あたたかな黄色の配色を基調とした座席シートが並ぶ。

都市と自然の移りゆく風景に溶け込みながら、毎日走り続ける特急車両が人々に親しまれ愛され続けるようなものになればと考えている。

Venice Biennale 2012 13th International Architecture Exhibition

Venice, Italy
2012

Sharjah Biennial 11, 2013

Sharjah, UAE
2013

Commissioned by Sharjah Art Foundation –SB11– 2013

*Exhibitions
2011–*

SANAA

KAZUYO SEJIMA + RYUE NISHIZAWA / SANAA

Towada Art Center, Towada, Aomori, Japan
2014

OSCAR NIEMEYER The Man Who Built Brasilia

Museum of Contemporary Art Tokyo, Tokyo, Japan
2015

Venice Biennale 2012
13th International Architecture Exhibition
In the year when the "Inujima Landscape Project" began, the history of Inujima, the Inujima "Art House project" and the transition of the landscape were summarized and displayed in several images. From multiple video monitors, various images were showed at the same time, so that the scenery of Inujima could be felt in the exhibition.

Sharjah Biennial 11, 2013
It is an installation in Sharjah in United Arab Emirates. In the historical courtyard of the old city, 28 transparent balls made of acrylic with a diameter of 1.8 m and one sphere with a diameter of 3.6 m were piled up to create a transparent space. While it is transparent, the refraction of the spherical surface overlaps in layers, un unusual scenery spreads in the courtyard.

Kazuyo Sejima + Ryue Nishizawa/SANAA
The SANAA exhibition will be held as part of the Towada Art Center's fifth anniversary project and the Office of Ryue Nishizawa is honored to design the space composition for the show. We have considered the spatial individuality of the art center and have decided to draw upon its resting place and corridors, as well as its exhibition rooms. The exhibits will include Sejima and Nishizawa's personal works as well as SANAA's projects, with the aim of expressing the expansion of SANAA's architectural world in mind. The format of the displays will be simple: models, plans, sketches, and films. All of these are tools which architects use for work on a daily basis and are the most basic language for architectural expression. By making use of these fundamental materials, we hope to show both how architects think and how imagination develops in an architecturally creative working environment.

Oscar Niemeyer
In the year of the 120th anniversary of diplomatic relations between Japan and Brazil, we designed for Oscar Niemeyer's first large retrospective exhibition in Japan at the Museum of Contemporary Art Tokyo.
By introducing "the life of Niemeyer" and exhibiting mainly models and drawings in chronologically "1940–1950", "1956–2007", "1970–2000", we intended a sequence that you can know the process Niemeyer had been lived. In the end of exhibition, the large 1/30-model of Ibirapuera Park was filled with the atrium, to make one feel this open and lively park throughout the body.

ヴェニス建築ビエンナーレ 2012
「犬島ランドスケーププロジェクト」が始まった年に，これまでの犬島の歴史や，犬島「家プロジェクト」，風景の移り変わりをいくつかの映像にまとめ展示した。複数のモニターから，様々な映像を同時に流し，犬島の情景が感じ取れるような展示とした。

シャルジャ・ビエンナーレ11，2013
アラブ首長国連邦シャルジャでのインスタレーションである。旧市街地の歴史ある中庭に，アクリルでできた直径 1.8m の球 28個と，直径 3.6m の球 1個を積み重ねながら透明な空間をつくった。透明でありながら，球面の屈折が幾重にも重なることで，いつもとは違う風景が中庭に広がる。

妹島和世＋西沢立衛／SANAA
十和田市現代美術館開館五周年記念事業として開催される SANAA 展の会場構成を，西沢立衛建築設計事務所で担当した。展覧会の会場としては，十和田市現代美術館の空間の個性を考えて，企画展示室だけでなく休憩スペース，回廊等を活用する展覧会とした。展示物は SANAA のプロジェクトと妹島，西沢個人のプロジェクトを同時に展示するというもので，それによって SANAA の建築世界の広がりを表現しようと試みた。展示物の形式は，模型と図面，スケッチ，動画という，どれも単純なものである。それらはどれも，建築家が仕事の現場で日常的に用いるツールであり，建築表現にとって最も基本的な言語である。そのような基本的材料を用いることで，建築家の考え方や，建築創造現場におけるイマジネーションの広がりを示せれば，と考えた。

オスカー・ニーマイヤー展
日本とブラジルの国交樹立120周年の年に，東京都現代美術館で日本におけるオスカー・ニーマイヤーの初の大回顧展の会場構成を行った。
「ニーマイヤーの一生」を導入とし，「1940～1950年」，「1956～2007年」，「1970～2000年」と時系列に模型とドローイングを中心に展示とすることで，ニーマイヤーが歩んできた過程を知ることができる空間構成とした。最後にアトリウムいっぱいにイビラプエラ公園を30分の1で表現し，開放的で生命感に溢れるこの公園を身体全体で感じられるようにした。

Exhibition

SANAA
2011年	– "Kazuyo Sejima + Ryue Nishizawa/SANAA"/ Zumtobel Light Center, Milan, Italy
2012年	– 13th International Architecture Exhibition/ Venice Biennale, Venice, Italy
2013年	– Sharjah Biennial 11, 2013/ Sharjah, UAE
	– "Kazuyo Sejima + Ryue Nishizawa/SANAA"/ Kumanokodo Nakahechi Museum of Art, Wakayama, Japan　妹島和世＋西沢立衛/SANAA展，熊野古道なかへち美術館，和歌山
2014年	– 14th International Architecture Exhibition/ Venice Biennale, Venice, Italy
	– "Kazuyo Sejima + Ryue Nishizawa/SANAA"/ Towara Art Center, Aomori, Japan　妹島和世＋西沢立衛/SANAA展，十和田市現代美術館，青森
2015年	– "Oscar Niemeyer"/ Museum of Contemporary Art Tokyo, Tokyo, Japan　オスカー・ニーマイヤー展，東京都現代美術館，東京
2016年	– 15th International Architecture Exhibition/ Venice Biennale, Venice, Italy
	– "A Japanese Constellation"/ MoMA, New York, U.S.A.
2017年	– Chicago Architecture Biennial/ Chiago Cultual Center, Chicago, U.S.A.
	– "Sejima Kazuyo SANAA × HOKUSAI"/ Sumida Hokusai Museum, Tokyo, Japan　「妹島和世　SANAA×北斎」，すみだ北斎美術館，東京

妹島和世
2012年	– "Kazuyo Sejima"/ Hitachi Station Information Center, Ibaraki, Japan　「Kazuyo Sejima 妹島和世」展 – 日立駅情報交流プラザ・オープニングイベント企画展，日立駅情報交流プラザ，茨城
2015年	– "Lina Bo Bardi" (supervisor: Kazuyo Sejima) / WATARI-UM, Tokyo, Japan　リナ・ボ・バルディ展（監修：妹島和世），ワタリウム美術館，東京

西沢立衛
2010-11年	– Pavilion Design of the 12th Istanbul Art Biennale Istanbul/ Istanbul, Turkey
2016年	– "The Architecture of Ryue Nishizawa" / Gallery of Hiroshi Senju Museum, Karuizawa, Nagano, Japan 西沢立衛建築展，軽井沢千住博美術館ギャラリー，軽井沢，長野県
	– Wooden Partition / Tokyo, Japan 「木のパーティション」，Okamura Design Space R，東京

Exhibition at GA gallery (Tokyo)

SANAA
2011-18年 – GA Japan 展（2011年，2013年，2014年，2016年，2017年），GA International 展（2011～2016年），STUDY MODELS KAZUYO SEJIMA / RYUE NISHIZAWA / SANAA（2015年）

妹島和世
2011-18年 – GA Japan 展（2012年），GA Houses Project 展（2011年）

西沢立衛
2011-18年 – GA Japan 展（2011年，2015年），GA Houses Project 展（2013～2017年）

*Furniture
2011–*

SANAA

Big Drop

2012

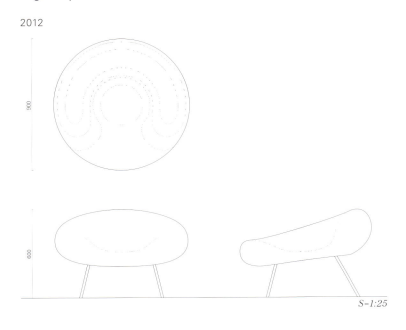

S=1:25

SANAA TABLE

2015

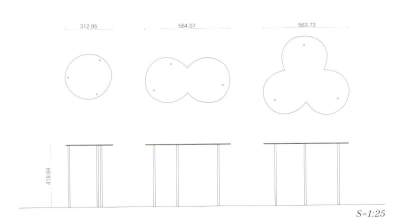

S=1:25

Trophy (Single Flower Vase)

2016

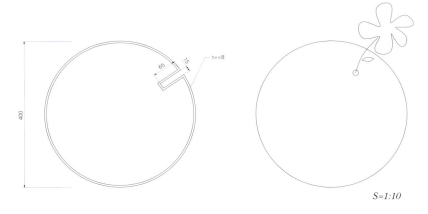

Inujima Chair

2016

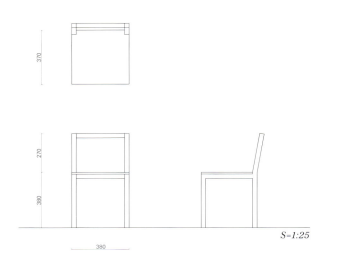

Lobby-chair

2017

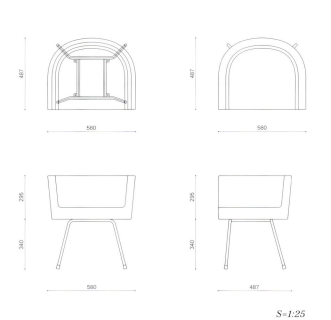

Furniture and Product

Big Drop
Enlarged original Drop (2004), a luxurious chair which is large enough to envelop people. Aluminum surface with a soft curve such as water droplet reflects the surrounding landscape.

SANAA TABLE
A table for SANAA Chair. The height of it is same as the SANAA Chair, with three sizes of S, M and L, and there are two types of finishings: mirror surface of stainless steel and galvanized steel. It is used as a side table in one or tea tables together, the layout according to usage creates one continuous horizontal plane.

Trophy (Single Flower Vase)
A trophy of sphere with a mirror finish of 8-mm-thick aluminum. It is shiny at first but gradually turns into a whitish mirror surface. It can be used as an ornament or a vase, since it rolls, you can fix it with stone or freely.

Inujima Chair
A chair for Inujima Life Garden (2016-). The seat height is 380 mm, which is lower than the usual chair to fit pergola of 2.3 meters-high, low and extends horizontally. Visitors sit on the chair to notice vegetations covering the ground, that is our intention to make furniture and landscape continuity.

Lobby-chair
A chair designed for entrance lobby and foyer of Shogin TACT Tsuruoka (Tsuruoka Cultural Hall). In order to produce the elegant approach to the theater, we made them with different colors and materials of 6 types in total.

Big Drop
Drop（2004年）を一回り大きくして人を包み込むような大きさのラグジュアリーな椅子。水滴のような柔らかなカーブを持つアルミニウムの表面が周囲の風景を映し出す。

SANAA TABLE
SANAA Chairと合わせて使うためにつくられたテーブル。SANAA Chairと高さを揃えており，S，M，Lの3サイズで，素材をステンレスの鏡面のものとスチールの亜鉛メッキのものがある。一つでサイドテーブルとして使ったり，合わせてティーテーブルとして使ったり，使い方に合わせたレイアウトが一つの連続した水平面をつくる。

Trophy（一輪挿し）
8mm厚のアルミの表面を鏡面仕上げにした球体状のトロフィーである。初めはピカピカだが，だんだんと白っぽい鏡面に変わっていく。置物や花瓶として使うこともできるが，丸くて転がってしまうので，石を置いて止めたり，置き方は自由である。

犬島のいす
「犬島 くらしの植物園」（2016年〜）のためにつくられた椅子。低く水平にのびたパーゴラの高さ2.3mに合うように，座面高さを通常の椅子より低い380mmとしている。植物園に訪れると，足元に草花が広がり，椅子に座ると植物の目線に近づくような，家具とランドスケープとが連続していくことを考えた。

Lobby-チェア
「荘銀タクト鶴岡（鶴岡市文化会館）」のエントランスロビーおよびホワイエにデザインした椅子。劇場へのアプローチを華やかに演出するために，色や素材の異なる計6種類の張地で製作した。

SANAA
2012年　−"Big Drop"／chair／空想舎
2015年　−"SANAA TABLE"／table／hhstyle
2015年　−"Trophy（一輪挿し）"／single-flower vase
　　　　−"犬島のいす"／chair
2017年　−"Lobby-チェア"／chair

西沢立衛
2015年　−"徳日邸の椅子"／chair
2015年〜−"(仮)SOFA"／sofa

List of Works 2011–18
作品リスト

SANAA 2011–18

2005–12
Louvre-Lens
Lens, France

Program: museum, park
Total floor area: 32,400m²
Site area: 200,000m²
Structure: reinforced concrete, steel frame
1 story, 2 basements

ルーヴル・ランス
所在地：フランス、ランス
設計：200508-0904　工事：200912-1212
建築主：Région Nord-Pas-de-Calais
主要用途：美術館、公園
Co-conceptors: IMREY CULBERT (general museograph), Catherine Mosbach (landscape)
ミュゼオグラフィ：Studio Adrien Gardère
ローカルアーキテクト：Extra Muros
構造コンセプト：SAPS/Sasaki and Partners
構造設計：Betom ingénierie,
Bollinger + Grohmann Sarl
設備：Betom ingénierie
環境：Transplan, Pénicaud Architecture Environment
主体構造・規模：RC造、鉄骨造／地上1階、地下2階
敷地面積：200,000m²
建築面積：12,800m²　延床面積：32,400m²

2006–12
Vitra Factory
Weil am Rhein, Germany

Program: assembly factory, furniture storage
Total floor area: 30,535m²
Site area: 47,000m²
Structure: steel frame braced by circular concrete facade
1 story, 1 basement

ヴィトラ・ファクトリー
所在地：ドイツ、ヴァイル・アム・ライン
設計：200606-0709
工事：200709-1212
建築主：Vitra
主要用途：組み立て工場、倉庫
共同設計：nkbak
ローカルアーキテクト：Mayer Bährle Freie Architekten BDA
構造：SAPS/Sasaki and Partners, Bollinger & Grohmann GmbH
設備：Herine & Walter
電気：Werner Schwarz GmbH
施工：Moser GmbH & Co. KG, Strabag
主体構造・規模：鉄骨造、RC造（外周壁）／地上1階、地下1階
敷地面積：47,000m²
建築面積：20,445m²　延床面積：30,535m²

2007–18
Paris Apartments
Paris, France

Program: housing
Total floor area: 14,252m²
(9,115m², residential area)
Site area: 4,650m²
Structure: steel frame
6 stories, 1 basement

パリ16区の公営集合住宅
所在地：フランス、パリ
設計：200704-0903
工事：201605-1808（予定）
建築主：ParisHabitat
主要用途：集合住宅
ローカルアーキテクト：Extra Muros
構造：SAPS/Sasaki & Partners（基本設計）, Bollinger + Grohmann GmbH
設備：Betom Ingénierie
環境：Hubert Penicaud
ランドスケープ：Extra Muros + SANAA
施工：Outarex.
主体構造・規模：鉄骨造／地上6階、地下1階
敷地面積：4,650m²
建築面積：2,127m²
延床面積：14,252m²（住宅部分／9,115m²）

2009–11
Shakujii Apartments
Tokyo, Japan

Program: housing (terraced house)
Total floor area: 482.58m²
Site area: 497.07m²
Structure: steel frame
2 stories, 1 basement

石神井アパートメント
所在地：東京都練馬区
設計：200906-1009
工事：201009-1108
建築主：個人
プロデュース：市川信明
主要用途：長屋
構造：佐々木睦朗構造計画研究所
設備：森村設計
施工：平成建設
主体構造・規模：鉄骨造／地上2階、地下1階
敷地面積：497.07m²
建築面積：285.09m²
延床面積：482.58m²

2010–15
Grace Farms
New Canaan, Conneticuit, U.S.A.

Program: multi-purpose hall, library, dining room, gymnasium, class room, art studio, and other
Total floor area: approx. 7,150m²
Site area: approx. 323,700m²
Structure: glue-laminated timber beams and steel columns
1 story, 1 basement

グレイス・ファームズ
所在地：アメリカ、コネティカット州、ニューケイナン
設計：201005-1306　工事：201306-1510
建築主：Grace Farms Foundation
主要用途：マルチパーパスホール、ダイニング、体育館、クラスルーム、アートスタジオ他
Project Direction : Paratus Group
Executive Architect : Handel Architects LLP
構造：SAPS/Sasaki and Partners, Robert Silman Associates
ランドスケープ：OLIN　環境：Transsolar
設備：BuroHappold Engineering
音響：HMBA, Nagata Acoustics
施工：Villa Construction, QSR Steel, Chicago Metal Rolled Products
主体構造・規模：鉄骨造 + 木梁架構／地上1階、地下1階
敷地面積：323,700m²
建築面積：7,710m²　延床面積：7,150m²

2010–13
Junko Fukutake Hall
Okayama, Okayama, Japan

Program: hall
Total floor area: 1,397.3m²
Site area: 135,327.00m²
Structure: steel frame
1 story

Junko Fukutake Hall（岡山大学J-Hall）
所在地：岡山県岡山市
設計：201009-1212
工事：201301-1310
建築主：福武純子
主要用途：ホール
構造：佐々木睦朗構造計画研究所
設備：森村設計
音響：ヤマハ
ランドスケープ：GAヤマザキ
施工：鹿島建設
主体構造・規模：鉄骨造、一部RC造／地上1階
敷地面積：135,327.00m²
建築面積：1,320.95m²
延床面積：1,397.3m²

2010–
La Samaritaine
Paris, France

Program: commercial, office, social housing, kindergarden, (hotel)
Total floor area: 55,000m²
Site area: 6,900m²
Structure: steel frame, reinforced concrete
8 stories, 3 basements

ラ・サマリテーヌ
計画地：フランス、パリ
設計：2010-2016
工事：2016-
主要用途：商業、事務所、集合住宅、幼稚園、(ホテル)
ローカルアーキテクト：SRA architectes
構造：AEDIS Ingenierie and RFR GO+
環境：Le Sommer Environment
歴史建築家：Cabinet Lagneau
住宅部設計：François Brugel
ファサード・エンジニア：RFR
音響：Acoustique et Conseil
積算：AE75
主体構造・規模：鉄骨造、RC造／地上8階、地下3階
敷地面積：6,900m²
建築面積：6,700m²
延床面積：55,000m²

2011
Competition for International High School of Nantes
Nantes, France

Program: classrooms, auditorium, restaurant, dormitories, 2 gymnasiums, teachers housing
Total floor area: 17,900m²
Site area: 51,000m²
Structure: steel frame, wood
1 story (school), 2 stories (auditorium+housing), 7 stories (other)

International High School of Nantes設計競技案
計画地：フランス、ナント
コンペ実施：201101
建築主：Regional Council of "Pays de la Loire"
主要用途：教室、講堂、食堂、体育館、教師用宿舎
ローカルアーキテクト：AIA architects
構造コンセプト：SAPS/Sasaki and Partners
構造：AIA engineering
設備：AIA engineering
ランドスケープ：SANAA
主体構造・規模：鉄骨造、木造／地上1階（学校）、地上2階（講堂+宿舎）、地上7階（その他）
敷地面積：51,000m²
建築面積：23,800m²
延床面積：17,900m²

2011
Competition for New Damascus National Museum
Damascus, Syria

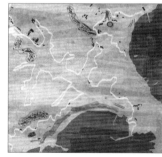

Program: museum
Total floor area: 34,200m²
Site area: 61,000m²
Structure: reinfoprced concret, steel frame
1 story, 1 basement

New Damascus National Museum設計競技案
計画地：シリア、ダマスカス
コンペ実施：201104
建築主：Office of the First Lady
主要用途：美術館
構造：SAPS/Sasaki and Partners
環境：ARUP
主体構造・規模：RC造＋鉄骨造／地上1階、地下1階
敷地面積：61,000m²
建築面積：26,800m²
延床面積：34,200m²

2011–14
Miyatojima Project
Higashimatsushima, Miyagi, Japan

Program: master plan

宮戸島の計画
計画地：宮城県東松島市
設計：201108-1403
プログラム：マスタープラン

2011–12
Home for All Miyatojima
Higashimatsushima, Miyagi, Japan

Program: community center
Total floor area: 118.55m²
Site area: 14,289.99m²
Structure: steel frame, wood frame (partly)
1 story

東松島市宮戸島のみんなの家
所在地：宮城県東松島市
設計：201110-1206
工事：201207-1210
主要用途：集会所
構造：佐々木睦朗構造計画研究所
施工：櫻井工務店、菊川工業、こあら
主体構造・規模：鉄骨造、一部木造／地上1階
敷地面積：14,289.99m²
建築面積：118.55m²
延床面積：118.55m²

2011
Skolkovo Innovation Center Guest Zone
Moscow, Russia

スコルコボ・イノベーションセンター・ゲストゾーン
計画地：ロシア、モスクワ
設計：2011
主要用途：マスタープラン/駅、ギャラリー、公園、ホテル
マスタープラン・建築設計：SANAA + OMA
構造：SAPS/Sasaki and Partners
環境：TRANSSOLAR

Program: masterplanning / station, gallery, park, hotel

2012
Competition for MECA (Maison de l'Économie Créative et de la Culture en Aquitaine)
Bordeaux, France

創造経済文化センター 設計競技案
計画地：フランス、ボルドー
コンペ実施：201202
建築主：Conseil Régional d'Aquitaine
主要用途：文化センター
構造：SAPS/Sasaki and Partners
環境：Transsolar
設備：Egis
ファサード：RFR
音響：Altia
コスト：Bureau Michel Forgue
主体構造・規模：RC造、鉄骨造/地上3階
敷地面積：10,400m²
建築面積：6,000m²
延床面積：12,100m²

2012–14
Junko Fukutake Terrace
Okayama, Okayama, Japan

Junko Fukutake Terrace
所在地：岡山県岡山市
設計：201204-1401
工事：201402-1412
建築主：福武純子
主要用途：カフェ
構造：佐々木睦朗構造計画研究所
設備：システムデザイン研究所
ランドスケープ：GAヤマザキ
施工：鹿島建設
主要構造・規模：鉄骨造、地上1階
敷地面積：326,245.57m²
建築面積：569.03m²
延床面積：569.03m²

Program: cafe
Total floor area: 569.03m²
Site area: 326,245.57m²
Structure: steel frame
1 story

2012–28
Shibuya Station Development Plan
Tokyo, Japan

渋谷駅地区駅街区開発計画
計画地：東京都渋谷区
設計：201204-2303　工事：202404-2803（予定）
建築主：東京急行電鉄、東日本旅客鉄道、東京地下鉄
主要用途：駅施設、事務所、店舗、展望施設、駐車場等
設計：渋谷駅周辺整備計画共同企業体
（日建設計、東急設計コンサルタント、ジェイアール東日本建築設計事務所、メトロ開発）
デザインアーキテクト：日建設計
隈研吾建築都市設計事務所
SANAA（中央・西棟北側外装、西棟東側外装、西口アーバンコア大屋根傘、中央棟国際交流施設外装、中央棟4階広場
※西口アーバン・コア屋根部分の基本コンセプト：佐々木睦朗構造計画研究所）
主体構造・規模：鉄骨造、RC造、SRC造
地上10階、地下2階（中央棟）、地上13階、地下5階（西棟）
建築面積：15,300m²
延床面積：約95,000m²（全体：約276,000m²）

Program: station, office, observatory, parking, etc.
Total floor area: approx. 95,000m²
Structure: steel frame, reinforced concrete, steel framecd reinforced concrete
10 stories, 2 basements (main building),
13 stories, 5 basements (west building)

2012
Competition for Menil Drawing Institute
Houston, U.S.A.

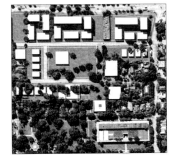

Menil Drawing Institute 設計競技案
計画地：アメリカ、ヒューストン
コンペ実施：201205
建築主：The Menil Collection
構造：SAPS/Sasaki and Partners
環境：ARUP
主体構造・規模：RC造、鉄骨造/地上2階
敷地面積：29,454m²
建築面積：4,754m²
延床面積：7,946m²

Program: museum
Total floor area: 7,946m²
Site area: 29,454m²
Structure: reinforced concrete, steel frame
2 stories

2012–21
Bezalel Academy of Arts & Design
Jerusalem, Israel

ベツァルエル・アカデミー・オブ・アート・アンド・デザイン
計画地：イスラエル、エルサレム
設計：201207-1806
工事：201602-2109（予定）
建築主：Bezalel Academy of Arts and Design
主要用途：大学
ローカルアーキテクト：Nir-Kutz
構造：Labaton & Partners
構造コンセプト：SAPS/Sasaki and Partners
ランドスケープ：SANAA（デザイン）+ Nir-Kutz（実施）
主体構造・規模：RC造（ポストテンション）地上4階、地下2階
敷地面積：13,500m²
建築面積：8,800m²
延床面積：50,000m²

Program: university
Total floor area: 50,000m²
Site area: 13,500m²
Structure: reinforced concrete (post tension)
4 stories, 2 basements

2012–17
Shogin TACT Tsuruoka (Tsuruoka Cultural Hall)
Tsuruoka, Yamagata, Japan

荘銀タクト鶴岡（鶴岡市文化会館）
所在地：山形県鶴岡市
設計：201208-1311
工事：201410-1708
建築主：鶴岡市
主要用途：多目的ホール
共同設計：新穂建築設計事務所、石川設計事務所
構造：ARUP
設備：総合設備計画
劇場計画・技術：本杉省三
音響：永田音響設計
舞台照明：尾部孟
施工：竹中工務店、菅原建設、鈴木工務店特定建設工事共同企業体
主体構造・規模：鉄骨造、RC造/地上3階、地下1階
敷地面積：13,096.84m²
建築面積：5,756.35m²
延床面積：7,846.12m²

Program: multi-purpose hall
Total floor area: 7,846.12m²
Site area: 13,096.84m²
Structure: steel frame, reinforced concrete
3 stories, 1 basement

2012
Competition for New National Stadium
Tokyo, Japan

新国立競技場 デザイン競技案
計画地：東京都新宿区
コンペ実施：201211
主要用途：スタジアム
共同設計：日建設計
構造：ARUP
主体構造・規模：鉄骨造、一部RC造/地上4階、地下3階
敷地面積：179,003.3m²
建築面積：65,500m²
延床面積：290,000m²

Program: sports comple
Total floor area: 290,000m²
Site area: 179,003.3m²
Structure: steel frame, reinforced concrete (partly)
4 stories, 3 basements

2013–14
Pergola
Okayama, Okayama, Japan

パーゴラ
所在地：岡山県岡山市
設計：201303-1306
工事：201309-1412
建築主：国立大学法人岡山大学
主要用途：休憩所
構造：佐々木睦朗構造計画研究所
施工：Nippo、鹿島建設
主体構造・規模：鉄骨造/地上1階
敷地面積：326,245.57m²
建築面積：198.92m²
延床面積：198.92m²

Program: rest space
Total floor area: 198.92m²
Site area: 326,245.57m²
Structure: steel frame
1 story

2013
Proposal for Odawara City Art and Culture Creation Center
Odawara, Kanagawa, Japan

小田原市芸術文化創造センター プロポーザル案
所在地：神奈川県小田原市
プロポーザル実施：201303
建築主：小田原市
主要用途：ホール
構造：佐々木睦朗構造計画研究所
設備：森村設計
主体構造・規模：鉄骨造、一部RC造/地上5階、地下1階
敷地面積：9,608.77m²
建築面積：7,300m²
延床面積：12,100m²

Program: hall
Total floor area: 12,100m²
Site area: 9,608.77m²
Structure: steel frame, partly reinforced concrete
5 stories, 1 basement

2013–19
Hitachi City Hall
Hitachi, Ibaraki, Japan

日立市新庁舎
所在地：茨城県日立市
設計：201304-1411（Ⅰ期）、201304-1606（Ⅱ期）
工事：201503-1704（Ⅰ期）、201704-1903（Ⅱ期）
建築主：日立市
主要用途：市庁舎
構造：ARUP
設備：総合設備計画
環境：ARUP
品質管理支援：三上建設事務所
施工：竹中・鈴縫・秋山・岡部特定建設工事共同企業体（1期）
主体構造：鉄骨造（免震構造）、RC造
規模：地上7階、地下1階
敷地面積：21,392.85m²
建築面積：7,892.69m²
延床面積：28,662.15m²

Program: city hall
Total floor area: 28,662.15m²
Site area: 21,392.85m²
Structure: steel frame, reinforced concrete
7 stories, 1 basement

2013–19
Bocconi University New Urban Campus
Milan, Italy

ボッコーニ大学新キャンパス
計画地：イタリア、ミラノ
設計：201307-1603　工事：201704-1909（予定）
建築主：Bocconi University
主要用途：大学
アーキテクトレコード：Costa Zanibelli Associati
ローカルアーキテクト：Progetto CMR
構造コンセプト：SAPS/Sasaki and Partners
構造：Studio di Ingegneria Pereira
技術協力：Politecnico di Milano
設備：Advanced Engineering s.r.l.
防災：Ing. Silvestre Mistretta
安全：Soluzioni s.r.l.
都市計画：FOA – Federico Oliva Associati
施工：Grassi & Crespi + Percassi
主体構造・規模：鉄骨＋RCスラブ/地上4階、地下1階
敷地面積：35,700m²　延床面積：65,000m²
建築面積：8,500m²（教育）、3,550m²（レクリエーション）

Program: university
Total floor area: 8,500m² (education), 3,550 (recreation)
Site area:35,700m²
Structure: steel columns + RC slab
4 stories, 1 basement

2013–
Taichung Green Museumbrary
Taichung, Taiwan, R.O.C.

Program: museum and library
Total floor area: 58,016m²
Site area: 26,108m²
Structure: steel frame, reinforced concrete
7 stories, 2 basement

Taichung Green Museumbrary
計画地：台湾, 台中市
設計：201308-2007　　工事：201803-2007(予定)
主要用途：美術館, 図書館
ローカルアーキテクト：Ricky Liu & Associates + Planners
構造コンセプト：SAPS/Sasaki and Partners
構造：Hsin-Yeh Engineering
ミュゼオグラフィ：長谷川祐子
設備・環境：Takenaka Corporation
空調：C.C. Lee & Associates
電気：We Can Electronical
ファサード：Sununity
照明：KILT Planning Office Inc.
図書館コンサルタント：Kuang-Mei Link, Ko-Chiu Wu
主体構造・規模：鉄骨造, RC造/地上7階, 地下2階
敷地面積：26,108m²
建築面積：7,850m²　延床面積：58,016m²

2013
Competition for Axel Springer Campus
Berlin, Germany

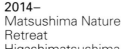

Program: office, campus
Total floor area: 71,292m²
Site area: 9,206m²

Axel Springer Campus 設計競技案
計画地：ドイツ, ベルリン
コンペ実施：201308
建築主：Axel Springer
主要用途：事務所, キャンパス共用空間
構造：SAPS/Sasaki and Partners
環境・空調：Transsolar
ファサードコンサルタント：Bollinger + Grohmann International GmbH (Kim Boris Löffler),
積算：Mayer-Bährle
敷地面積：9,206m²
建築面積：8,137m²
延床面積：71,292m²

2013
Competition for Nobel Center
Stockholm, Sweden

Program: museum, auditorium
Total floor area: 27,979m²
Site area: 17,114m²
Structure: aluminum lattice system

Nobel Center 設計競技案
計画地：スウェーデン, ストックホルム
コンペ実施：201309
建築主：Nobelhuset AB
主要用途：博物館, オーディトリアム
構造：佐々木睦朗構造計画研究所
環境・空調：Transsolar
主体構造：アルミ・ラティス・システム
敷地面積：17,114m²
建築面積：4,591m²
延床面積：27,979m²

2013–14
Home for All Tsukihama
Higashimatsushima, Miyagi, Japan

Program: fishing workshop, rest space
Total floor area: 72.00m²
Site area: 232.00m²
Structure: steel frame
1 story

宮戸島月浜のみんなの家
所在地：宮城県東松島市
設計：201310-1404
工事：201405-1407
建築主：月浜海苔組合, 月浜鮑組合
主要用途：漁業用作業場, 休憩所
構造：佐々木睦朗構造計画研究所
施工：シェルター・カーペンターズ
主体構造・規模：鉄骨造/地上1階
敷地面積：232.00m²
建築面積：72.00m²
延床面積：72.00m²

2013–19
Huaxin Financial Plaza
Shanghai, China

Program: office, commersial
Total floor area: 57,648m²
Site area: 14,412m²
Structure: reinforced concrete
14 stories

上海金融センター
計画地：中国, 上海市
設計：2013-17
工事：2016-19(予定)
建築主：China Fortune Properties (Group) Co., Ltd & Shanghai Westbund Development (Group) Co., Ltd
主要用途：事務所, 商業
ローカルアーキテクト/構造/ランドスケープ：同済大学建築設計研究院(集団)有限公司
照明：ARUP Shanghai
ファサードコンサルタント：CIMA Project Consultancy Co.Ltd., Shanghai
主体構造・規模：RC造/地上14階
敷地面積：14,412m²
建築面積：4,990m²
延床面積：57,648m²

2014–16
Maru
Kanazawa, Ishikawa, Japan

Program: art work
Total floor area: 26.38m²
Site area: 26,016.68m²
Structure: stainless steel

まる
所在地：石川県金沢市
設計：201402-1502
工事：201506-1611
建築主：金沢市
主要用途：アート
構造：ARUP
施工：竹中工務店
主体構造：ステンレススチール造
敷地面積：26,016.68m²
建築面積：26.38m²
延床面積：26.38m²

2014–
Matsushima Nature Retreat
Higashimatsushima, Miyagi, Japan

Program: short stay facility
Structure: reinforced concrete, steel frame

松島自然の家
所在地：宮城県東松島市
設計：201411-1512(第1期), 201604-1803(予定, 第2期)
工事：201501-1603(第1期)
建築主：宮城県
主要用途：短期宿泊施設
共同設計：盛総合設計
構造：佐々木睦朗構造計画研究所
設備：森村設計
主体構造・規模：RC造, 鉄骨造/地上2階

2014–
Auckland Castle Walled Garden Project
Auckland, U.K.

Structure: steel frame
2 stories

オークランド・キャッスル・ウォールド・ガーデン
計画地：イギリス, オークランド
設計：2014-
主要用途：
構造：ARUP
主体構造・規模：鉄骨造, RC造/地上2階

2014
Competition for Tuiliere Stadium, Lousanne
Lousanne, Switzerland

Program: stadium
Total floor area: 10,376m²
Site area: 50,000m²
Structure: reinforced concrete, steel frame (roof)
2 stories, 1 basement

Tuiliere Stadium, Lousanne 設計競技案
計画地：ローザンヌ, スイス
コンペ実施：201408
主要用途：スタジアム
主体構造・規模：RC造, 鉄骨造(屋根)/地上2階, 地下1階
構造・環境：ARUP
スタジアムコンサルタント：Arup sport(ロンドン)
敷地面積：50,000m²
建築面積：7,150m²
延床面積：10,376m²
(スタジアム/9,295m², オフィス/1,080m²)

2014
Competition for Beethoven Fertspielhaus
Bonn, Germany

Program: music hall
Total floor area: 9,593m²
Site area: 6,467m²
Structure: reinforced concrete, steel frame
2 stories, 2 basements

Beethoven Fertspielhaus 設計競技案
計画地：ドイツ, ボン
コンペ実施：201409
主要用途：音楽ホール
設計：磯崎新+SANAA
ローカルアーキテクト：Hikaru Hane
構造：SAPS/Sasaki and Partners, Bollinger + Grohmann Ingenieure
環境：Transsolar
ファサード：Emmer Pfenninger Partner AG
劇場：theater projekte daberto + kollegen
コスト：emproc GmbH Kostenmanagement für Immobilien
主体構造・規模：RC造, 鉄骨造/地上2階, 地下2階
敷地面積：6,467m²
建築面積：2,753m²
延床面積：9,593m²

2014
Competition for Tour M2
Paris, France

Program: office
Total floor area: 40,000m²
Site area: 36,800m²

Tour M2 設計競技案
計画地：フランス, パリ
設計：2014
建築主：GENERALI, SAINT-GOBAIN
主要用途：事務所
ローカルアーキテクト：Collectif 07
構造：AEDIS
環境・ファサードコンサルタント：RFR éléments
空調・衛生：INEX
積算：Bureau Michel Forguexx
敷地面積：36,800m²
建築面積：2,616m²
延床面積：40,000m²

2015–16
Naoshima Port Terminal
Naoshima, Kagawa, Japan

Program: waiting area, bicycle parking space, toilet
Total floor area: 101.66m²
Site area: 323.08m²
Structure: wood frame (waiting area, bicycle parking space), concrete block (toilet)
1 story

直島港ターミナル
所在地：香川県香川郡直島町
設計：201501-1601
工事：201602-1610
建築主：直島町
主要用途：待合所, 駐輪場, トイレ
構造：ARUP
施工：建築工房おおやま
主体構造・規模：木造(待合所, 駐輪場), コンクリートブロック造(トイレ)/地上1階
敷地面積：323.08m²
建築面積：101.66m²
延床面積：101.66m²

2015
Proposal for Redevelopment Plan for Takarazuka Garden Fields
Takaraduka, Hyogo, Japan

Program: garden, complex
Total floor area: 3,540m²
Site area: 10,200m²
Structure: steel frame, partly reinforced concrete
1 story

宝塚ガーデンフィールズ跡地利用基本計画 プロポーザル案
計画地：兵庫県宝塚市
プロポーザル実施：201503
主要用途：庭園、複合施設
構造：佐々木睦朗構造計画研究所
主体構造・規模：鉄骨造、一部RC造/地上1階
敷地面積：10,200m²
建築面積：3,540m²
延床面積：3,540m²

2015–
Shiga Museum of Modern Art
Otsu, Shiga, Japan

Program: museum
Total floor area: 15,200m²
Site area: 91,633m²
Structure: steel frame, reinforced concrete
2 stories, 1 basement

滋賀県立近代美術館・新生美術館
計画地：滋賀県大津市
設計：201504–
建築主：滋賀県
主要用途：美術館
構造：佐々木睦朗構造計画研究所
設備：森村設計
ランドスケープ：GAヤマザキ
主体構造・規模：鉄骨造、RC造/地上2階、地下1階
敷地面積：91,633m²
延床面積：15,200m²

2015–21
Sydney Modern Project
Sydney, New South Wales, Australlia

Program: art gallery
Total floor area: 16,000m²
Site area: 28,196m²
Structure: steel frame
5 stories

シドニー・モダン・プロジェクト
計画地：オーストラリア、シドニー
設計：201505-1811
工事：201901-2112（予定）
建築主：Art Gallery of New South Wales
主要用途：アートギャラリー
ローカルアーキテクト：Architectus
構造：ARUP
設備：Steensen Varming
ファサードコンサルタント：Surface
ランドスケープ：McGregor Coxall
主体構造・規模：鉄骨造/地上5階
敷地面積：28,196m²
建築面積：8,668m²
延床面積：16,000m²

2015
Proposal for Improvement Plan for Kyoto Municipal Museum of Art
Kyoto, Kyoto, Japan

Program: museum
Total floor area: 6,600m² (proposal area)
Site area: 28,196m²
Structure: reinforced concrete
2 stories, 2 basementsl

京都市美術館再整備 プロポーザル案
計画地：京都市左京区
プロポーザル実施：201508
主要用途：美術館
構造：佐々木睦朗構造計画研究所
設備：森村設計
主体構造・規模：RC造/地上2階、地下2階
敷地面積：24,331m²
延床面積：6,600m²（増築・改築提案部）

2015–
New National Gallery, Liget Budapest
Budapest, Hungary

Program: art gallery
Total floor area: 50,000m²
Site area: 19,707m²
Structure: reinforced concrete, steel frame
5 stories, 2 basements

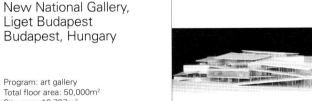

新国立美術館 リゲット・ブダペスト
計画地：ハンガリー、ブダペスト
設計：201511-2020（予定）
工事：2018-2020（予定）
主要用途：アートギャラリー
建築主：Városliget Zrt.
ローカルアーキテクト：Bánáti + Hartvig Építész Iroda
構造コンセプト：SAPS/Sasaki and Partners
構造：Exon2000 Kft.
環境コンセプト：Transsolar
ランドスケープ：Mio Watanabe Design Office
設備：ZWP Ingenieur - AG
電気：IB Schwarz
積算：Spányi Partners
主体構造・規模：RC造、鉄骨造/地上5階、地下2階
敷地面積：19,707m²
延床面積：50,000m²

2016
Competition for Museum of the 20th Century
Berlin, Germany

Program: museum
Total floor area: 26,637m²
Site area: 10,200m²
Structure: reinforced concrete, steel frame
1 story, 2 basements

Museum of the 20th Century 設計競技案
計画地：ドイツ、ベルリン
コンペ実施：201601
主要用途：美術館
ローカルアーキテクト：HANE Architects
構造：SAPS/Sasaki and Partners + Bollinger-Grohmann
環境：Transsolar
ランドスケープ：Bureau Bas Smets
ファサードコンサルタント：Bollinger-Grohmann
積算：Emproc GmbH
主体構造・規模：RC造、鉄骨造/地上1階、地下2階
敷地面積：10,200m²
延床面積：26,637m²

2017–
Sanya MOCA Project
Sanya, Hainan, China

Program: master plan, museum
Total floor area: 100,000m² (master plan), 41,000m² (museum)
Site area: 66,976m² (master plan), 20,721m² (museum)

三亜MOCAプロジェクト
計画地：中国、海南
設計：201701–
工事：-2020（予定）
建築主：Hainan Zhonghai San Bangyou Real Estate Development Co., Ltd.
主要用途：マスタープラン、美術館
敷地面積：66,976m²（マスタープラン）、20,721m²（美術館）
延床面積：100,000m²（マスタープラン）、41,000m²（美術館）

2017
Proposal for Akita Cultural Center
Akita, Akita, Japan

Program: theater
Total floor area: 21,500m²
Site area: 13,225m²
Structure: steel frame, reinforced concrete
3 stories, 2 basements

秋田県・市連携文化施設 プロポーザル案
計画地：秋田県秋田市
プロポーザル実施：201704
主要用途：劇場
共同設計：三上建築事務所、小野建築研究所
構造：佐々木睦朗構造計画研究所
設備：森村設計
主体構造・規模：鉄骨造、RC造/地上3階、地下2階
敷地面積：13,225m²
延床面積：21,500m²

2017
Proposal for Shinano Museum
Nagano, Nagano, Japan

Program: museum
Total floor area: 10,000m² (new building)
Site area: 29,130m²
Structure: steel frame, reinforced concrete
2 stories, 1 basement

信濃美術館 プロポーザル案
計画地：長野県長野市
プロポーザル実施：201705
主要用途：美術館
構造：佐々木睦朗構造計画研究所
設備：森村設計
ランドスケープ：GAヤマザキ
主体構造・規模：鉄骨造、RC造/地上2階、地下1階
敷地面積：29,130m²
延床面積：10,000m²（新築）、1,698m²（改修）

2017–
Shizuoka City History Museum
Shizuoka, Shizuoka, Japan

Program: museum
Total floor area: 5,000m²
Site area: 8,400m²
Structure: steel frame, steel framed reinforced concrete
4 stories, 1 basement

静岡市歴史博物館
計画地：静岡県静岡市
設計：201711-1803（基本設計、予定）
建築主：静岡市
主要用途：博物館
構造：佐々木睦朗構造計画研究所
設備：森村設計
主体構造・規模：SRC造、RC造/地上4階、地下1階
敷地面積：8,400m²
建築面積：2,050m²
延床面積：5,000m²

2017–
Suzhou Shishan Square Art Theater and Museum
Suzhou, China

Program: theater
Total floor area: 19,660m²
2 stories, 2 basements

蘇州獅山広場芸術劇場
計画地：中国、蘇州市
設計：2017–
建築主：Administrative Committee Of Suzhou National New & Hi-Tech Industrial Development Zone
主要用途：劇場
構造：SAPS/Sasaki and Partners
環境：Transsolar
設備：Transplan
音響：永田音響設計
劇場計画・技術：本杉省三
照明：ARUP
規模：地上2階、地下2階
建築面積：12,571m²
延床面積：19,660m²

KAZUYO SEJIMA 2011–18

2004–11
Hitachi Station and Free-Corridor
Hitachi, Ibaraki, Japan

Program: station, free passage, cafe
Total floor area: 1,849.97m² (station), 1,559.00m2 (corridor), 212.00m² (interaction facility)
Site area: 2,984.27m² (station + corridor), 2,727.59m² (interaction facility)
Structure: steel frame
2 stories

日立駅自由通路及び橋上駅舎
所在地：茨城県日立市
設計：200401-0803　工事：200807-1104
建築主：日立市、東日本旅客鉄道
主要用途：駅舎、自由通路、カフェ
デザイン監修：妹島和世建築設計事務所
設計：ジェイアール東日本建築設計事務所、東日本旅客鉄道水戸支社
構造協力：佐々木睦朗構造計画研究所
施工：東鉄工業水戸支店
主体構造・規模：鉄骨造／地上2階
敷地面積：2,984.27m²（駅舎・自由通路）、2,727.59m²（交流施設）
建築面積：1,600.95m²（駅舎）、1,559.00m²（自由通路）、212.00m²（交流施設）
延床面積：1,849.97m²（駅舎）、1,559.00m²（自由通路）、212.00m²（交流施設）

2008–11
Shibaura Office (Shibaura House)
Tokyo, Japan

Program: office
Total floor area: 950.61m²
Site area: 244.33m²
Structure: steel frame
5 stories

芝浦のオフィス(SHIBAURA HOUSE)
所在地：東京都港区
設計：200804-1003　工事：201004-1106
建築主：Shibaura House
主要用途：事務所
構造：佐々木睦朗構造計画研究所
設備：森村設計
施工：清水建設
主体構造・規模：鉄骨造／地上5階
敷地面積：244.33m²
建築面積：202.21m²
延床面積：950.61m²

2009–14
Soneiji Cemetery Pavillion "Muyuju-rin"
Ichikawa, Chiba, Japan

Program: temple, watering place, foyer, terrace
Total floor area: 1,473.89m²
Site area: 11,326m²
Structure: alluminium alloy
1 story

總寧寺永代供養施設「無憂樹林」
所在地：千葉県市川市
設計：200901-1308　工事：201309-1405
建築主：總寧寺
主要用途：お堂（永代供養墓）、水場、ホワイエ、テラス
構造：佐々木睦朗構造計画研究所
設備：森村設計
アルミ圧体：高橋工業
施工：栄港建設（建築）、オーク建設（設備）
主体構造・規模：アルミニウム合金造／地上1階
敷地面積：11,326m²
建築面積：1,241.83m²
（既存部分：1,176.27m²、増築部分65.56m²）
延床面積：1,473.89m²
（既存部分：1,435.71m²、増築部分38.18m²）

2009–16
Sumida Hokusai Museum
Tokyo, Japan

Program: museum
Total floor area: 3,278.87m²
Site area: 1,254.14m²
Structure: steel frame
4 stories, 1 basement

すみだ北斎美術館
所在地：東京都墨田区
設計：200905-1405　工事：201407-1604
建築主：墨田区
主要用途：美術館
構造：佐々木睦朗構造計画研究所
設備：森村設計
施工：大林・東武谷内田建設JV
主体構造・規模：鉄骨造／地上4階、地下1階
敷地面積：1,254.14m²
建築面積：699.9m²
延床面積：3,278.87m²

2009–11
Tsuchihashi House
Tokyo, Japan

Program: private house
Total floor area: 72.04m²
Site area: 49.62m²
Structure: steel frame
3 stories, 1 basement

土橋邸
所在地：東京都
設計：200906-　工事：-2011
建築主：個人
主要用途：住宅
構造：佐々木睦朗構造計画研究所
施工：平成建設
主体構造・規模：鉄骨造／地上3階、地下1階
敷地面積：49.62m²
建築面積：29.74m²
延床面積：72.04m²

2010–13
Kyoto Apartments (Nishinoyama House)
Kyoto, Japan

Program: housing
Total floor area: 1,260.00m²
Site area: 1,767.94m²
Structure: steel frame, reinforced concrete (partly)
2 stories, 1 basement

京都の集合住宅 (NISHINOYAMA HOUSE)
所在地：京都府京都市
設計：201003-1206
工事：201207-1310
建築主：長谷ビル
主要用途：共同住宅
構造：佐々木睦朗構造計画研究所
設備：鴻池組
施工：鴻池組
主体構造・規模：鉄骨造、一部RC造／地上2階、地下1階
敷地面積：1,767.94m²
建築面積：879.17m²
延床面積：1,260.00m²

2010–14
Nakamachi Terrace
Kodaira, Tokyo, Japan

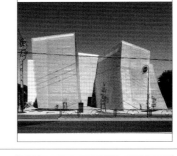

Program: library, community center
Total floor area: 1,453.27m²
Site area: 993.77m²
Structure: steel frame, reinforced concrete (partly)
3 stories, 1 basement

なかまちテラス（小平市仲町公民館・仲町図書館）
所在地：東京都小平市
設計：201010-1202
工事：201212-1410
建築主：小平市
主要用途：図書館、公民館
構造：佐々木睦朗構造計画研究所
設備：森村設計
施工：大成建設
主体構造・規模：鉄骨造、一部RC造／地上3階、地下1階
敷地面積：993.77m²
建築面積：361.94m²
延床面積：1,453.27m²

2011–14
Yoshida Printing Inc. Tokyo HQ
Tokyo, Japan

Program: office, tenant
Total floor area: 3,197.00m²
Site area: 1,124.77m²
Structure: reinforced concrete and steel framecd reinforced concrete (basement), steel frame (above ground part)
4 stories, 1 basement

ヨシダ印刷東京本社
所在地：東京都墨田区
設計：201105-1304
工事：201305-1404
建築主：ヨシダ印刷
主要用途：事務所、テナント
構造：佐々木睦朗構造計画研究所
設備：総合設備計画
施工：鹿島建設
主体構造・規模：鉄骨造、一部RC造／地上4階、地下1階
敷地面積：1,124.77m²
建築面積：676.51m²
延床面積：3,197.00m²

2011–14
Dangozaka House
Tokyo, Japan

Program: private house
Total floor area: 50.38m²
Site area: 40.64m²
Structure: wood frame
2 stories

団子坂の家
所在地：東京都
設計：201110-1306
工事：201307-1402
建築主：個人
主要用途：住宅
構造：ARUP
施工：工藤工務店
主体構造・規模：木造／地上2階
敷地面積：40.64m²
建築面積：24.25m²
延床面積：50.38m²

2011–13
Inujima "Art House Project" phase II A-Art House, C-Art House
Okayama, Okayama, Japan

Program: art (A), gallery(C)
Total floor area: 107.56m² (C)
Site area: 581.02m² (A), 651.36m² (C)
Structure: acrylic (A), wood frame (C)
1 story (C)

犬島「家プロジェクト」2　A邸、C邸
所在地：岡山県岡山市
設計：201112-1204
工事：201205-1302
建築主：公益財団法人 福武財団
主要用途：アート作品（A邸）、展示場（C邸）
構造：佐々木睦朗構造計画研究所（A邸）、シマムラ建築工房（C邸）
設備：科学応用冷暖研究所
施工：第一工芸、総合管理、日プラ、藤原工業、ADFアヤベ、ダイダン
主体構造・規模：アクリル造（A邸）、木造（C邸）／地上1階（C邸）
敷地面積：651.36m²（C邸）
建築面積：157.09m²（C邸）
延床面積：107.56m²（C邸）

2012–
House in Quebradas
Los Vilos, Chile

Program: weekend house
Total floor area: 210m²
Site area: 6,000m²
Structure: steel frame
1 story, 1 basement

チリの住宅
計画地：チリ、ロスビロス
設計：201210-1810（予定）
工事：2018-
建築主：個人
主要用途：住宅
構造：ARUP
主体構造・規模：鉄骨造／地上1階、地下1階
敷地面積：6,000m²
建築面積：230m²
延床面積：210m²

2013
Proposal for New Museum of Modern Art, Toyama
Toyama, Toyama, Japan

Program: museum
Total floor area: 9,750m²
Site area: 12,600m²
Structure: steel frame, reinforced concrete
3 stories, 1 basement

新富山県立近代美術館 プロポーザル案
所在地：富山県富山市
プロポーザル実施：2013
建築主：富山県
主要用途：美術館
構造：佐々木睦朗構造計画研究所
設備：森村設計
主体構造・規模：鉄骨造、RC造/地上3階、地下1階
敷地面積：12,600m²
建築面積：6,000m²
延床面積：9,750m²

2014–21
Japan Women's University Mejiro Campus
Tokyo, Japan

Program: university
Total floor area: 6,180m² (library), 5,500m² (classroom & research)
Site area: 3,378.45m² (library), 23,620.00m² (classroom & research, student's cafeteria)
Structure: reinforced concrete (library, classroom & research), steel frame (student's cafeteria)

日本女子大学目白キャンパス
計画地：東京都文京区　建築主：日本女子大学
設計：201409-1709(図書館棟)、201409-(教室・研究室棟)
工事：201710-1902(予定、図書館棟)
主要用途：大学(図書館、教室・研究室棟、新学生棟)
構造：佐々木睦朗構造計画研究所＋清水建設
設備：森村設計、清水建設
ランドスケープ：GAヤマザキ
共同設計：清水建設(実施・監理)　施工：清水建設
主体構造：RC造(図書館棟、教室・研究室棟)、鉄骨造(新学生棟)
敷地面積：3,378.45m²(図書館棟)、23,620.00m²(教室・研究室棟、新学生棟)
建築面積：1,941.56m²(図書館棟)、1,460.0m²(教室・研究室棟)
延床面積：6,180m²(図書館棟)、5,500m²(教室・研究室棟)

2015–
Osaka University of Arts, Art Science
Kanan, Osaka, Japan

Program: university
Total floor area: 3,137.5m²
Site area: 209,854.26m²
Structure: steel frame, reinforced concrete
2 stories, 1 basement

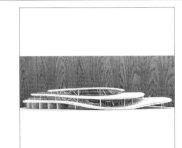

大阪芸術大学アートサイエンス学科棟
計画地：大阪府南河内郡河南町
建築主：学校法人塚本学院
設計：201509-1706
工事：201707-1810(予定)
主要用途：大学
構造：佐々木睦朗構造計画研究所
設備：森村設計
施工：大成建設
主体構造・規模：鉄骨造、RC造/地上2階、地下1階
敷地面積：209,854.26m²
建築面積：2,684.2m²
延床面積：3,137.5m²

2015–
Inujima Landscape Project Inujima Stay, Inujima Life Garden
Okayama, Okayama, Japan

Program: short stay facility, garden
Total floor area: 84.16m² (pergola)
Site area: 500m² (stay), 4,502.97m² (life garden)

犬島ランドスケーププロジェクト
犬島ステイ、犬島 くらしの植物園
計画地：岡山県岡山市
設計：2015-(ステイ)、2016-(くらしの植物園)
建築主：公益財団法人福武財団
主要用途：宿泊施設(ステイ)、パーゴラ・カフェ小屋(くらしの植物園)
敷地面積：500m²(ステイ)、4,502.97m²(くらしの植物園)
建築面積：84.16m²(パーゴラ)

2016
Spring
Daigo, Ibaraki, Japan

Spring (KENPOKU ART 茨城県北芸術祭)
所在地：茨城県久慈郡大子町
設計：201601-1609
工事：201609-1610
主要用途：展示、足湯
コーディネーション：エヌ・アンド・エー(茨城県北芸術祭実行委員会 東京事務局)
施工：髙橋工業
主体構造：アルミ造
敷地面積：4,443m²
建築面積：78.5m²

Program: art, footbath
Total floor area: 78.5m²
Site area: 4,443m²
Structure: alluminium alloy
1 story

2018
New Express Train

新型特急車両
発注者：西武鉄道
プログラム：電車
基本デザイン監修：妹島和世
テキスタイル協力：安東陽子
照明協力：豊久将三
運行開始：2018年度予定

Program: limited express train

RYUE NISHIZAWA 2011–18

2006–11
Garden & House
Japan

ガーデン＆ハウス
所在地：日本
設計：200604-0910
工事：-201107
主要用途：住宅およびオフィス
構造：structured environment
設備：システムデザイン研究所
施工：平成建設
主体構造・規模：RC造/地上4階
敷地面積：37.84m²
建築面積：24.66m²
延床面積：66.03m²

Program: house, office
Total floor area: 66.03m²
Site area: 37.84m²
Structure: reinforced concrete
4 stories

2007–11
Hiroshi Senju Museum Karuizawa
Karuizawa, Nagano, Japan

軽井沢千住博美術館
所在地：長野県北佐久郡軽井沢町
設計：200706-0905
工事：200906-1101
主要用途：美術館
構造：佐々木睦朗構造計画研究所
設備：環境エンジニアリング
照明コンサルティング：遠藤照明
サイン：菊池敦己事務所
施工：清水・笹沢建設共同企業体
主体構造・規模：鉄骨造、一部RC造/地上1階
敷地面積：6,183.45m²
建築面積：1,918.82m²
延床面積：1,818.42m²

Program: museum
Total floor area: 1,818.42m²
Site area: 6,183.45m²
Structure: steel frame, reinforced concrete (partly)
1 story

2009–14
United Church of Christ in Japan, Ikuta Church
Kawasaki, Kanagawa, Japan

日本キリスト教団 生田教会
所在地：神奈川県川崎市
設計：200909-1307
工事：201306-1409
主要用途：教会
構造：佐々木睦朗構造計画研究所
設備：環境エンジニアリング
音響コンサルタント：ヤマハ
施工：辰
家具：イヨベ工芸社
主体構造・規模：鉄骨造/地上2階
敷地面積：581.18m²
建築面積：221.56m²
延床面積：393.92m²

Program: church
Total floor area: 393.92.m²
Site area: 581.18m²
Structure: steel frame
2 stories

2010–12
Treform
Tokyo, Japan

トレフォルム
所在地：東京都豊島区
設計：201002-1101
工事：201101-1203
主要用途：共同住宅(賃貸)
建築：千葉学建築計画事務所(E棟)、小川晋一都市建築設計事務所(N棟)、西沢立衛建築設計事務所(W棟)
構造：金箱構造設計事務所
設備：環境エンジニアリング
施工：安藤建設
企画：タカギプランニングオフィス
主体構造・規模：RC造/地上5階、地下1階
敷地面積：1,939.92m²
建築面積：1,146.18m²
延床面積：5,601.21m²

Program: apartment
Total floor area: 5,601.21m²
Site area: 1,939.92m²
Structure: reinforced concrete
5 stories, 1 basement

2010–11
Pavilion Design of the 12th Istanbul Art Biennale
Istanbul, Turkey

第12回イスタンブールビエンナーレ会場
所在地：トルコ、イスタンブール
設計：201012-1106
工事：201107-1109
主要用途：展覧会場
ディレクター：bige oder
キュレーター：adriano pedrosa、jens hoffman
構造：小山内 博輔
ローカルアーキテクト：duygu dogan
施工：ozsoy insaat
主体構造：鉄骨造
延床面積：9,500m²

Program: exhibition space
Total floor area: 9,500m²
Structure: steel frame

2011–14
Terasaki House
Kanagawa, Japan

寺崎邸
所在地：神奈川県
設計：201111-1306
工事：201307-1406
主要用途：住宅
構造：ARUP
設備：システムデザイン研究所
施工：栄港建設
主体構造／規模：鉄骨造、木造／地上1階、地下1階
敷地面積：160.19m²
建築面積：61.94m²
延床面積：56.38m²

Program: private house
Total floor area: 56.38m²
Site area: 160.19m²
Structure: steel frame, wood frame
1 story, 1 basement

2012–13
Fukita Pavilion in Shodoshima
Shodoshima, Kagawa, Japan

小豆島の蒼田パヴィリオン
所在地：香川県小豆郡小豆島町
設計：201212-1307
施工：201304-1307
主要用途：休憩所
構造：ARUP
施工：鹿島建設
主体構造／規模：鉄骨造／地上1階
建築面積：184.08m²
延床面積：191.44m²

Program: rest space
Total floor area: 191.44m²
Structure: steel frame
1 story

2012–
House in Los Vilos
Los Vilos, Chile

ロスビロスの住宅
計画地：チリ、ロスビロス
設計：2012-
工事：201604-
主要用途：住宅
構造：Luis Soler P.& Asociados、金田充弘、櫻井克哉
主体構造／規模：コンクリート造／地上1階
敷地面積：7,200m²
建築面積：497.65m²
延床面積：322.35m²

Program: weekend house
Total floor area: 322.35m²
Site area: 7,200m²
Structure: concrete
1 story

2012
Shinkenchikusha Kasumigaseki Office
Tokyo, Japan

新建築社霞が関オフィス
所在地：東京都千代田区
工事：-2012
主要用途：オフィス
延床面積：475.5m²

Program: office
Total floor area: 475.5m²

2013
Roof and Mashroom Pavilion
Kyoto, Japan

森の屋根ときのこ
所在地：京都府京都市
設計：201304-1305
工事：201306-1307
主要用途：屋外作品（仮設パヴィリオン）
構造：ARUP
施工：山本興業
企画：Water and Art
家具：nendo
主体構造／規模：木造／地上1階
建築面積：57.72m²
延床面積：57.72m²

Program: temporary pavilion
Total floor area: 57.72m²
Structure: wood frame
1 story

2013–
Kokusai Soushoku Headquarters
Tokyo, Japan

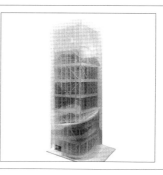

国際装飾本社
所在地：東京都渋谷区
設計：201312-1603
工事：201604-1705
主要用途：オフィス
構造：佐々木睦朗構造計画研究所
主体構造／規模／鉄骨造／地上8階
敷地面積：153.34m²
建築面積：61.73m²
延床面積：472.64m²

Program: office
Total floor area: 472.64m²
Site area: 153.34m²
Structure: steel frame
8 stories

2013–
House in Marbella
Marbella, Chile

マルベーリャの住宅
計画地：チリ、マルベーリャ
設計：2013-
主要用途：住宅
構造：金田充弘
主体構造／規模：鉄骨造、地上1階、地下1階
敷地面積：1,290m²
建築面積：310m²
延床面積：250m²

Program: weekend house
Total floor area: 250m²
Site area: 1,290m²
Structure: steel frame
1 story, 1 basement

2014
Cawaii Bread & Coffee
Tokyo, Japan

カワイイブレッド＆コーヒー
所在地：東京都中央区
設計：201402-1405
工事：201405-1407
主要用途：飲食店
構造協力：小山内博樹
施工：ライテスト
店舗面積：46m²

Program: shop
Total floor area: 46m²

2014–
Jining Museum
Jining, China

済寧市美術館
計画地：中国、済寧市
設計：201410-1611
工事：201612-18（予定）
主要用途：美術館
プロジェクト・マネージメント：Shanghai Ruishe Architectural Design
構造・設備コンセプト：ARUP
構造・設備：East China Architectural Design & Research Institute
ランドスケープ：Shanghai Yuanjing Architecture Studio
ランドスケープ・コンセプト：GAヤマザキ
施工：China State Construction Engineering Corporation Limited
主体構造／規模：鉄骨造／地上1階、地下1階（機械室）
敷地面積：131,281.47m²
建築面積：14,232.76m²
延床面積：12,314m²

Program: museum
Total floor area: 12,314m²
Site area: 131,281.47m²
Structure: steel frame
1 story, 1 basement

2014–18
O House
Tokyo, Japan

O邸
計画地：東京都
設計：201411-1610
工事：201611-1803（予定）
主要用途：住宅
構造：小松宏年構造設計事務所
設備：システムデザイン研究所、Transsolar
施工：工藤工務店
主体構造／規模：鉄骨造／地上2階、地下1階
敷地面積：73.19m²
建築面積：43.00m²
延床面積：96.42m²

Program: private house
Total floor area: 96.42m²
Site area: 73.19m²
Structure: steel frame
2 stories, 1 basement

2014–
Morimoto House
Aichi, Japan

森本邸
計画地：愛知県
設計：201411-
主要用途：住宅
構造：小松宏年構造設計事務所
プロデュース：ミサワホームAプロジェクト
主体構造／規模：木質パネル工法＋木造／地上2階
敷地面積：371m²
建築面積：80m²
延床面積：108m²

Program: private house
Total floor area: 108m²
Site area: 371m²
Structure: wooden-panel building method, wood frame
2 stories

2015–
House in Kyoto
Kyoto, Japan

京都の住宅
計画地：京都府
設計：201501-
主要用途：住宅
構造：ARUP
設備：ARUP
施工：熊倉工務店
主体構造／規模：鉄骨造／地上2階
敷地面積：156.98m²
建築面積：125m²
延床面積：190m²

Program: private house
Total floor area: 190m²
Site area: 156.98m²
Structure: steel frame
2 stories

272

2015–16
Tokuda House
Kyoto, Japan

徳田邸
所在地：京都府
設計：201504-1512
工事：201505-1604
主要用途：住宅、オフィス
構造：桃李舎
施工：アトリエ九間
主体構造・規模：木造・地上2階
敷地面積：93m²
建築面積：63.5m²
延床面積：88.2m²

Program: private house, office
Total floor area: 88.2m²
Site area: 93m²
Structure: wood frame
2 stories

2016
Okamura Design Space R "Wooden Partition"
Tokyo, Japan

Okamura Design Space R「木のパーティション」
計画地：東京都千代田区
設計：201601-
工事：-201608
主要用途：インスタレーション
構造：金田充弘
制作：西沢立衛建築設計事務所、ライテスト
主体構造：木造
面積：181.73m²

Program: installation
Area: 181.73m²
Structure: wood

2016
Shodoshima-Fukutake House
Shodoshima, Kagawa, Japan

小豆島・福武ハウス一部改修工事
所在地：香川県小豆郡小豆島町
設計：201604-1605
工事：201606-1608
主要用途：展覧会会場
構造：小松宏年構造設計事務所
施工：ARTISAN、炭山電器
面積：405m²

Program: exhibition space
Area: 405m²

2016–17
Atelier
Tokyo, Japan

アトリエ
計画地：東京都
設計：201606-1609
工事：201610-1701
主要用途：事務所
構造協力：小山内博樹
施工：ライテスト
延床面積：240.6m²

Program: office
Total floor area: 240.6m²

2016–
I House
Nagano, Japan

I邸
計画地：長野県
設計：201607-1802（予定）
工事：201803-1811（予定）
主要用途：住宅
構造：小松宏年構造設計事務所
設備：システムデザイン研究所
主体構造・規模：RC造、鉄骨造・地上2階
敷地面積：497m²
建築面積：108m²
延床面積：163m²

Program: private house
Total floor area: 163m²
Site area: 497m²
Structure: reinforced concrete, steel frame
2 stories

2016–
Inujima Landscape Project "Stay 01", "Stay 02"
Inujima Stay
Okayama, Okayama, Japan

犬島ランドスケーププロジェクト
ステイ01、ステイ02／犬島ステイ
計画地：岡山県岡山市
設計：201611-1701（ステイ01）
201703-1707（ステイ02）
工事：201702-（ステイ01）
主要用途：滞在場所
構造：シマムラ建築工房
施工：カナオカ（ステイ01）、遠藤建工（ステイ02）
主体構造・規模：木造・地上1階
建築面積：24m²（ステイ01）、16m²（ステイ02）
延床面積：24m²（ステイ01）、16m²（ステイ02）

Program: short stay facility
Total floor area: 24m² (stay 01), 16m² (stay 02)
Structure: wood frame
1 story

2017–
Louna Music Hall Project
Guizhou, China

楼納音楽ホールプロジェクト
計画地：中国、貴州省
設計：201704-
主要用途：音楽ホール
構造：ARUP
主体構造・規模：RC造・地上1階
敷地面積：1,800m²
建築面積：1,800m²

Program: music hall
Site area: 1,800m²
Structure: reinforced concrete
1 story

Monograph and Published Writing

SANAA

2011年
- 「GA ARCHITECT "KAZUYO SEJIMA + RYUE NISHIZAWA 2006-2011"」A.D.A. EDITA Tokyo
- 「SANAA, Kazuyo Sejima + Ryue Nishizawa 2008/2011」EL CROQUIS, No.155, Spain

2013年
- 「妹島和世＋西沢立衛読本—2013」A.D.A. EDITA Tokyo

2014年
- 「SANAA SEJIMA & NISHIZAWA 2007-2015」AV Monographs, Spain

2015年
- 「SANAA, Kazuyo Sejima + Ryue Nishizawa 2011/2015」EL CROQUIS, No.179/180, Spain

妹島和世

2015年
- 「PLOT 07　Kazuyo Sejima」A.D.A. EDITA Tokyo
- 「JA 99 "家　妹島和世"」新建築社

西沢立衛

2011年
- 「豊島美術館写真集」millegraph（西沢立衛〈建築〉, 内藤礼〈アート〉, 鈴木研一〈写真〉）

2012年
- 「続・建築について話してみよう」王国社

2013年
- 「a+u　Ryue Nishizawa」新建築社
- 「けんちくワークブック Workbook of Architecture」平凡社
- 「PLOT 04　Ryue Nishizawa」A.D.A. EDITA Tokyo

2016年
- 「NISHIZAWA cuatro obras + ochoalcubo」Ediciones ARQ

Awards

SANAA

1998年
- Prize of Architectural Institute of Japan, Tokyo, Japan (for Multimedia Workshop, Ogaki, Gifu)　日本建築学会賞（国際情報科学芸術アカデミー マルチメディア工房）

2000年
- Erich Schelling Architekturpreis, Kalsruhe, Germany　エーリッヒ・シェーリング建築賞／ドイツ

2002年
- Arnold W. Brunner Memorial Prize in Architecture, American Academy of Arts & Letters, New York, U.S.A.　アーノルド・W・ブルナー記念建築賞／アメリカ
- Architecture Award of Salzburg Vincenzo Scamozzi, Salzburg, Austria　ザルツブルグ建築賞 V・スカモッツィ賞／オーストリア

2004年
- Golden Lion for the Most Remarkable Work in the Exhibition Metamorph in the 9th International Architecture Exhibition, la Biennale di Venezia　ヴェネツィア・ビエンナーレ国際建築展金獅子賞受賞

2005年
- 46th Mainichi Newspapers Arts Award, Architecture Category (for 21st Century Museum of Contemporary Art, Kanazawa)　第46回毎日芸術賞建築部門受賞（金沢21世紀美術館）
- Rolf Schock Prize in Category of Visual Arts, Sweden　ロルフ・ショック賞ビジュアル・アーツ部門受賞／スウェーデン

2006年
- Prize of Architectural Insititute of Japan, Tokyo, Japan (for 21st Century Museum of Contemporary Art, Kanazawa)　日本建築学会賞（金沢21世紀美術館）

2007年
- Premio Mario Pani 2007 (Mario Pani Award), Mexico City, Mexico　マリオ・パニ賞／メキシコ
- Kunstpreis Berlin (Berlin Art Prize), Berlin, Germany　ベルリン美術賞／ドイツ

2010年
- Pritzker Architecture Prize 2010, U.S.A.　プリツカー建築賞2010／アメリカ

2013年
- Prix de l'Équerre d'Argent, France (for Louvre Lens)　銀の定規賞／フランス（ルーヴル・ランス）

2014年
- Daylight Award, Switzerland (for ROLEX Learning Center)　Daylight Award／スイス（Rolex ラーニングセンター）

2016年
- Mies Crown Hall Americas Prize, U.S.A. (for Grace Farms)　Mies Crown Hall Americas Prize／アメリカ（グレイス・ファームズ）
- American Institute of Architecture Honor Award, U.S.A. (for Grace Farms)　American Institute of Architecture Honor Award／アメリカ（グレイス・ファームズ）

妹島和世

1988年
- Kashima Prize, SD Review 1988 (for Platform I, Platform II)　SD Review 1988 鹿島賞（PLATFORM I. PLATFORM II）

1989年
- Yoshioka Prize, The Japan Architect (for Platform I)　第6回新建築住宅特集新人賞・吉岡賞（PLATFORM I）

1992年
- Young Architect of the Year, Japan Institute of Architects (for Saishunkan Seiyaku Women's Dormitory)　新日本建築家協会新人賞'92（再春館製薬女子寮）

1994年
- Grand Prize, Commercial Space Design Award'94 (for Pachinko Parlor I, Pachinko Parlor II)　'94商環境デザイン賞大賞（パチンコパーラー I, パチンコパーラー II）

1995年
- Kenneth F. Brown Asia Pacific Culture and Architecture Design Award, University of Hawaii (for Saishunkan Seiyaku Women's Dormitory)　ケネス・F・ブラウン環太平洋地域文化建築賞（再春館製薬女子寮）

2006年
- Minister of Education's Art Encouragement Prize, Tokyo, Japan　芸術選奨文部科学大臣賞美術部門
- Japan Architecture Award (for House in Plum Grove)　日本建築大賞（梅林の家）

2007年
- International Fellowship of RIBA/Royal Institute of British Architects　王立英国建築家協会国際フェロー

2009年
- StellaRe Prize, Turin, Italy　ステラ・レ賞／イタリア
- Erna Hamburger Prize, Lausanne, Switzerland　エルナ・ハンバーガー賞／スイス

2010年
- Officier de l'Ordre des Arts et des Lettres, France　芸術文化勲章オフィシエ／フランス

2015年
- Murano Togo Prize, Tokyo, Japan (for Inujima "Art House Project")　村野藤吾賞（犬島「家プロジェクト」）
- American Academy of Arts and Letters, New York, U.S.A.　American Academy of Arts and Letters／アメリカ
- Medal with Purple Ribbon, Tokyo, Japan　紫綬褒章

西沢立衛

1999年
- Yoshioka Prize, The Japan Architect (for Weekend House)　第15回新建築住宅特集新人賞・吉岡賞（ウィークエンドハウス）

2000年
- First Prize in Residential Architecture, Tokyo Society of Architects & Building Engineers (for Weekend House)　東京建築士会住宅建築賞金賞（ウィークエンドハウス）

2001年
- Kashima Prize, SD Review 2001 (for Ichikawa Apartment)　SD Review 2001 鹿島賞（市川アパートメント）

2005年
- Young Scientists' Prize, Commendation for Science and Technology by Minister of Education, Culture, Sports, Science and Technology　文部科学大臣表彰若手科学者賞

2011年
- Officier de l'Ordre des Arts et des Lettres, France　芸術文化勲章オフィシエ／フランス

2012年
- Prize of Architectural Institute of Japan, Tokyo, Japan (for Teshima Art Museum)　日本建築学会賞作品賞（豊島美術館）
- Murano Togo Prize, Tokyo, Japan (for Teshima Art Museum)　村野藤吾賞（豊島美術館）

Staff list

SANAA *SANAA*

—

妹島和世 *Kazuyo Sejima*
西沢立衛 *Ryue Nishizawa*

—

棚瀬純孝 *Yoshitaka Tanase*
ユミコ・ヤマダ *Yumiko Yamada*
山本力矢 *Rikiya Yamamoto*

—

長谷川高之 *Takayuki Hasegawa*
片桐広祥 *Hiroaki Katagiri*
ルーシー・スタイルズ *Lucy Styles*
北澤伸浩 *Nobuhiro Kitazawa*
湯浅崇史 *Takashi Yuasa*
フランチェスカ・シンガー *Francesca Singer*
八木麻乃 *Asano Yagi*
リカルド・カンナタ *Riccardo Cannata*
ニコロ・ベルティノ *Nicolo' Bertino*
宮崎茉里奈 *Marina Miyazaki*
李恵利 *Lee Hyeri*
セレーナ・ディ・ジュリアーノ *Serena Di Giuliano*
ヒョンスー・キム *Hyunsoo Kim*
宮崎侑也 *Yuya Miyazaki*
柳田里穂子 *Rihoko Yanagida*
劉嘉名 *Liu Jiaming*
パット・ポンティーカーユ *Pat Pongteekayu*
何嘉珍 *Amira Ho*
ジュリア・ボヴォレンタ *Giulia Bovolenta*
杉原由樹子 *Yukiko Sugihara*
小田切駿 *Hayao Odagiri*
エクトル・バランテス・モンテス *Héctor Barrantes Montes*
常國文萌 *Ayame Tsunekuni*
エイミー・ヘミン・ジャン *Amy Hyemin Jang*
亀井由紀子 *Yukiko Kamei*
ジャニス・リム *Janice Rim*
レジーナ・ヴェスト・タン *Regina Vest Teng*
フランチェスカ・ジェルヴァズッティ *Francesca Gervasutti*
アダム・ヴォスバーグ *Adam Vosburgh*
村田徹 *Toru Murata*
アンナ・バーヒリナ *Anna Bakhlina*
エンリコ・アルメリン *Enrico Armellin*
グリアー・はな *Hana Greer*
ファディー・ハダッド *Fady Haddad*
吉井梢 *Etsuko Yoshii*
秋元梢 *Kozue Akimoto*
中野理恵 *Rie Nakano*

妹島和世建築設計事務所 *Kazuyo Sejima & Associates*

—

妹島和世 *Kazuyo Sejima*

—

棚瀬純孝 *Yoshitaka Tanase*
山本力矢 *Rikiya Yamamoto*
松澤一応 *Ichio Matsuzawa*
池田賢 *Satoshi Ikeda*
降矢宜幸 *Takayuki Furuya*
平木紀子 *Noriko Hiraki*
福原光太 *Kota Fukuhara*
横前拓磨 *Takuma Yokomae*
伊東加恵 *Kae Ito*
原田直哉 *Naoya Harada*

—

元所員 *former staff*
長尾亜子 *Ako Nagao*
西沢立衛 *Ryue Nishizawa*
和田圭子 *Keiko Wada*
船木幸子 *Sachiko Funaki*
時森康一郎 *Koichiro Tokimori*
吉村寿博 *Toshihiro Yoshimura*
細矢仁 *Jin Hosoya*
小島善文 *Yoshifumi Kojima*
堀直樹 *Naoki Hori*
桑田豪 *Go Kuwata*
菊池宏 *Hiroshi Kikuchi*
大成優子 *Yuko Onari*
フェナ・ハクマ・ワグナール *Fenna Haakma Wagenaar*
ヨナス・エルディング *Jonas Elding*
フロリアン・アイデンバーグ *Florian Idenburg*
西村嘉哲 *Yoshinori Nishimura*
福屋粧子 *Shoko Fukuya*
川嶋貫介 *Kansuke Kawashima*
近藤哲雄 *Tetsuo Kondo*

アナ・ロプリオレ *Anna Lopriore*
ニコル・ベルガンスキー *Nicole Berganski*
石上純也 *Junya Ishigami*
林順孝 *Yoritaka Hayashi*
内山敬子 *Keiko Uchiyama*
吉田孝司 *Koji Yoshida*
日高恵理香 *Erika Hidaka*
中坪多恵子 *Taeko Nakatsubo*
今村水紀 *Mizuki Imamura*
菊池裕 *Yutaka Kikuchi*
平木敦子 *Atsuko Hiraki*
加藤研 *Osamu Kato*
トシヒロ・オオキ *Toshihiro Oki*
篠原勲 *Isao Shinohara*
西山由花 *Yuka Nishiyama*
浴啓造 *Keizo Eki*
ハビエル・ハッダッド・コンデ *Javier Haddad Conde*
長島未帆 *Miho Nagashima*
太田定治 *Sadaharu Ota*
アンドレアス・クラヴチック *Andreas Krawczyk*
松岡聡 *Satoshi Matsuoka*
田村裕希 *Yuuki Tamura*
ヨハンナ・マイヤー・グローブリュッゲ *Johanna Meyer-Grohbrugge*
山下貴成 *Takashige Yamashita*
周防貴之 *Takashi Suo*
吉田昌平 *Shohei Yoshida*
サム・チェリマイエフ *Sam Chermayeff*
アンジェラ・パン *Angela Pang*
野口直人 *Naoto Noguchi*
鍛冶瑞子 *Mizuko Kaji*
ジャンヌ・フランソワ・フィッシャー *Jeanne-Francoise Fischer*
マリエケ・クムズ *Marieke Kums*
ルイ・グレゴ *Louis Grego*
マティアス・ハーテル *Matthias Haertel*
河内尚子 *Naoko Kawachi*
ロイック・エンゲルハド *Loic Engelhard*
イングリッド・モエ *Ingrid Moye*
カタリーナ・カナス *Catarina Canas*
レア・イポライト *Lea Hippolyte*
トミー・ハドック *Tommy Haddock*
アビタル・ゴウラリー *Avital Gourary*
ジャック・ホーガン *Jack Hogan*
マーク・デュジョン *Marc Dujon*
ボブ・ヴァン・デン・ブランデ *Bob van den Brande*
小野寺匠吾 *Shogo Onodera*
ブラッドリー・フレイザー *Bradley Fraser*
井手口航 *Wataru Ideguchi*
福原智子 *Tomoko Fukuhara*
ギヨム・ショプラン *Guillaume Choplan*
アラテ・アリザガ・ヴィラルバ *Arrate Alizaga Villalba*
菊本貴晩 *Takaaki Kikumoto*
工藤浩平 *Kohei Kudo*
佐竹知子 *Tomoko Satake*
小村晴美 *Harumi Komura*
瀬川慧理 *Eri Segawa*
モハメッド・マンスール *Mohammed Mansoor*

西沢立衛建築設計事務所 *Office of Ryue Nishizawa*

—

西沢立衛 *Ryue Nishizawa*

—

松井元靖 *Motoyasu Matsui*
藤澤賢一 *Kenichi Fujisawa*
内藤慶太 *Keita Naito*
横山拓矢 *Takuya Yokoyama*
徳野由美子 *Yumiko Tokuno*
東出優子 *Yuko Higashide*
舘真弘 *Masahiro Tachi*
植田有紗 *Arisa Ueda*
エミリー・ブリン *Emilie Brin*
金丸真由美 *Mayumi Kanemaru*

—

元所員 *former staff*
岡田公彦 *Kimihiko Okada*
大井裕介 *Yusuke Ooi*
髙橋一平 *Ippei Takahashi*
中坪多恵子 *Taeko Nakatsubo*
宝田麻里子 *Mariko Takarada*
尾野克矩 *Katsunori Ono*
松田彩加 *Ayaka Matsuda*
北林さなえ *Sanae Kitabayashi*

Photography Credits

Except as noted: GA photographers

—

Courtesy of SANAA: p.46, p.4˝, p.99, p.121, p.127 left, p.128 left, p.129, p.135, p.144, p.162, p.163, p.179, p.206, pp.218-219, p.224, pp.224-225, p.239, p.241, p.252, p.253, p.267 right bottom, p.269 top
Courtesy of Kazuyo Sejima & Associates: p.76, p.111, p.148, p.149, p.204, p.205, p.210-211, p.211, p.229 below, p.230, p.271 left third from top
Courtesy of Office of Ryue Nishizawa: p.146, p.161, p.176, p.177, p.189, p.192, p.193, p.194, p.195, p.196, p.217, p.231, p.242, p.247, p.254, p.271 right bottom, p.272 left fourth from top

—

Hisao Suzuki: p.110

Drawing and Rendering Credits

Except as noted: courtesy of architects

—

ARFORIA: p.98 left
Cyrille Thomas: p.98 right, p.99 bottom left, p.99 bottom right, p.121 above left, pp.168-169, p.171, pp.232-233, p.256, p.257

English Translations

*Lisa Tani: pp.8-15, p.30, pp.*60-161*
Satoko Hirata: p.72
Erica Sakai: p.16, p.34, p.35, p.48, p.64, p.67, p.77, p.82, p.87, p.91, p.99, p.101, pp.106-107, p.110, p.113, p.114, p.120, p.122, p.126, p.127, p.128, p.129, p.130, p.134, p.138, p.146, p.149, pp.154-155, p.162, p.164, p.169, p.173, p.176, pp.178-179, p.182, p.184, p.187, p.189, p.192, p.196, p.198, pp.200-202, p.205, p.209, pp.220-221, p.224, pp.229-230, p.236, p.239, p.242, p.244, p.247, p.248, p.250, p.253, p.254, p.256
Joyce Lam: p.212
Nanami Kawashima: p.216
Courtesy of Towada Art Center: p.262 left third from top
Courtesy of architects: pp.20-21, p.46, p.54, p.61, p.91, p.142, p.206, p.232

GAアーキテクト
〈妹島和世　西沢立衛　SANAA　2011-2018〉

2018年1月25日発行

企画：二川由夫
編集：山口真
撮影：GA photographers
序文：妹島和世, 西沢立衛
ロゴ・デザイン(GA)：細谷巌
デザイン：関拓弥
発行者：二川由夫
印刷・製本：大日本印刷株式会社
発行・制作：エーディーエー・エディタ・トーキョー
151-0051 東京都渋谷区千駄ヶ谷3-12-14
TEL.(03)3403-1581(代)

禁無断転載

ISBN978-4-87140-436-5 C1352